Christian Kaunert and Kamil Zwolski
The EU AS A GLOBAL SECURITY ACTOR
A Comprehensive Analysis beyond CFSP and JHA

Marina Kolb
THE EUROPEAN UNION AND THE COUNCIL OF EUROPE

Finn Laursen (*editor*)
DESIGNING THE EUROPEAN UNION
From Paris to Lisbon

Pontus Odmalm
THE PARTY POLITICS OF THE EU AND IMMIGRATION

Dimitris Papadimitriou and Paul Copeland (*editors*)
THE EU's LISBON STRATEGY
Evaluating Success, Understanding Failure

David Phinnemore
THE TREATY OF LISBON
Origins and Negotiation

Claudia Sternberg
THE STRUGGLE FOR EU LEGITIMACY
Public Contestation, 1950–2005

Yves Tiberghien (*editor*)
LEADERSHIP IN GLOBAL INSTITUTION BUILDING
Minerva's Rule

Liubomir K. Topaloff
POLITICAL PARTIES AND EUROSCEPTICISM

Amy Verdun and Alfred Tovias (*editors*)
MAPPING EUROPEAN ECONOMIC INEGRATION

Richard G. Whitman and Stefan Wolff (*editors*)
THE EUROPEAN NEIGHBOURHOOD POLICY IN PERSPECTIVE
Context, Implementation and Impact

Sarah Wolff
THE MEDITERRANEAN DIMENSION OF THE EUROPEAN UNION'S INTERNAL SECURITY

Jan Wouters, Hans Bruyninckx, Sudeshna Basu and Simon Schunz (*editors*)
THE EUROPEAN UNION AND MULTILATERAL GOVERNANCE
Assessing EU Participation in United Nations Human Rights and Environmental Fora

Ozge Zihnioglu
EUROPEAN UNION CIVIL SOCIETY POLICY AND TURKEY
A Bridge Too Far?

Palgrave Studies in European Union Politics
Series Standing Order ISBN 978–1–403–99511–7 (hardback) and
ISBN 978–1–403–99512–4 (paperback)
(*outside North America only*)

You can receive future titles in this series as they are published by placing a standing order. Please contact your bookseller or, in case of difficulty, write to us at the address below with your name and address, the title of the series and one of the ISBNs quoted above.

Customer Services Department, Macmillan Distribution Ltd, Houndmills, Basingstoke, Hampshire RG21 6XS, UK.

The Party Politics of the EU and Immigration

Pontus Odmalm

Department of Politics and International Relations, University of Edinburgh, UK

First published 2014 by
PALGRAVE MACMILLAN

Palgrave Macmillan in the UK is an imprint of Macmillan Publishers Limited, registered in England, company number 785998, of Houndmills, Basingstoke, Hampshire RG21 6XS.

Palgrave Macmillan in the US is a division of St Martin's Press LLC, 175 Fifth Avenue, New York, NY 10010.

Palgrave Macmillan is the global academic imprint of the above companies and has companies and representatives throughout the world.

Palgrave® and Macmillan® are registered trademarks in the United States, the United Kingdom, Europe and other countries.

ISBN 978–0–230–36774–6

This book is printed on paper suitable for recycling and made from fully managed and sustained forest sources. Logging, pulping and manufacturing processes are expected to conform to the environmental regulations of the country of origin.

A catalogue record for this book is available from the British Library.

A catalog record for this book is available from the Library of Congress.

Contents

List of Tables and Figures   vi

Acknowledgements   vii

1 The Changing Nature of Party Competition   1

2 Competing in Multidimensional Party Spaces   8

3 (Almost) Contesting the EU and Immigration (1945–1990)   30

4 'Pulled' or 'Pushed'? Increased Ideological Uncertainty on the EU and Immigration 'Issues'   63

5 The Changing Modes of Party Competition (1991–2010)   97

6 The Death of Ideology, or Ways of Dealing with an Increased State of Flux   112

Notes   117

Bibliography   146

Interviews   165

Index   167

Tables and Figures

Tables

4.1 Type of ideological 'pull' (grouped by country)   65
4.2 EU (confirmed cases in bold)   95
4.3 Immigration (confirmed cases in bold)   96

Manifesto positions (EU)
5.1 Belgium – Flanders   98
5.2 Belgium – Wallonia   98
5.3 Britain   99
5.4 The Netherlands   99
5.5 Sweden   99

Manifesto positions (Immigration)
5.6 Belgium – Flanders   100
5.7 Belgium – Wallonia   100
5.8 Britain   100
5.9 The Netherlands   100
5.10 Sweden   101
5.11 Manifesto positions and expected modes of competition: EU (1991–2010)   101
5.12 Manifesto positions and expected modes of competition: immigration (1991–2010)   102
5.13 De facto modes of competition/EU (aggregate %)   104
5.14 De facto modes of competition/immigration (aggregate %)   104
5.15 Modes of competition: party/frequency/total nr of elections (EU)   104
5.16 Modes of competition: party/frequency/total nr of elections (immigration)   105

Figures

4.1 Average Manifesto Positions (1991–2010)   64

Acknowledgements

The precise origins of this book are difficult to trace, but I am fairly sure that the ideas that underpin it evolved from several discussions with Paul Taggart on how to classify party positions. These ideas later developed into a funding proposal to the ESRC's 'First Grants' scheme, which I was very fortunate to secure and very grateful for (RES-061-25-0195). The book would not have been possible to write without the fantastic advice and feedback I got from numerous friends and colleagues (Elizabeth Bomberg, Christina Boswell, Ailsa Henderson, Charlie Jeffery, Luke March and Wilfried Swenden). I am also very grateful for the comments I received from various discussants and workshop participants over the years (Tim Bale, Gregg Bucken-Knapp, Alexander Caviedes, James Hampshire, Jonas Hinnfors, Dirk Jacobs, Sarah de Lange, Charles Lees, Laura Morales, Martin Schain, Andrea Spehar and Richard Whitaker). Special thanks go to Randall Hansen and the Centre for European, Russian and Eurasian Studies (University of Toronto) for the several invitations to present my work and to Betsy Super for her great assistance over the course of the project. The research undertaken for this book owes a lot to the Belgian, British, Dutch and Swedish MPs who so generously gave up their time to speak to Betsy and me in 2009–2013. And, finally, a world of thanks goes to Sarah and Maya for their continuous support and love throughout this process. This book is dedicated to them.

1
The Changing Nature of Party Competition

Party systems across Europe have become increasingly complex and volatile (Enyedi and Deegan-Krause, 2010). New questions have emerged – with the attendant formation of 'new' parties – which have often come to challenge the status quo of party competition (Harmel and Gibson, 1995; Franklin, 1992). This change is said to manifest itself in the increased prominence of lifestyle, value and environmental questions that have taken the political conversations in a post-material direction over recent decades (Bomberg, 2002; Davis and Davenport, 1999; Knutsen, 1990; Inglehart, 1971). But this volatility also relates to those novel questions that have entered the party-political agendas and which do not always have an obvious dimensional fit or any equally obvious modes of framing (see e.g. Chong and Druckman, 2007; Rydgren, 2005; Taggart, 1995). And simultaneously, the party-electorate linkages show increasing signs of dissonance and friction (Walgrave and Nuytemans, 2009; Hobolt, 2008; Jones and Baumgartner, 2005), and parties are also said to be increasingly difficult to distinguish from one another. The behaviour of the voters has in turn echoed these developments and points to how competence and an ability to deliver seem to be more important than ideological proximity for their choice of party (Green and Hobolt, 2008; Holian, 2004; van der Brug, 2004).

These changes raise several pertinent questions for the political scientist. Does ideology matter in the political 'game' (Fukuyama, 1992)? Do parties offer a choice between different societal outcomes anymore (Stokes, 1963)? And, if so, are these choices significantly different from one another (Petrocik, 1996)? If one answers these in the negative, then this leads to an additional set of queries that need to be addressed. Should we have entered an era of visionary decline (Elff, 2007), what is it that then drives party conflict? And why are some parties still more likely than others to experience an internal ideological turmoil?

1

Electoral competition has previously been explained by the different spatial positions that parties occupy (Downs, 1957), the assumption being that these *ideological* location(s) would translate into specific – and different – policy solutions. Conflict has therefore tended to revolve around competing ideas of 'the good society'. Similarly, the electoral dynamics that parties are subjected to (Deschouwer, 2013; Adams and Somer-Topcu, 2009; Adams and Merrill, 1999), and how they have responded (either pro- or re-actively) to certain exogenous 'shocks' (Adams et al., 2004; Budge, 1994), have also been put forward to explain the identified modes of party competition.

However, such explanations assume that the party-political landscapes have remained relatively stable, and that certain fault lines continue to be relevant for parties and electorates alike. But as increasingly noted, party systems appear to be in a state of flux (see e.g. Poguntke, 2012; Broughton and Donovan, 1999; Mair, 1989), and the political mainstream may therefore find that their traditional stances – and solutions – are no longer viable. These questions are of course important for the more general understanding of how party competition has evolved and changed over time, and, indeed, 'parties', 'ideologies' and 'elections' continue to be key topics for the comparative scholar (see e.g. Budge et al., 2001; Inglehart and Klingemann, 1987; Budge and Farlie, 1983; 1978; Rose, 1964). But they are equally important questions to address when trying to explain (and make sense of) how parties engage with, and negotiate, issues that often fall outside of the traditional dimensions of conflict. While much of the post-war period was characterised by uni-dimensional types of competition concerning the distribution, and ownership, of societal resources, this *material* cleavage is said to be less dominant today and subsequently also less relevant than it was, say, 40 years ago (Jansen et al., 2013). In parallel, however, a new set of issues have emerged, which are characterised by their more *post-material* nature (Kitschelt, 1988; Inglehart, 1971). One would, perhaps, expect these changes to have generated *more* room for conflict, given the plurality of cleavages that are now present, yet paradoxically, there also appears to be an increased level of agreement on certain *societal outcomes* (e.g. the continuation of the welfare state or protecting the environment). Therefore, what is said to have changed is how parties intend to *achieve* these mutually desirable goals. This suggests that party competition, at the very least, has been affected by these socio-political changes but possibly also that it has changed fundamentally. Where parties were previously more likely to put forward a set of competing visions, they can now be described to be more concerned with portraying competence, claiming ownership over particular issues and convincing the electorate that they are more capable than their opponent(s) are at delivering on these *valence* issues (Clark, 2009; Green, 2007; Bale, 2006; Stokes, 1963).

Yet, explaining the modes of competition on some of these 'new' sources of conflict continues to be difficult to do. The European Union (EU) and immigration 'issues' are in many ways indicative of the changes that have taken place regarding party competition (see e.g. Breunig and Luedtke, 2008; Harmsen and Spiering, 2004; Hooghe et al., 2002; Faist, 1994). They have not only contributed to this state of flux but have also added further complexity to an already complex situation of trying to understand party systems and party placements (Benoit and Laver, 2007). It somewhat relates to the delicate balancing act that parties need to perform when these questions develop into contested 'issues'. Both areas are of frequent electoral concern, media frenzy and sustained challenge by, particularly, the populist radical right (PRR) (see e.g. Hampshire, 2013; Hayton, 2010; Boswell and Hough, 2008; Hunger, 2001; Mudde, 1999; Karapin, 1999; Freeman, 1997; Kitschelt and McGann, 1995), which often means that there is ample room for the political mainstream to get it electorally 'wrong'. But they are also questions that pose internal difficulties for parties since there is not always any obvious *ideological* lynchpin to hang their position(s) on (see also Spies and Franzmann, 2011). At the same time, parties have also struggled with a growing sense of ideological crisis as the political conversation has shifted from 'visions' over to 'competence' (and occasionally back again). Should certain questions thus fall outside of the so-called 'old' and 'new' dimensions of conflict, then they may very well give rise to intra-party, as well as inter-party, tension as parties attempt to get the new calculus right. The adopted party stances are usually categorised along a 'Europhile – Eurosceptic', or 'Liberal – Restrictive', continuum (see e.g. Alonso and Claro da Fonseca, 2013; Kopecky and Mudde, 2002), but such classifications may not necessarily lend themselves to be equated with the positions that parties hold on either of these 'old' or 'new' divides (Smith, 2008; Hooghe and Marks, 2007). A mismatch is therefore likely to develop between the 'issue' and the 'ideological' positions that parties have, and one that can be traced back to the multifaceted nature of *both* issues. But if this is the case, then what would drive electoral conflict and competition on the EU and immigration 'issues'? Since parties are usually motivated by office-, policy- or vote-seeking objectives, they also tend to respond to those questions that will allow them to achieve such aims (Enyedi and Deegan-Krause, 2010; Green-Pedersen, 2004; Karp and Banducci, 2002). Given how saliency levels and the electoral 'threat' of the PRR have witnessed a significant incline across many West European states (Ennser, 2012), a reasonable assumption would thus be that the party attention paid to both issues would show a similar development. But although parts of the mainstream have continuously campaigned on an EU and/or immigration ticket, others have not. Due to their ideologically ambiguous nature, issues of *dimensional* fit and *societal* impact should be likely to emerge, and mainstream parties may therefore struggle to identify the most appropriate frame to use (Helbling et al., 2010; Chong and Druckman, 2007). Furthermore, should one accept the multidimensionality of the political space, then this may very well subject parties to a set of *conflicting ideological 'pulls'* (Odmalm, 2011) as they attempt to establish and internally negotiate this frame. For centre-right parties, the tension involves weighing free-market ideals against national sovereignty/value conservatism, whereas for the centre-left, it concerns notions of welfare state/labour market protectionism pitted against ideals of international solidarity and human rights (Hinnfors et al., 2011; Bale, 2008). Should parties frame the EU and/or immigration according to the 'wrong' stream, it is likely to bring unwanted attention and criticism, from their mainstream as well as from their more radical competitors, and thereby detract attention from parties' core competencies and electoral priorities (Green-Pedersen and Odmalm, 2008). But such discrepancies may not necessarily be a problem should ideology, indeed, be 'dead' and should the role of parties have shifted from 'popular vehicles of representation' to 'competent implementers' (see e.g. van Biezen, 2012; Petrocik, 1996; Katz and Mair, 1995; Schattschneider, 1960; 2009). However, if parties struggle to accommodate their issue position/s with their overall ideological orientation, then this would suggest that the death of ideology is, perhaps, exaggerated and that it still continues to play some form of role in political life and discourses.

This book therefore sets out to investigate these complicated relationships by adopting a comparative perspective. More specifically the focus is on those mainstream actors that occupied the Belgian, British, Dutch and Swedish party systems between 1991 and 2010. The period in question includes several key developments and events where parties should have been subjected to increased (re)framing pressures, and one would therefore expect these strains to also be reflected in their respective manifestos. On the one hand, the EU witnessed numerous 'critical junctures' that have come to affect its original raison d'être (e.g. the signings of the Amsterdam and Maastricht Treaties; the establishment of the single market; Schengen taking effect; the further enlargement eastwards becoming a tangible, and later, a de facto reality; the introduction of the Euro; and the 'Community' tag being replaced by the 'Union' ditto) (see further Bache et al., 2011; Cowles and Smith, 2000). And on the other hand, immigration pressures were building up, the PRR was becoming increasingly credible as an electoral challenger and the prevailing philosophies of integration were being challenged (see e.g. Dahlström and Esaiasson, 2011; Mudde, 2007; Bevelander, 2004; Breugelmans and van de Vijver, 2004; Vink and Meijerink, 2003; Geddes, 2000; 2003). The choice of cases, and the time frame covered, will thus be particularly illuminating for further probing how the political mainstream has tried to engage with, and negotiate, two of the most contested areas in contemporary European politics.

In some respects, they constitute a 'usual suspects' list in the EU and immigration literatures. The ambivalent relationships that the British and Swedish parties have had with the former have been extensively covered (see e.g. Crowson, 2011; Archer, 2000), whereas the more Euro-friendly situation in the Low Countries has tended to receive less attention (although see e.g. Abts et al., 2009; Hylarides, 2001). Equally, a substantial body of literature exists that references these cases and their respective approaches to immigration and/or integration (e.g. Shain, 2008; Boswell, 2003; Page Moch, 2003; Castles and Miller, 2003; Castles and Davidson, 2000). As such, they show a high degree of variation not only regarding their 'party-based Euroscepticism' (Taggart and Szczerbiak, 2008; Lubbers and Scheepers, 2005) but also in terms of the sources and composition of newcomers, and in the levels of conflict that the immigration 'issue' has endured (see e.g. Roggeband and Vliegenthart, 2007; Rydgren, 2002; Castles and Miller, 2003).

Since it first emerged as an 'issue' in the post-war period, the British party politics of the EU has witnessed significant positional shifts, whereas in Sweden, a more stable domestic/foreign policy dilemma came to dominate political debates and served to split the party system into (fairly even) pro- and anti-camps. In Belgium and the Netherlands, conversely, the EU managed to remain a largely uncontested issue for a remarkably long period of time. The immigration 'issue' shows similar levels of variation. In terms of flows and types, Britain, Belgium and the Netherlands form a postcolonial cluster, which is juxtaposed by Sweden who has had higher numbers of asylum seekers and family reunification migrants. And the way that it has played out during elections differs remarkably. While the British and Dutch parties have come to adopt

an increasingly confrontational approach, immigration has rarely registered as an election issue in neither Belgium nor Sweden. Some of
these cases also experienced the sudden rise – and equally sudden success – of various types of PRR challengers, but this has come with quite
different responses from the mainstream players (see e.g. Norris, 2005;
Mudde, 1999; 2004; Perlmutter, 1996; Betz, 1994). Although there have
indeed been instances where mainstream parties have tried to co-opt or
even outdo these 'threats' (Britain, the Netherlands), there have also
been signs that point in the opposite direction when they have not
deviated from the official party line on, for example, asylum and family reunification (Sweden), or where the reductionist position has been
largely redundant since this was already the consensus understanding
(Belgium).

That said, systematic comparisons have been scarce and studies tend
to adopt either a binary-study or a case-study approach (be that either
country or 'issue'). Studying the four countries in tandem, and using
the same analytical lens, allows for an assessment of whether the EU
and immigration – as party-politically relevant issues – are dependent, or
largely independent, of the above externalities. While these factors are
likely to have had some form of effect on how the mainstream has chosen to engage (or not) with the two 'issues', the book's main emphasis
is on their ability to handle and negotiate these conflicting 'pulls', and
whether any similarities found can help us to understand the changing dynamics of party competition in Western Europe. The empirical
data are based on a novel way of coding party manifestos, and a substantial set of qualitative interviews (conducted with MPs and party
strategists), which are invoked to address the following questions: has
the political mainstream resolved the ideological strains that are likely to
emerge when competing in multidimensional party spaces? If not, has
this resulted in a higher frequency of ownership claims being present in
their party manifestos?

The key findings suggest that competition has become increasingly
dependent on processes internal to the parties themselves rather than
being a reaction to particular cues in the external political environment.
At the same time, however, the issues' ideological uncertainties have
been likely to increase levels of indecisiveness regarding what strategies to pursue, and when to make the EU and/or immigration a top
election priority. The role of ideology may have changed but perhaps
not in the desired way. Rather than offering clarity and a firm directional steer, it has instead added to the complexity and nuance of an
already complex political context. This further helps to explain the

identified party behaviour, which increasingly stresses competence and a successful track record of delivery.

The book is structured as follows. Chapter 2 maps the changing nature of the societal cleavages and what consequences these changes have had for party competition. The chapter's final section discusses the novel coding scheme that is used for the manifesto analysis and qualifies its approach in relation to the existing datasets – the *Comparative Manifestos Project* (CMP) and the *Chapel Hill Expert Survey* (CHES). This section also provides further details on the interviews that were conducted. Chapter 3 offers an historical overview of the relationships that each case has had with the EU and immigration – from the postwar years up until the late 1980s – and highlights some of the key sources of contestation that both areas have tapped into and that, to some extent, continue to fuel the debates today. Thus, it 'sets the scene' for chapters 4 and 5, which in more detail examine how the political mainstream has engaged, negotiated and competed on these issues during the increasingly politicised period between 1991 and 2010. These analytical and empirical chapters discuss *party competition in the multidimensional space* (Chapter 4) and the *changing modes of party competition* (Chapter 5). Finally, chapter 6 relates the book's conclusions to the broader implications they have for studying the *party* politics of the EU and immigration.

2
Competing in Multidimensional Party Spaces

Numerous attempts have been made to classify parties along some form of left-right continuum using either party publications; expert judgements or voters' self-placements to identify these locations (Budge, 2000; 2001; Gabel and Huber, 2000; Giljam and Oscarsson, 1996; Inglehart and Klingemann, 1987). While it has become a standard vocabulary in the field, the meaning of 'left-right' is said to be so diverse that it is 'multifaceted at best, elusive at worst' (Arian and Shamir, 1983: 139). This elusiveness stems from prevailing discrepancies regarding the essence of the party-ideological space (Huber and Inglehart, 1995). The literature is thus characteristically divided on the topic. Some suggest that a 'new', post-material divide has come to *supersede* the 'old', material cleavage (Flanagan and Lee, 2003; Inglehart, 1997; Knutsen, 1990; 1995a; 1995b; see also Clark and Lipset, 1991), while others consider the key change to be the *meaning* of these 'left-right' divide(s) (Jahn, 2010; Kriesi et al., 2006). And while a further grouping has come to accept the *existence* of multidimensional dimensions, they also disagree on the nature – and salience – of these divisions (Linhart and Shikano, 2009; Kitschelt and McGann, 1995; van der Brug, 2004; Evans et al., 1996; Daalder, 1984; Budge and Farlie, 1978). However, what the above camps appear to be in agreement on is how a majority of the West European polities were structured around *disagreements* for much of the post-war period, especially regarding the remit of state involvement in the economy. Parties on 'the left', for example, tended to favour higher levels of collective ownership, taxation and labour market regulation compared to parties on 'the right' (hereafter labelled the *State Interventionist* (SI) – *Free Market* (FM) axis).[1] Later on, these differences came to relate to certain lifestyle choices, the nature of democracy and/or to state-individual relationships (Della Porta and Diani, 2006; Inglehart, 1971), but have increasingly come to connect with issues of national identity (due to growing immigration pressures) and sovereignty (due to EU membership/further integration) (Hooghe et al., 2002). Yet, levels of conflict also appear to have subsided, particularly relating to certain economic issues, as parties on the left have begun to accept the (occasional) benefits of the market economy (Franzmann and Kaiser, 2006; Kitschelt, 2004). These developments are not only a concern for the interested scholar but have also come to affect the dynamics of party competition (Clark, 2009; Hobolt, 2008; Dalton, 2002; Budge et al., 2001). On the one hand, the inter- and intra-party relationships have changed as the political conversation is said to have shifted from 'visions' to 'competence' (Green and Hobolt, 2008; Holian, 2004) and, on the other hand, the party-electorate linkages have come under increased strain caused by the increased diversification of actors, issues and modes of competition (Mair, 1989; 2008).

What, then, has happened since Lipset and Rokkan (1967) famously found the societal divides to have become 'frozen' around four central cleavages (church/state, centre/periphery, urban/rural and owner/worker)? Inglehart (1971; 1990; 1997; 2008), for one, has suggested that increased levels in economic affluence and increased levels of physical security have had an impact on voters' values, which, in turn, have come to influence their electoral priorities. Once the basic – *material* – needs were met, the associated values would then be replaced by higher order – and *non-material* – concerns of, for example, social equality, personal freedom(s) and quality of life issues. By identifying this development, Inglehart offered a causal link between the electorate's changing values and their changing political behaviour. These 'new' preferences would then not only be reflected in a different ranking of issues but also in an electoral demand for 'new' parties. The 'silent revolution' (Inglehart, 1977) of the mid-to-late 1960s meant that a different set of social and political norms began to emerge, which in turn became associated with an array of issues that not necessarily corresponded to the 'frozen' left-right divides. The origins of this novel cleavage can be traced back to the time when the 'new social movements' started to mobilise around issues of cultural liberalism and social justice (Della Porta and Diani, 2006; Inglehart, 1997). The conventional understandings of the non-economic divides were thus challenged and eventually grew into a 'new' line of conflict between culturally liberal and conservative/authoritarian positions. And while it was initially limited to certain lifestyle questions, it has become increasingly tied to a variety of non-material questions, ranging from the environment to personal freedom issues to nationalism and to the structure of democratic decision-making (Massetti, 2009; Elff, 2007; Dalton, 1996; Lane and Ersson, 1991).

But whether post-materialism, in fact, constituted a 'new' and distinct cleavage has been the topic of intense debate (Davis and Davenport, 1999). Kitschelt and McGann (1995; see also Kitschelt, 1994; 2000), for example, found few differences, especially on economic issues, between the 'old' and the 'new' parties and instead suggest that the 'new' area of contestation relates to a libertarian/authoritarian split that runs *diagonally* through the SI – FM dimension. This divide, they argue, has become the main source of dispute since preceding disagreements regarding state involvement in the economy have, by and large, been settled. Kriesi et al. (2006) raise similar objections. While the political space is still understood to involve a plurality of cleavages, what has changed is 'the *meaning* [emphasis added] of the conflicts associated with these two dimensions' (2006: 924). This 'new' meaning is said to stem from the clashes between the 'winners' and the 'losers' of globalisation, which, in turn, has come to structure competition along two (reinterpreted) cleavages: one *economic* and the other *socio-cultural*. Although 'old' conflicts between pro-state and pro-market positions continue to be present, it is the way that the political actors have come to perceive them that has been the key change. The winners – the well-educated and certain employers – tend to adopt a more pro-market and internationalist stance, whereas the losers, who see their job situation under threat, have often gravitated towards a more pro-state position, which tends to be protectionist as well as nationalist. Although their labels may indeed have changed, these fault lines also appear remarkably static in that the overarching issue is still about the role of the state (albeit in different spheres). However, for reasons of parsimony, Hooghe et al.'s (2002) terminology – *GAL/TAN* (green/alternative/libertarian – traditional/authoritarian/nationalist) – will be used when referring to this non-economic dimension.

These changes have thus presented the study of electoral competition with a series of challenges. Does multidimensionality give rise to any specific challenges once parties engage with atypical questions (such as the EU and/or immigration)? And if so, what effects have they had on strategies and tactics? The literature has typically focused on whether conflict takes place along single, dual or multiple cleavages (Jahn, 2010; Enyedi, 2008), and on the evolving role of ideology in the political 'game'. Van der Brug and van Spanje (2009), for example, suggest that party conflict continues to be, by and large, uni-dimensional and that it still is, broadly, connected to the SI – FM divide. The reasons for this concern the institutional constraints that parties are subjected to, and especially those stemming from the electoral system that they compete in. Additional cleavages may very well exist, but since parties are often required to form coalitions, particularly in proportional systems, they tend to cooperate with those parties that they are the closest to on the dimension of conflict they consider to be the most salient one. And since voters often consider SI – FM questions such as taxes, unemployment and the labour market to be 'the most important issues' facing the country, parties tend to prioritise these questions as well. The 'old' cleavage has therefore continued to be the dominant one, and parties will often downplay more challenging questions so as to avoid any potential coalition splits. Opposition parties, conversely, tend to be less affected by such constraints but will, equally, not have many incentives to politicise less salient issues since they can make coalition building unfeasible. While such conclusions would suggest that the SI – FM dimension, and its associated issues, are still relevant for parties and party competition, Green-Pedersen (2007) finds that West European parties have been paying less and less attention to these questions over time. Others have found that parties and electorates appear to be more concerned with the managerial aspects of political life rather than with any broader visionary quests (Thomassen, 2005). But such findings are, however, challenged elsewhere, and there have also been signs that parties are trying to re-establish themselves as ideological actors (see e.g. Jansen et al., 2013; Corbetta et al., 2009).

Competing on the EU and immigration 'issues' could therefore be less problematic for the political mainstream, and subsequently also less divisive, should contestation (still) be uni-dimensional, and should the Europhile – Eurosceptic/Liberal – Restrictive axes (still) map onto an SI – FM continuum. But such assumptions also leave some important questions unanswered. If a single fault line continues to characterise the political landscapes, why would the centre-left, but not the centre-right, be 'caught between ideology and strategy' when competing on immigration? (Alonso and Claro da Fonseca, 2012: 866; see also Hinnfors et al., 2011; Bale et al., 2010; Bale, 2008; 2003; Lahav, 1997). And why would both party families have moved closer together regarding their views on the EU? (Crum, 2007).

What is suggested herein is that not only are party systems themselves characterised by multidimensionality and a diversity of actors/issues/modes of competition but so are the EU and immigration 'issues'. This presents mainstream parties with a series challenges rooted in the multifaceted and cross-cutting nature of *both* issues. This can in turn lead to a variety of framing dilemmas (Lahav and Courtemanche, 2012; Wagner, 2012; Aspinwall, 2002) such that parties are likely to get it electorally 'wrong' and further confound party supporters with the impression of evasiveness, or limping from one strategy to the next (Scheffer, 2011). Consequently, should parties attempt to internalise 'new' questions into 'old' cleavages (Hooghe et al., 2002; Marks and Wilson, 2000), this may prove exceptionally difficult if there is intra-party disagreements regarding, for example, issue fit and societal impact. These potential obstacles may in turn run the risk of crystallising any inherent ideological tensions and bring them to the fore (Börzel and Risse, 2008; van Kersbergen and Krouwel, 2008) with the result of adverse electoral outcomes and a continued sense of loss of direction being likely outcomes. Should one therefore subscribe to the existence of multiple dimensions, and if parties adopt positions on more than one, will this then subject them to a set of conflicting ideological 'pulls' (Odmalm, 2011)?

These strains are likely to emerge when party stances on the *SI – FM* continuum run counter to their positions on the *GAL – TAN* divide. But certain positional combinations should work together more harmoniously since they provide corresponding cues on the role and remit of the state. Therefore, the degree of 'pull' could be weaker for some parties than it is for others. In other words, if parties get the balance 'right' – through a combination of either FM/GAL or SI/TAN positions – then they should be less likely to experience any significant degree of conflict on the two issues compared to what parties with an SI/GAL or FM/TAN profile will go through. The latter couplings will effectively have got the balance 'wrong' and should therefore be more likely to experience increased levels of uncertainty and internal struggle.

Such volatile ideological relationships have often been characteristic of the mainstream's dealings with the EU *and* immigration. When the SI-wings, usually present in social democratic and reformed left parties, identified the EU as a 'capitalist club', the GAL-factions, often present in Green and reformed left parties, saw increased opportunities to handle borderless problems such as environmental pollution and human trafficking. And where the FM contingents, usually present in conservative and liberal democratic parties, understood the European project to bring an expanding market base and increased opportunities for trade, the TAN-wings, often present in conservative and Christian democratic parties, feared the sustained erosion of national identity and sovereignty (Crum, 2007; Hooghe et al., 2002).

Immigration presents similar challenges. The SI-wings have often perceived it to be a wedge into their working-class constituencies since increasing the supply of newcomers has been said to contribute to undercut wages and bypass any collectively bargained salary levels (Givens and Luedtke, 2004). But for the GAL-wings, a more liberal tendency is often present because of their commitment to internationalism and a 'no borders' understanding of the world (Riaño and Wastl-Walter, 2006). A similar dilemma has also affected parties with an FM/TAN profile. The stronger the FM element is, the more liberal the stance has tended to be, given prevailing views on state-market relations. Such a position has often considered the market, rather than the state, to be 'better' at handling and determining the appropriate levels of immigration. For the TAN-wings, on the other hand, more state involvement has usually been preferred since immigration taps into concerns over national identity, crime and social order.

The risk of getting caught in an ideological deadlock could thus be significant as different factions struggle over the appropriate way to frame the EU and immigration 'issues'. These struggles may lead not only to further fractionalisation and fragmentation but also to positions being adopted that border those of their more radical competitors (see also van Spanje, 2010). The degree of ideological dissonance may of course not be the only factor that determines whether parties are conflicted (or not). Other types of institutions, especially the electoral systems that parties function in, may equally affect their behaviour (Dalton, 2002) and the degree of 'pull' that they experience. Should this be the case, then the British data, in particular, will reflect this as well with fewer instances of *ideological* strain compared to what is expected to be present in the remaining cases that have a system of proportional representation (PR). That is, the system-level differences should be more pronounced than the party-family, or ideologico-positional, differences that may exist across the board. While the book's primary aim is to analyse how parties have engaged with two key areas of contestation in Western Europe (Boswell, 2003; Taggart, 1998), it also goes beyond the pure case study (George and Bennett, 2005). If those parties that are expected to be 'pulled' do, in fact, *not* perceive these strains to pose much of a problem, then this will also allow for more general conclusions to be made regarding the extent to which ideology (still) matters to parties and for party competition.

This leads us to the first set of hypotheses that the book will explore:

H1. Parties with an SI/GAL or FM/TAN combination are *more* likely to experience conflicting ideological 'pulls' on the EU/immigration.

H2. Parties with an FM/GAL or SI/TAN combination are conversely *less* likely to experience such strains.

H3. Parties in a first-past-the-post (FPTP) system are *less* likely to experience *any* 'pulls' (SI/GAL *or* FM/TAN) compared to parties in PR systems.

If these propositions are supported, what implications will they have for party competition? Parties have certain objectives in mind when they engage in electoral competition and will try to achieve these goals by anticipating an optimal position along one or more dimensions of conflict. Their respective ideologies are one factor that can determine particular locations (Merrill, 1995; Downs, 1957), but the institutional context that parties function may be just as influential. The centripetal forces of FPTP systems should thus push parties towards the median voter position, whereas in the centrifugal PR systems parties should be more evenly spread out (Cox, 1990; Sartori, 1976).[2] The choice of party/candidate is then said to link in with the degree of proximity to the voter. Such reasoning has traditionally been applied to, and tested on, a variety of SI/FM and GAL/TAN issues but whether a similar logic also applies to positions on the EU and immigration has been less obvious. On the one hand, parties' issue placements have not always followed the pattern anticipated by their 'old' or 'new' left-right positions (Benoit and Laver, 2007). And on the other, most mainstream parties have tended to settle somewhere along a continuum of 'Eurosceptic' positions, and advocated for regulated yet properly managed immigration policies rather than for a complete stop (Taggart and Szczerbiak, 2008; Green-Pedersen and Krogstrup, 2008).

Competition may therefore not necessarily revolve around the different sets of choices that parties offer to the electorate (e.g. leaving or remaining a member/liberalising or restricting entry regulations). It may equally be about the means used to achieve the same goals (e.g. making the EU work 'better' for [country], or ensuring the effective control of borders), and which party that is considered to be the most competent at delivering on these mutually desired outcomes. This shift in strategy connects to broader trends identified elsewhere and which posit that parties are increasingly in agreement on key issues. The political struggle has thus moved from the 'positional' to the 'valence' dimension (Stokes, 1963). To emphasise the different alternatives on offer may therefore be a largely redundant option since increasing levels of issue consensus mean that parties are judged on performance delivery and perceived competence through 'the linking of the parties with some condition that is positively or negatively valued by the electorate' (ibid., p 373; see also van der Brug, 2004). But drawing attention to an issue on which there is more or less full agreement may not always be an optimal vote winning strategy (Jones and Baumgartner, 2005; Riker, 1996; Carmines and Stimson, 1993). Therefore, parties tend to focus on particular differences, especially in terms of *how* they intend to achieve these goals. Accordingly, it will be more advantageous to frame their 'choice' as party A is 'better' than parties B and C at delivering on the issue (Bélanger and Meguid, 2008; Holian, 2004; Petrocik, 1996). When it comes to making the electoral calculus, it is the party's past performance and credibility on the issue(s) that will be important for voters. Parties therefore tend to be selective and emphasise questions, or particular aspects of the question, which they are seen to 'own' while de-emphasising others (Budge and Farlie, 1983). This further means that two behavioural patterns are likely to emerge. Following a *principle of dispersion,* the party that is negatively associated with the valence issue will attempt to draw attention *away* from it even though voters may still rank it highly. And as per a *principle of dominance,* parties will instead push an issue where they have the electorate on their side (Riker, 1996). That said, the presence of ownership struggles does not necessarily mean the absence of positional competition (Green-Pedersen and Krogstrup, 2008) or even that positions are adopted, which signal neither 'competence' nor 'choice'. The latter approach would suggest that parties merely acknowledge the issue's importance but will not further specify how they intend to 'solve' or 'deal' with it.

Any scarcity of 'choice' options would partially be explained by this virtual convergence of positions, yet it may also relate to the diverse nature that both 'issues' undoubtedly inhabit. They often tend to cut across several policy and ideological domains, which, in turn, have made it difficult for parties to establish societal impact and on which cleavage to pin the 'issues' down to. This problem of fit has consequently generated different accounts in the literature. On the one hand, party attitudes towards the European project are said to be a function of their *domestic* SI – FM positioning. The former grouping tends to be more benign as long as the EU is understood to act as a constraint on the market forces. The latter, on the other hand, has 'only' come to accept 'Europe' should it serve to free up the market. But the EU has also been characterised as being a largely orthogonal issue, which does not necessarily have any connection to the SI – FM dimension, or parties' positions therein. As such, this would explain the somewhat counterintuitive positions that are adopted by some parties in some countries.

A third explanation suggests different ideological positions to reflect party stances on a *subset* of EU capabilities (Hooghe et al., 2002; Hix, 1999; Hix and Lord, 1997). To determine what type of 'issue' that immigration constitutes has been equally problematic since it not only has economic consequences but also affects ideas and perceptions of what the receiving state is, and should be, as a nation.

But as alluded to above, both issues can also be said to display certain valence characteristics. At some point or the other, most mainstream parties have expressed some form of Eurosceptic sentiment but only a minority of these have come to adopt a more hard-line approach and/or advocated for a country exit (Katz, 2008; Taggart and Szczerbiak, 2002; Taggart, 1998). Similarly, following the oil crisis in 1973, a consensus developed on halting most types of labour migration, but this was also coupled with an understanding that asylum and family reunification would continue to be potential paths of entry (Freeman, 2006; Castles and Miller, 2003). Yet, parties have also disagreed on the appropriate loci for deciding on the demand for these (skilled) labour migrants (individual firms vs. employment agencies), and whether the initial screening of asylum seekers is more effectively handled by private actors (or not) (Hinnfors et al., 2011; Banks, 2000).

Once politicised, then, it suggests competition to revolve around party A convincing the electorate that it is more competent than party B is to 'handle the EU', or how party A is the only party that can be trusted on delivering a 'responsible management of borders'. But not all parties will behave in this way. Should ideology (still) matter, in the sense of providing conflicting cues on the two 'issues', then this may also prompt parties to engage in ownership struggles. Such tactics may then enable parties to bypass any of the potential obstacles that are likely to emerge from these conflicting 'pulls', which, in turn, may jeopardise their electoral objectives. 'The winner takes it all' pressure that is present in FPTP systems may equally incentivise parties to emphasise their ability to deliver rather than to offer a choice on either 'issue'.

This leads us to an additional set of hypotheses:

H4. When issue positions converge, parties frame their stances in 'Ownership' discourses.

H5. When they diverge, positions will be framed in 'Choice' discourses.

H6. Parties subject to conflicting ideological 'pulls' are more likely to use ownership discourses than parties that are not.

H7. Parties in FPTP-systems are more likely to engage in ownership struggles than parties in PR dittos.

Manifesto analysis and interview data

In order to establish party locations in the two-dimensional space (*SI – FM* and *GAL – TAN*), and what their issue positions are (*EU* and *Immigration*), a manifesto analysis[3] has been carried out for the following parties (grouped by family) (Ennser, 2012; Camia and Caramani, 2012):

1. Religious/Christian democratic: Belgium – *Christen-Democratisch en Vlaams* (CD&V); *Centre Démocrate Humaniste* (CDH); the Netherlands – *Christen-Democratisch Appèl* (CDA); Sweden – *Kristdemokraterna* (KD)
2. Conservative: Britain – *Conservative Party* (Cons.); Sweden – *Moderata Samlingspartiet* (M)
3. Liberal/Social liberal: Belgium – *Mouvement Réformateur* (MR); *Open Vlaamse Liberalen en Democraten* (Open Vld); Britain – *Liberal Democrats* (Lib Dems.); the Netherlands – *Politieke Partij Democraten 66* (D'66); *Volkspartij voor Vrijheid en Democratie* (VVD); Sweden – *Folkpartiet Liberalerna* (FP); *Centerpartiet* (CP)
4. Socialist/Social democratic: Belgium – *Parti Socialiste* (PS); *Socialistische Partij Anders* (Sp.a); Britain – *Labour Party* (Lab.); the Netherlands – *Partij van de Arbeid (PvdA)*; *Socialistische Partij* (SP); Sweden – *Sveriges Socialdemokratiska Arbetareparti* (SAP); *Vänsterpartiet* (V)
5. Green: Belgium – *Écologistes Confédérés pour l'organisation de luttes originales* (Ecolo); *Groen Agalev* (GA); the Netherlands – *Groen-Links* (GL); Sweden – *Miljöpartiet De Gröna* (MP)

Although 'issue' impact is often discussed at both sub- and supra-national levels, deciding on which direction to pursue is usually taken at the federal/national stage. And by and large, these negotiations will be between those parties defined as 'mainstream' rather than as 'radical' or as 'extreme' (Adams et al., 2004; Meguid, 2005). The main focus is thus placed on those parties that are likely to be the 'dominant force[s] in the formation of government' (Ackland and Gibson, 2013: 235), or act as a 'junior' partner in this process (either as a full-blown coalition member or as an informal supporter in parliament), and who should therefore be in a position to influence policy and/or the agenda. This has, however, meant that a number of equally interesting actors have been excluded. These were predominantly of the regionalist kind (e.g. the *Scottish Nationalist Party* and the *Plaid Cymru* (Britain), or those that were classified as radical/extremist/far-right in the literature (e.g. *UKIP, BNP* (Britain), *Vlaams Belang* (Belgium), *Lijst Pim Fortuyn, Partij voor de Vrij*heid (the Netherlands) and the *Sverigedemokraterna* (Sweden)) or parties that were particularly small in size, especially in Britain (e.g. the *Democratic Unionist Party* and the *Greens*) but also in the Netherlands (e.g. *Partij voor de Dieren* and *Staatkundig Gereformeerde Partij*).

Party manifestos have served as a central data source for the conducted study since they 'assess the importance of current political problems, specify the party's *position* [emphasis added] on them, and inform the electorate about the course of action the party will pursue when elected' (Klingemann, 1987: 300). Both 'issues' are of course debated and discussed elsewhere too but manifestos have the added advantage of putting forward the *aggregate party position*, and are as such well suited for investigating the degree of conflict in comparative perspective (Green-Pedersen, 2007). However, one should be careful to equate 'manifesto' with 'actual party position' or, even, 'party direction' (Dinas and Gemenis, 2010; Franzmann and Kaiser, 2006; Pelizzo, 2003) and there may also be discrepancies regarding positions 'during elections', and positions 'when in government/parliament' (see e.g. Aspinwall, 2007). Indeed, conducting 'elite surveys of party politicians' (Benoit and Laver, 2007: 90) could have allowed these locations to be identified as well. But as the 'final word' prior to an election, manifestos are nevertheless what parties present to the electorate and also provide the general framework for subsequent policy proposals (Gemenis, 2012; Walgrave and Nuytemanns, 2009).

To establish party placements along the SI – FM, GAL – TAN and 'issue' dimensions, the starting point has been the model developed by Pellikaan et al. (2003; see also Odmalm, 2012; De Lange, 2007). Their measurement tool builds on Kitschelt and McGann's ideas of the two-dimensional space and seeks to capture degrees of conflict on key variables. The SI – FM dimension is thus defined as 'opposition// ... //between statements favouring the "political redistribution" of economic resources// ... //and statements favouring the "market allocation" of resources' (1995: 1). As per De Lange (2007), the following indicators have been used: (1) privatisation, (2) public sector, (3) welfare and social security system, (4) labour market, (5) taxation, (6) budget deficit and (7) trade and enterprise policies.

A hand-coded content analysis (Patton, 2002; Mayring, 2000) was then carried out using keywords to identify the quasi-sentences associated with each individual category (e.g. 'private', 'public' or 'pensions'). Should the statements 'predominantly indicate that a party was in favour of state intervention [it] receive[d] a score of (−1) on that specific issue' (2007: 420), exemplified by the following quotes:

> Alternatives and diversity – against commercialisation and privatisation.
>
> (V, 1991) ['Privatisation']

> We will immediately introduce an emergency programme of investment in the infrastructure and in public works in order to get companies and people back to work.
>
> (Lib Dems, 1992) ['Public Sector']

> [A]dditional health insurance should never replace the basic provision of health care.
>
> (CD&V, 2007) ['Welfare and Social Security System']

Conversely, when the statements suggested to be in favour of more market influence, a score of (+1) was given.

> The state is the biggest owner of businesses in Sweden. FP and the Alliance aim to privatise a couple of these enterprises.
>
> (FP, 2006) ['Privatisation']

> Open VLD wants the government to act mainly as the regulator of public services
>
> (Open VLD, 2007) ['Public Sector']

> [B]e allowed the opportunity to build up supplementary pensions in addition to the statutory one.
>
> (MR, 2003) ['Welfare and Social Security System']

Should the statements be unclear or ambiguous, on the other hand, a score of 0 was allocated as per the following excerpts:

> Modern government has a strategic role not to replace the market but to ensure that the market works properly. Other competitors in Europe and elsewhere recognise that industrial policy must be at the heart of economic policy. It is the government's responsibility to create the conditions for enterprise to thrive.
>
> (Labour, 1992) ['Privatisation']

> [E]nhance public transportation but also make the administration and public service provision more efficient.
>
> (CDH, 1995) ['Public Sector']

Financing of the health care sector should be done by everyone through taxation but the execution//...//should be characterised by diversity

(M, 2010) ['Welfare and Social Security System']

But for some of the indicators, the 'more state-more market' – dichotomy did not always work. Therefore, a few adjustments have been made. On indicators four and seven, a score of (−1) was given should the manifesto indicate a preference for more regulation, and (+1) should it prefer less (e.g. 'The market economy must be regulated//...//we want to introduce a 6-hour working day//...//' (V, 1994) (−1); 'New Labour believes in a flexible labour market that serves employers and employees alike. But flexibility alone is not enough. We need "flexibility plus"' (Labour, 1997) (+1)).

On indicator five, if the statement favoured raising taxes, a score of (−1) was given, whereas lowering taxes was scored (+1) (e.g. '[T]he decision to abolish tax on wealth should be revoked' (SAP, 1994) (−1); 'We will be a tax-cutting government.' (Conservatives, 2001) (+1)). And on indicator six, a statement that advocated for more public spending was given a score of (−1), whereas if it suggested less, it was scored (+1) (e.g. '[I]t is neither realistic nor wise to assume that the hole in our budget can be fully closed during a government's four year term. If we cut so much at once, the probability of a "double dip" recession is great' (SP, 2010) (−1); 'Reduce the budget deficit that has grown during the past administration' (VVD, 2010) (+1)).

Operationalising the GAL – TAN dimension proved somewhat more complicated. These challenges stem from how it 'encompasses several political questions' (De Lange, 2007: 420), and how it suffers from a lack of consensus regarding what the key indicators should be (see e.g. Franklin and Rudig, 1992; Inglehart, 1990). De Lange, however, points to how Kitschelt's three elements (citizenship/ethnocultural relations, individual freedoms and collective decision-making) are central to this dimension of conflict and has thus suggested the following scheme:

1. Citizenship/ethnocultural relations

   (a) *Immigration* (support for an inclusive and universalistic society (−1), support for an exclusive and particularistic society (+1))
   (b) *Integration of Cultural Minorities* (support for an inclusive and universalistic society (−1), support for an exclusive and particularistic society (+1))

2. Individual freedoms

   (a) *Diversity of Lifestyles* (support for individual freedom (−1), support for a moral government (+1))
   (b) *Ethical Legislation* (support for individual freedom (−1), support for a moral government (+1))

3. Collective decision-making

   (a) *Direct Representation* (support for more direct representation and more participation in the decision-making process (−1), support for appointed representation and hierarchical decision-making procedures (+1))
   (b) *Participation in Decision-Making* (support for more direct representation and more participation in the decision-making process (−1), support for appointed representation and hierarchical decision-making procedures (+1))

Nevertheless some challenges are still present, especially regarding the wording of some of these indicators. 'Immigration' and 'Integration of Cultural Minorities', for example, are used to measure 'Citizenship/Ethnocultural Relations', yet they appear to be more relevant for stances on 'Integration' *only* and do not necessarily capture 'Immigration' as such. There is also some inherent ambiguity with the term 'Integration' since it may *also* capture positions on 'Nationalism' and/or 'National Identity'. To dichotomise 'Diversity of Lifestyles' as 'support for individual freedom/moral government' may equally run the risk of not capturing the full range of *diversities* that exist or the impact that parties perceive them to have on society.

And, crucially perhaps, neither indicator captures the key GAL – TAN concern of 'Environmental Protection' versus 'Economic Growth'. Therefore, the second scale has also been modified, so it clearly covers 'Integration', 'The Environment' and 'National Identity' in addition to the existing categories of 'Individual Freedoms' ('Diversity of Lifestyles'/ 'Ethical Legislation') and 'Modes of Collective Decision-Making' ('Direct Representation'/'Participation in the Decision-Making').

These subsequent adjustments have thus meant a slightly different scoring system to that proposed by De Lange:

1) Diversity of lifestyles: positive (−1) or negative (+1)

Equality between men and women, equal rights and opportunities for all//...//tolerance and the right to be different.

(MR, 2003) (−1)

Those who come to the Netherlands//...//are in a society where the Judeo-Christian, and a humanist tradition and culture colour society. This means that a Western culture and the Western values are leading for Dutch society.

(CDA, 2010) (+1)

2) Supports: individual freedom (−1) or a moral government (+1)

Everyone has the right to a private sphere//...//[i]t should be a cornerstone in a free and democratic society.

(MP, 2010) (−1)

Labour will appoint an anti-drugs supremo to co-ordinate our battle against drugs across all government departments. The 'drug czar' will be a symbol of our commitment to tackle the modern menace of drugs in our communities.

(Labour, 1997) (+1)

3) Supports: direct (−1) or appointed representation (+1)

[M]ore referendums increase citizens' possibilities to influence and strengthen democracy//...//more power to local authorities.

(MP, 2002) (−1)

Mayors and commissioners remain appointed by the Crown.

(CDA, 2002) (+1)

4) Supports: individual participation (−1) or hierarchical modes of decision-making (+1)

[M]ore participatory democracy, where citizens are actively involved in public debate

(GA, 2010) (−1)

PS, however, considers community issues, which constitute a danger to the unity of our country, to be likely to bias the participatory process.

(PS, 2007) (+1)

5) National identity: less (−1) or more important to preserve (+1)

We want to protect the rights and opportunities for our national minorities to develop their own culture and language.

(V, 2002) (−1)

Revive Britain's sense of community.

(Lib Dems, 1997) (+1)

6) Supports: an inclusive and universalistic (−1) or exclusive and particularistic (+1) society

It is SP's view that everything possible should be done to help these people to integrate into our society.

(SP, 1994) (−1)

English language tests for everyone who wants to stay permanently.

(Labour, 2005) (+1)

7) More important: environmental protection (−1) or economic growth (+1)

Increasing taxes on environmentally damaging activities is not only desirable but also necessary.

(CP, 1994) (−1)

Expand airport and transport options// ... //everyone is concerned about the economy, it is important to innovate and grow.

(VVD, 2006) (+1)

Two additional 7-point scales were then set up to measure positions on the EU and immigration 'issues'. As elaborated on earlier, only a minority of parties can be said to 'fit' neatly into either a soft or hard 'Eurosceptic' category (Taggart, 1998; Taggart and Szczerbiak, 2008). They should instead fall somewhere along a continuum ranging from Eurosceptic to pragmatic to Euroenthusiastic (Kopecky and Mudde, 2002). And the manifestos should also be likely to vary regarding the 'enthusiasm' that is expressed for the different *aspects* of the European project (Hooghe et al., 2002). With these points in mind, the EU scale was designed so as to capture levels of confrontation in the following key areas:

(1) membership, (2) function of the EU, (3) integration, (4) the Euro, (5) common foreign policy, (6) enlargement and, finally, (7) Constitution/treaties

The scoring system has been comparatively straightforward and based on statements that portray an overall *Negative* view (−1)

The current drive for a political; monetary; economic and military union is only in the interests of business.

(SP, 1994) [Membership]

The EMU is an undemocratic construction//...//it is not run by the elected representatives but by independent central bankers that follow dogmatic treaty texts.

(V, 1998) [Euro]

– or an overall *Positive* view (+1)

Europe is essential for our prosperity and for our security.

(CD&V, 2010) [Membership]

Labour is pledged to do all it can to enable the first group of applicant countries to join in time to take part in the next European Parliamentary elections in 2004.

(Labour, 2001) [Enlargement]

A similar situation is likely to apply to the immigration 'issue' as well. That is, it should be rare to find instances where the aggregate sum amounts to either an exclusively 'liberal' or an exclusively 'restrictive' position. It is rather expected to fall somewhere between these two poles. It is equally expected that these positions will vary depending on what *type* of migrants that the parties are more liberal or more restrictive towards. To then capture the full range of newcomers, seven categories have been identified. These cover the 'typical' (e.g. 'Asylum Seeker/Refugees') to the 'atypical' migrant ('Retirement').

(1) asylum seekers/refugees, (2) labour, (3) family reunification, (4) unaccompanied minors, (5) students, (6) retirement and (7) immigration (in general)[4]

Apart from 'Immigration (in general)' and 'Student Migration', the same scoring system has been used throughout: (−1) if the statement indicated a more liberal approach and (+1) if it suggested a more restrictive one. For example, FP's statement in 2010 – 'Sweden should be open to labour migrants' – was given a score of −1, whereas SP's line in 2002 – 'No short-sighted imports of foreign labour' – was allocated a score of (+1). The two exceptions were scored depending on whether they were considered to have a positive (−1) or a negative (+1) impact on the receiving society.[5] And again, should statements be unclear or ambiguous (on either scale), a score of (0) is given, exemplified by CDA's 2010 view on 'Labour Migration':

Admission of migrant workers should be based upon the needs of the Dutch labour market.

and by GL's 2006 statement on 'Enlargement':

The European Union took on the promise that Turkey and the countries of the Western Balkans could join if they meet the entry requirements.

This measurement technique thus differs from that of the CMP and CHES (Bakker et al., 2012; Hooghe et al., 2010; Steenbergen and Marks, 2007; Budge et al., 2001; Ray, 1999; Laver and Hunt, 1992). While the CMP data directly reflect the stated party positions and have generated a rich time-series set (Budge and Pennings, 2007), they also contain significant methodological 'noise' since the economic and social policy positions are conflated into one, unified left-right dimension, which may exaggerate positions as well as the moves that parties make between elections (Benoit and Laver, 2007). The CHES data have tried to avoid the 'mathematically constrained nature of the saliency-based CMP left-right measure' (ibid: 103) by asking country experts to classify parties on four substantive dimensions – economic, social, loci of decision-making and environmental policy – plus a 'direct measure of party positions on a general left-right scale' (ibid.: 91). Although this method allows for more measurement flexibility, the survey is also limited by its current lack of comparative *time* points. Furthermore, the key finding suggests that 'the substantive meaning of left-right is not constant' (ibid.: 103) and, as such, appears to be highly dependent on context. This raises further questions as to what type of (comparative) conclusions can actually be drawn if the tools are not able to 'travel' between the cases.

   In contrast, the measurement technique used within is less constrained by context and also offers a more nuanced view on the key 'issue' variables. Although the CMP covers, for example, 'Membership' and 'Enlargement', it does not include any specific indicators on the 'Euro', or a 'Common Foreign Policy'. And the indicators used for immigration – 'Underprivileged Minority Groups' and 'Multiculturalism: Positive/Negative' – again do not capture such positions as much as they do integration. The CHES data, conversely, provide more detail (especially on the EU) but are also mainly concerned with 'leadership' rather than 'party' positions. And while the 2010 survey includes a general indicator on 'Immigration', it has previously been understood as 'Asylum' *only* and will as such miss to pick up any of the other categories of newcomers.

The calculations made for this book have however been compared with the CMP and CHES results for general directional fit, and the average party positions tend to fall in the same ideological sphere as the two comparative benchmarks. And none of the calculations fall into the 'CMP says "right", CHES says "left" category'. The estimations do, however, allocate some parties with a higher score. One reason for this discrepancy is because the SI – FM dimension (i.e. 'old' Left-Right) is defined in strictly economic terms, whereas for the CMP, for example, it is 'a general scale dealing with social-economic policy positions' (Benoit and Laver, 2007: 100). And since party positions are understood to be the sum of the proportion of right-wing categories minus the left-wing ones, they will naturally end up being closer to the midway point. To further ensure coding consistency, a series of inter-reliability checks were carried out. The relevant manifesto statements were initially scored by the author, or the research assistant, and then passed on to the other to score 'blind'. Some differences were identified through this process, for example, one coder would allocate a score of (+1), whereas the other would give it a (0). These instances tended to arise when the concerned quasi-sentences were particularly lengthy, thus prompting a discussion, and occasional re-coding, of the score given.

Quantifying manifestos in this way provides a positional range where the closer to (−7) the aggregate score is, the more SI/GAL/EU: negative/liberal the party's stance will be. In contrast, the closer to (+7) the score is, the more FM/TAN/EU: positive/restrictive will the position be. To then establish which parties that should be more and less likely to experience any conflicting ideological 'pull', the average SI – FM and GAL – TAN position has been taken for the 22 elections that have been studied. The respective party locations are plotted in a two-dimensional scatter diagram (see Figure 4.1), and grouped together depending on positional configuration (see Table 4.1).

To assess the party management of these 'pulls', a substantial number of semi-structured interviews were carried out with MPs or with party strategists in the four case countries (67 in total). They centred on a set of pre-arranged themes (*ideology, policy position(s)* and *party competition*) but also allowed for follow-up questions to be asked should the answers be vague or off-topic (Devine, 2002). To get as representative a view as possible, a purposive sample was drawn from those elites that were assumed to have particular knowledge of the three themes (Patton, 2002). The selection criteria included past, and current, memberships of committee/s (e.g. labour market or home affairs), position/s held (e.g. political secretary or committee chair) and time as an MP. Due to issues of access (particularly in the British case), a 'snow-balling' technique was also employed (Biernacki and Waldorf, 1981), which subsequently led to some former MPs and party strategists being approached. To minimise any steering effect that the interviewer may have had on the interviewee, open-ended questions were employed and asked in a balanced fashion (e.g. 'some parties would describe themselves as being for more state intervention in the market, while others favour more market freedom. How would you describe [party] in these terms?'). The interviews were then transcribed by the author and the research assistant and followed a 'denaturalist' approach, which removed any 'idiosyncratic elements of speech (e.g., stutters, pauses, nonverbals, involuntary vocalizations)' (Oliver et al., 2005: 173–74). And prior to being incorporated into Chapter 4, all quotes were checked for relevance and fit.

As an additional ethical precaution, all interviewees were informed that the data would be anonymised for future publications. They were also given the option to view a copy of the transcript. In a minority of cases, they suggested changes to be made. These primarily related to incorrect spelling of names and places rather than to any misinterpretation or representation of what had been discussed. Some of the validity concerns, which were likely to emerge when using qualitative data, were able to be 'controlled' for, while others proved more difficult. The material was returned 'over and over again to see if the constructs, categories, explanations, and interpretations ma[d]e sense' (Patton, 2002: 339), and special attention was paid to the latter when the quotes were applied. But the data were also revisited to try and identify emerging patterns, for example, did different interviewees portray their party's ideology in a similar fashion? Were the effects of the EU or immigration understood differently depending on age and/or role in party? Yet other aspects, for example, 'how accurately the account represent[ed] participants' realities of the social phenomena' (Creswell and Miller, 2000: 124), were more challenging as it had to be accepted that the information provided was a truthful account of these 'realities'. As such, the conducted research has made use of 'mixed methodology' (quantifying manifestos, semi-structured interviews) as well as 'mixed modelling' techniques when combining the two approaches across all stages of the research process (Tashakkori and Teddlie, 1998).

And finally, the number of interviews breakdown is as follows:

- Belgium: CD&V (2), Ecolo (1), GA (2), MR (1), PS (3), Sp.a. (2), Open VLD (2), CDH (0)[6]
- Britain: Labour (4), Liberal Democrats (5) and Conservative (9)

- The Netherlands: CDA (4), D'66 (1), GL (1), PvdA (3), SP (2), VVD (3)
- Sweden: V (4), MP (2), SAP (4), CP (4), FP (3), KD (2), M (3)

The quantitative element of the manifesto analysis has also made it possible to establish degrees of positional convergence *or* divergence (see Tables 5.1 to 5.10). In turn, this enabled certain predictions to be made for the *expected* types of competition that are likely to be present ('Ownership'; 'Choice', or 'Neither Ownership nor Choice') (see Tables 5.11 and 5.12). To establish the de facto modes of competition, some further calculations were then made (see Tables 5.13 to 5.16). If the manifesto framed either 'issue', and its associated sub-categories, using either 'Ownership'; 'Choice' or 'Neither Ownership nor Choice' discourses, the relevant box was ticked regardless of the number of times such language was present. For a statement to qualify as 'Choice', the quasi-sentence would include keywords such as 'vision' or 'wants', for example –

'Our vision is of a European Union that is decentralised, democratic and diverse'

(Lib Dems, 1997)

'MR wants a common [European] policy on legal immigration which allows the Union to meet the demands of the labour market.'

(MR, 2010)

To qualify as an 'Ownership' statement, conversely, the sentence would include more authoritative language such as 'must' or 'has to', or where the discourse very clearly signalled the party's level of competence or sustained commitment to 'issue', for example –

'Sweden must become a full member of the EC as soon as possible.'

(FP, 1991)

'Asylum claims are back down to early 1990s levels, and the cost of asylum support to the taxpayer has been cut by half in the last six years.'

(Labour, 2010)

And finally, to be scored in the 'Neither Ownership nor Choice' category, the statement would include matter-of-fact, or fairly non-committed positions, for example –

'Belgians have their hopes but they also have concerns about the state of the EU.'

(PS, 2007)

'Britain is made up of many ethnic communities. Conservatives believe that we are richer and stronger for it.'

(Conservatives, 2001)

The qualitative aspect, on the other hand, provides a more in-depth exploration of the justifications that were made to the adopted positions (see Chapter 5 for further discussion of these outcomes).

3
(Almost) Contesting the EU and Immigration (1945–1990)

As suggested in the introductory chapter, there has been ample variation regarding the degree and the sources of conflict surrounding the two 'issues'. This variation is said to connect not only to historical reasons but also to some context specific factors. Although bubbling beneath the surfaces, neither the EU nor immigration managed to fully develop into key election issues for much of the post-war period, even though several of the necessary conditions were in place. This chapter outlines the trajectories that Belgium, Britain, the Netherlands and Sweden followed up until the late 1980s, and accounts for the explanations found in the literature as to why the 'issues' never quite took off. These reasons are often linked to the external environment that the respective parties functioned in, and had to relate to (e.g. the instigator role played the Low Countries, Britain's changing position on the world stage, Sweden's commitment to neutrality, the changing patterns of international migration, the changing interpretations of citizenship and the emergence of the populist radical right). Although important for assessing the relative levels of politicisation, they also downplay the *internal* ideological processes which are likely to affect the complicated relationships these parties have had with both 'issues'.

Belgium (the EU)

To mention 'Belgium' and 'diverging views on the EU' in the same sentence is somewhat of a misnomer, and as an 'issue' it has by and large been an uneventful affair (Abts et al., 2009). Indeed, she is one of the few member states to *not* have experienced much party or public hostility towards the European project (Taggart and Szczerbiak, 2008). This remarkable level of enthusiasm can be traced back to instigator role that

Belgium had and how a clear distinction between 'the national' and 'the supra-national' was rarely made. Since the 'political and administrative heart of the EU beats in Brussels' (Deschouwer, 2009: 219–220), membership has often been taken for granted and there has consequently been few opportunities for 'Europe' to develop into an area of contention.

A similar type of supporting statements that tended to characterise the other early member states has generally applied to Belgium as well. 'Europe' was, in a sense, always there, and whether Belgium should be in or out was never really an issue (Deschouwer and van Assche, 2005; 2008). The question of membership, however, was a very much elite-driven process and one which was met by a largely supportive – yet uninterested – public. Early fears that related to any potential sovereignty trade-offs, or any pre-Treaty of Rome skittishness, were soon replaced by strong levels of support. As such, the number that has considered the EC/EU to be 'a good thing' has often been close to, or above, the 50% mark (Jadot, 2012), and continued to be well above the European averages for a remarkably long period of time (Deschouwer and van Assche, 2008).

The anticipated economic benefits also managed to trump any prevailing concerns of handing over 'too much' sovereignty to the supra-state level (Eichenberg and Dalton, 1993; Anderson and Kaltenthaler, 1996), and having become increasingly orientated towards an Atlantic defence strategy, 'Europe' became something beneficial, if not crucial, to be part of. Following the acceptance of the Treaty of Rome, any significant degree of party-based Euroscepticism has been virtually non-existent and certainly not present prior to the debates on the Maastricht Treaty. However, the cautiousness that was expressed in the immediate post-war period was not unlike that found in the Netherlands. For example, Prime Minister van Acker had not been eager to join the European Coal and Steel Commission (ECSC) and had to be convinced by foreign affairs minister, Spaak. But this early, and arguably very mild, hesitation soon gave way to very strong levels of support, which meant that by the time that the ratification debates came around, the then prime minister was complaining about the *lack* of debate (Deschouwer and van Assche, 2008).

But in contrast to their Dutch neighbours, the Belgian approach always appeared in a distinctly 'European' framework. During the first European Parliament election in 1979, for example, parties made explicit references to which left/right coalition they were a member of, and the Socialist Party even created a poster of candidate van Miert next to pictures of the Dutch prime minister, den Uyl, and the German prime minister, Willy Brandt. While discourses of being 'in the national interest' had contributed to shape party positions, they also appeared to be mixed in with a very Europeanist understanding of Belgium's relationship with the EC/EU, which consequently came to blur the distinction between the 'national' and the 'supra-national' elections. Competition, as much as there was any, therefore, became characterised by a contest between the supporters and the even more strident supporters of Europe (Deschouwer and van Assche, 2008). The list *E-NON* was the exception and actively campaigned on an anti-EU ticket but they only managed to achieve a very small percentage of votes. This left *Vlaams Blok* (VB) to be the sole electorally viable Eurosceptic party but their position was – in comparative context – on the softer side of Euroscepticism. But this stance was of secondary (or even tertiary) importance in relation to its other policy positions, and did not properly develop until the early 1990s. The Belgian party politics of the EC/EU has thus been so uneventful that it has received short shrift in the academic literature.

Belgium (immigration)

When a majority of the parties discussed in this book have either converged on a liberal position (Sweden), or become increasingly polarised (Britain, the Netherlands), the Belgian mainstream managed to reach consensus around a 'doctrine of zero-immigration' (Martiniello, 2003: 225). The emphasis was therefore placed on reducing, preventing and reversing the flows as much as possible (Koopmans et al., 2005; Jagers and Walgrave, 2007; van Spanje and van der Brug, 2007).

The Belgian 'politics of immigration' very much developed in tandem with the changing patterns of post-war migration while it has also echoed some of the responses found elsewhere in Europe (Mielants, 2006). But they have been equally influenced by a particular domestic context. The 'consociational' approach had been a response to the prevailing linguistic and religious cleavages (Deschouwer, 2009), yet these 'pillars' had begun to crumble by the 1960s and as such initiated an institutional shift that would eventually lead to the current federal system. Politically, it was the 'centrifugal forces' of the Belgian party system that would come to play a significant role here. This has further meant that a different set of 'philosophies of integration' (Favell, 1998) have been pursued in French-speaking Wallonia compared to Flemish-speaking Flanders, and (perhaps not surprisingly) a mash of the two in bilingual Brussels (Ireland, 2000).

These region-specific approaches are therefore best understood with reference to the Dutch multicultural *and* the French assimilationist model (Koopmans, 2010). Against this background, and at a time of relative calm regarding Flemish-Waloon relations, the ethno-nationalist VB gained a foothold in local and regional elections. It was their success in the late 1980s that finally pushed the federal government into formulating a more systematic policy of integration. While Belgium shares a number of characteristics with the other countries in this book (e.g. migration patterns and trends, levels of issue saliency and the rise and success of populist radical right (PRR) challengers), there have also been some key differences in terms of how the immigration 'issue' has played out in electoral and party politics.

Similar to the resistance found in the Netherlands, public and political discourses had been slow to recognise the de facto state of affairs (Loobuyck and Jacobs, 2006; Joppke and Morawska, 2003). The Belgian 'age of migration' (Castles and Miller, 2003) has its origins in the nineteenth-century recruitment of Southern Europeans to the burgeoning mining industries. As such, the post-war flows can be seen as a continuation of these historical patterns that had developed earlier on. Identifying the survival of these industries to be central to the economic success of the nation, the Belgian government entered into a series of bilateral agreements with countries around the Mediterranean basin. However, the extent to which work permits were available did often fluctuate dramatically depending on domestic economic developments and the associated unemployment levels (Ireland, 2000; Florence and Martinello, 2005). Following its formal end in 1974, small-scale asylum flows came to replace these labour migrants and thus preceded the larger wave(s) that were to follow in the 1990s (Messina, 2007). These changes were however not entirely independent phenomena. Rather, it was the closing of the 'front-door' – *labour* – route that led to alternative means of entry, such as asylum and undocumented migration becoming all the more important as the sources of newcomers.

Belgium also presents a deviant case in this context, especially regarding asylum seekers, when adopting some rather stringent approaches to entry followed by a very liberal understanding of access to certain parts of the welfare state (Baldwin-Edwards, 1991; Luedtke, 2011). Under the 1980 Aliens Act, authorities can detain any asylum applicant that does not appear to have the necessary documentation, or who originates from a country with low recognition rates. This detention can last up to the two months usually taken for the admissibility decision to be made. But once an application is deemed admissible, claimants are able to enjoy certain freedoms, usually only applicable to legally settled migrants, for example, provisional work permits, freedom of movement, some choice regarding place of residence (depending on the stage of the application procedure) and access to education and health care. These provisions are of course not always met in practice and the choices regarding housing often depend on the applicants' ability to find accommodation at market prices (Vanheule and Witlox, 2010; Banks, 2000).

Furthermore, the Treaty of Rome did come to have important consequences for the stock of (European) labour migrants. Since a significant number originated from the soon-to-be-member-states, these workers were able to change their legal (if not sociological) identity from 'migrant' to 'EU national' with the attendant workers' rights (Florence and Martinello, 2005; Martinello and Rea, 2003). As Belgium was also party to the Schengen Agreement, which endeavoured to move each signatory state towards the abolition of border controls, this made the free movement of *labour* a more practicable reality (Geddes, 2000). In more recent decades, however, inter-EU mobility has figured little on the political agendas. The notable exception relates to the debates on whether (or not) to extend voting rights to resident foreign nationals, which has become entangled with the overall question of whether (or not) to introduce similar rights to the resident *EU* migrants (Jacobs, 1999).

While border control, asylum procedures and the rules governing citizenship acquisition are all reserved for the federal government, the broader spectrum of integration policies take place in an institutionally different and remarkably more complex context since they involve both regional and local governments (Martiniello, 2012). In the postwar period, voluntary organisations played a prominent role in the provision of social services to migrants, but these duties were gradually ceded to councils set up in the different regions. The adopted policies would then come to reflect either a Dutch multicultural (Flanders) or French assimilationist (Wallonia) approach (Martinello and Rea, 2003; Yanasmayan and Foblets, 2010). By 1989, this complicated (and some would even suggest incoherent) framework was not only eclipsed but also perpetuated by the Royal Commissioner for Policy on Immigrants, which was announced in response to the electoral gains made by VB. (Downs, 2001; Fennema, 2000).

Since a relatively small number of (colonial) migrants had made any claims to citizenship, naturalisation policies were not considered to be in any need of change and therefore remained virtually intact until the 1980s. The extent to which migrants had any additional claims to labour market access, rights and privileges – beyond those already provided through their work permits – was through the status of being an EU citizen. The changes made in 1984, preceded by initial reforms relating to residency rules, were the first to affect nationality legislation since 1932. These new rules established the rights for children born in Belgium with parents of foreign origin to citizenship. However, unlike the Dutch reforms made around the same time, they did not result in any additional voting rights (Martinello and Rea, 2003; Dronkers and Vink, 2012), nor were they accompanied by any additional integration 'tests' (Corluy et al., 2011). The concerns about extending franchise, based on residency, were embedded within broader Flemish worries that residents from the other EU states could potentially sway a political advantage towards the French-speaking communities (Ireland, 2000; see also Teney et al., 2010).

These nationality changes were further accompanied by the implementation of the International Convention on the Elimination of all forms of Racial Discrimination (ICERD). Although it had been already ratified in 1975, it was not until 1981 that the Belgian government actually implemented this legislation (the so-called 'Moreau law'). The law prohibited incitement to discrimination, segregation, hatred and violence, and publication with the intention to practise discrimination, but the punishments meted out were not as severe as, for example, in France or Germany. Furthermore, the law was only applied 14 times between 1981 and 1992[1] (Van Donselaar, 1995).

As mentioned above, social service provisions were often organised through the voluntary sector, and especially through the religious ones, but the trade unions also came to play a crucial role in this process (van Rie et al., 2011). The (Catholic) unions had been particularly effective, compared to their socialist counterparts, in recruiting the South European migrants. But they also went beyond merely recruiting and integrating new members; they were also active participants when opposing the government's efforts to expel unemployed foreigners in the late 1960s. While the unions were divided along confessional/secular lines, they nevertheless shared a commitment to back migrant claims to social, economic and political rights. However, by the late 1960s, the state-organised councils were beginning to play a more prominent role. The Consultative Council on Immigration (CCI) was set up in 1965 to 'create the conditions permitting the integration and assimilation of the families of migrant workers into the Belgian community' (Ireland, 2000: 251). The CCI was composed of representatives of central ministries, regional economic councils and those provinces that contained a high number of migrants. Simultaneously, however, provincial service councils had been set up in some Walloon cities, which were then followed by similar efforts in Flanders. After gaining increased autonomy over cultural affairs in 1971, certain labour market and 'welcome' policies were devolved to the regions, which then started to play an increasingly important role in these areas (Phalet and Swyngedouw, 2003). The Walloon approach was informed by not only the French 'model' but also a more localised concept of assimilation that emphasised the political dominance of the nation-state (Martinello, 1995; Ireland, 2000). Thus, integration policies became embedded in broader discourses of what the Belgian nation should be as well as within a Walloon position that foregrounded assimilation over preserving migrants' cultural identities. The traditional strength of PS in Wallonia further helps to explain this relative hesitation towards ideas of multiculturalism. Instead of being measures that targeted specific groups, what emerged were broader policies in housing, unemployment and health care which aimed to reduce – *overall* – levels of inequality. As such, class-based notions of group identity *and* assimilationist models became the key policy determinants. Although *Front National* posted modest electoral gains in both regions during the 1980s, their presence was at most sporadic and, compared to the success of VB, relatively unimportant for the broader policy developments (Swyngedouw, 1998).

The Flemish approach, on the other hand, has had more in common with the multiculturalist policies found north of the border. Having initially rejected the presence of an 'ethnic identity' in its policy formulation, a Dutch-style model soon developed, which contained specific programmes targeted at certain migrant communities. The presence, and importance, of the strong Catholic institutions informed this more culturally based notion of identity, which was independent from immigration issues as such. A more explicit multicultural stance was therefore able to be adopted. Such a position was said to correspond 'better' to the pre-existing notions of group identity politics and the prevailing linguistic communities, while it also highlighted the societal benefits that these models could bring to the integration process itself.

In 1977, the Flemish Oversight Committee for Migration Development (VOCOM) was set up to coordinate these activities but was later replaced by the Flemish Council for Migrants (VHRM) in 1982. Though relatively modest in influence, their long-lasting impact was through the formation of local integration centres, which provided additional services (through the local public administration) or helped to set up non-profit *migrant* associations (Ireland, 2000).

Swyngedouw (1998) has been more critical of the Flemish approach. Noting initially that these policies primarily aimed to provide for the integration of the underprivileged, he then suggests that local political conditions, a total absence of visions and the use of the funds provided for programmes *other* than their original purposes resulted in a set of incoherent policies, which had little or no effect at all. Rather than providing for more effective integration, they in fact contributed to the 'ghettoisation' process and further isolation of the minority communities (see also Koopmans, 2010; Ålund and Schierup, 1991). In Brussels, the policy framework reflected the presence and influence of both linguistic communities, resulting in a patchwork system with both assimilationist and multicultural programmes, which further complicated an already-complex system (Ireland, 2000).

While the Flemish, Walloon and Brussels regions were busy pursuing 'their own' approach to integration, immigration – as a political and electoral issue – was beginning to gestate. With roots in wartime collaboration, paramilitary organisations and in the extreme right-wing politics of the 1960s, VB began as a break-off movement from the *Volksunie* (VU) in the late 1970s (Swyngedouw, 1998). Their electoral campaigns were initially based around 'classic' populist themes – appealing to (Flemish) nationalism, favouring lower taxes and fighting political corruption but immigration soon emerged as a winning issue, and by the late 1980s, it had become the dominant question for the party (Pauwels, 2011; Downs, 2001).

VB's strategy in Antwerp, for example, started with targeting rundown working-class neighbourhoods that showed high levels of crime and unemployment and (preferably) also with a high number of migrants and ethnic minorities (Swyngedouw, 1998; Ireland, 2000; Fitzmaurice, 1992). The party then pursued a 'blame the migrants' line for any number of social ills that had been identified, with clear policy solutions of repatriation and to further bring down numbers (Martinello and Rea, 2003). Their electoral success was initially limited to a few key cities, but VB aimed to build a core constituency of young, secular and lower/middle-class voters who were mainly informed by the parties' immigration and Flemish independence positions. The 1988 election was crucial for VB. It was the first time that they managed to break the 10% threshold, which was followed by further gains in other Flemish cities, notably Ghent and Brussels (De Cleen, 2009). It was also the first election in which it had more explicitly emphasised the immigration 'issue' – as opposed to independence – and which further contributed to solidify VB's position as an anti-immigrant party of the ethno-nationalist variety. Following these gains, the Belgian government announced the Royal Commission for Policy on Immigrants to start a four-year term. The commission was to pay special attention to education and to further foster integration but was also to work on a broader package of improving the structural conditions for migrant political participation, making the terms for nationality more flexible[2], standardising the system of subsidies to ethnic organisations and developing a Belgian-style Islamic 'pillar' (Bousetta, 2009; Ireland, 2000).

The behaviour of the Belgian mainstream thus displays some variation from the more general observations made by, for example, Freeman (1995) and van Spanje (2010). Although the immigration 'issue' remained a relatively low electoral priority throughout the 1980s, all Flemish parties had agreed not to cooperate with VB in May 1989. Yet, this position only held until the following June when a number of mainstream parties abrogated (Swyngedouw, 1998), and unlike the 'cordon sanitaire' adopted elsewhere (Penninx, 2005), the electoral success of VB contributed to the pursuit of divergent responses from the political mainstream and came to precipitate a more direct policy response.

Britain (the EU)

Given the recent crystallisation of positions, it is easy to overlook the ambivalent history that the British parties have had with the EC/EU (Menon, 2004). Both Labour and the Conservatives have made numerous shifts, and sometimes quite drastically so, which often meant that they have tended to reverse mirror each other. When Labour opposed the Single European Act in 1986, the Conservatives supported it, and following the Maastricht Treaty when the EC/EU became a 'Thatcherite bugbear' (Heffernan, 2001: 181), Labour started to became more pro-European.

Yet, there has also been a significant degree of overlap despite their positions diverging on domestic and international issues. Thus, parties may start out being moderately 'Eurofriendly', especially when taking up office, only to end up being suspicious and hostile once (re)entering opposition (Aspinwall, 2000; Evans, 1998). This 'awkward relationship' traces back to the multitude of 'Europes' that emerged in the post-war period, and which coincided with Britain's flagging position as a world power and with the uncertainty as to what her role should be in this new Europe. While several continental countries perceived cooperation to be crucial, it was just one of many options that Britain could pursue. This opened up for an assembly of positions, which further meant that 'Britain could afford to be Eurosceptic' (Spiering, 2004: 137). Although Heath, for example, believed that Britain's future was tied to that of the other European countries, his successors, from Wilson to Major, pursued a position of 'quarrelsome obstructionism' (Denman, 1996: 243). However, this uneasy relationship was also characterised by strong Labour antipathies and one that culminated in the 1983 pledge to free Britain from a number of Community treaties.

The necessity to retain a strong economy and linking 'Empire' to 'World Trade' was initially seen as a way of not getting too entangled in Europe, but it was also an option that would enable Britain to adopt an arbiter position. Yet, certain post-war developments had however put the role of world leader in flux. The colonies were beginning to move towards independence, which further meant that the trade patterns were beginning to change as well. Joining 'Europe' would thus become part of a wider strategy of maintaining Britain's role as a key player on the world stage. Membership was therefore seen as economically unavoidable if Britain was to survive as a global actor (Crowson, 2011). While this early rationale was based on a somewhat crude cost-benefit analysis, any potential impact on sovereignty tended to be downplayed, and would only emerge as a real source of conflict once Britain was forced out of the Exchange Rate Mechanism in the early 1990s (Gifford, 2009).

Trying to establish a coherent view of these positions has therefore proved a notoriously difficult task to accomplish. Not only have scholars struggled to find suitable definitions to work with (see e.g. Taggart, 1998; Kopecky and Mudde, 2002; Flood, 2009; Harmsen and Spiering, 2004; Leconte, 2010) but British parties have also, with the exception of the Liberal Democrats (Russell et al., 2002), often been fractionalised into small, internal blocs displaying varying degrees of scepticism. Crowson (2011), for example, suggests that Labour was split into three parts: a fundamentalist left, a revisionist right and non-aligned centre. The Conservatives have been equally splintered but conversely characterised by a large 'agnostic' centre flanked by extreme enthusiasts and hard-core opponents. And for the latter party especially, the post-membership period came with increased tensions between the camps that strongly disapproved of the European project (since if would weaken national sovereignty) and those that strongly supported it (since it would strengthen Britain's economic standing). But the more the EC/EU's competencies grew, the more problematic, and the more paradoxical, these strands became. Since there was a strong *ideological* preference for a 'globalist, deregulatory and supply-side national economic policy', this view brought it at odds with 'the inbuilt "social market" bias of the EU's macro-economic system' (Baker, 2001: 277). But at the same time, the Conservatives were also sympathetic to further cooperation on foreign policy issues since there was 'no question of any surrender of sovereignty' (Gowland et al., 2010: 107). The Labour Party was just as torn, and these strains had subsequently prompted Wilson to agree on a referendum on membership in 1975. The source of concern bordered Conservative fears of losing sovereignty, but the Cabinet was also divided over how much the EC/EU's supranational aims would impede on the government's scope for action. And added to this mix of positions was how the party's left wing viewed the Union as a 'capitalist club' and a congregation that would significantly hinder the workers' movement and further impede on Labour's nationalisation programme (Forster, 2002).

Spiering (2004) points to how prevailing institutions, and in particular the 'first-past-the-post' system, invited parties to adopt polarised positions (see also Usherwood, 2002), which meant that they would constantly position themselves as each other's opposites in order to cement these latent divides. However, the anti-marketeers – in both parties – were able to unite since they were equally unhappy with how the EC/EU could impact on, amongst other areas, parliamentary sovereignty. Baker (2001) and Gifford (2009), conversely, stress sovereignty to be the key aspect in order to understand this complicated relationship. Since Britain's experience of World War II had re-legitimised, rather than de-legitimised, the state, the need for any further integration was perceived to be a largely redundant issue.

The referendum was anticipated to yield a victory for the 'No' side since the anti-marketeers had initiated it, and the opinion polls signalled significant support for such a stance. However, competition proved to be an unequal affair since the 'Yes' camp had greater financial resources and was backed by the political mainstream (Wilson, Thatcher and Thorpe) as well as by the press and the business world. The outcome was thus positive with a two-to-one majority that favoured a continuation of membership. But this victory was however short-lived since neither Labour's internal divisions nor the national debate over Britain's membership had been fully resolved. Once the party's left wing gained more influence, they were then able to push a harsher anti-marketeer agenda. For example, the CAP was considered to be an expensive farce, Britain's contribution to the budget was seen as monstrously unfair and calls were made for tougher bargaining stances and for major Treaty revisions. If not, it would be necessary to consider a withdrawal. Between 1981 and 1983, the idea of a negotiated withdrawal became official Labour policy. But as the EC/EU developed into a predominantly *political* rather than *economic* affair, the Conservative and Labour positions also began to shift. When the former saw 'creeping Euro-federalism', increased protectionism and loss of sovereignty, the latter envisioned 'an alliance of independent nations choosing to co-operate to achieve goals they [could not] achieve alone' with the additional benefits of increased environmental protection and of consumers' rights (Heffernan, 2001: 181; Leconte, 2010).

Britain (immigration)

To be able to grasp the various positional shifts that took place in the post-war period, a good starting point is the British Nationality Act (Mycock, 2009; see also Statham and Geddes, 2006; Messina, 1989). Introduced by the Labour government in 1948, the act was a dual response: on the one hand, to the struggles for independence in the colonies, and on the other, to domestic calls for increased sovereignty (Hansen, 1999). Although the act distinguished between British subjects (citizens of the United Kingdom and its colonies) and Commonwealth citizens, it confirmed the right to enter and settle in the United Kingdom for *both* groups (Solomos, 2003; Schain, 2008). The bill was opposed by the Conservatives due to how it could potentially affect the role of the Empire. By upgrading what, in effect, was a form of local citizenry to 'full' British citizenship, the latter would become diluted and thus likely to threaten the unity of the Commonwealth. Concerns were also raised as to how these provisions could be used to discriminate against *different* Commonwealth citizens (Layton-Henry, 1980). This opposition was partly due to the Conservative's pride in Britain's imperial past but also tapped into some of the anticipated problems associated with removing the right to entry for those citizens who had served the Empire in its various wars. However, the effect of the act was not so much a movement of aliens towards a sovereign territory but rather a movement of citizens *within* an imperial polity (Hampshire, 2005). For a period of almost 15 years, persons born in colonial countries were formally permitted to enter and settle without restrictions because they were citizens of the United Kingdom *and* its Colonies. This was not the principal aim of the act, however. It was rather a constitutional exercise, which neither Labour nor the Conservatives predicted any of the British subjects to actually take advantage of.

As emigration from Britain grew, encouraged by economic as well as mobility pull-factors, questions were being asked regarding the effects that further immigration would have. James Harrison (Labour) suggested the need to control colonial entrants due to concerns over accommodation and integration issues, whereas Cyril Osborne (Conservative) referenced increasing levels of disease and crime. There is disagreement in the literature of the extent to which Labour and Conservative governments disapproved of (New) Commonwealth migration. Layton-Henry (1980) suggests that questions of control received little attention because of the complicated negotiations that were involved in the transition process from Empire to Commonwealth. The Conservatives, in particular, were sceptical towards any restrictions since these were likely to jeopardise the future – post-independence – relationships with these countries. At the same time, the party perceived Caribbean migrants to be relatively 'unproblematic' since they were quickly absorbed into the expanding labour markets. To contrast, Solomos (2003) argues that the 1948–1962 period was in fact *not* characterised by a laissez-faire approach but rather by an increasingly racialised debate, which involved several attempts of finding ways to stop these migratory flows. Dummett and Nicol (1990) echo this point and suggest that both sets of governments tended to adopt very similar views on immigration control and sought to find ways of restraining coloured immigration while, of course, not excluding migrants 'of good type'. Further complexity stemmed from the act itself, which made it difficult to establish who was a citizen (and who was not), and how citizenship acquisition was to be determined (Dummett, 2005). Moreover, both Labour and Conservative governments faced ample resistance from the colonial offices when trying to impose restrictions on those people wanting to *leave* the colonies (Spencer, 1997). Furthermore, the civil service was split on the issue. The treasury, in particular, had identified economic benefits from a more liberal approach, whereas other home departments wanted more controls to be imposed fearing increased societal unrest and turmoil.

But opposition to these unregulated flows was beginning to take root. Since these migrants primarily came for labour purposes, their settlement patterns tended to cluster around a few industrial centres. The Conservative leadership may have been reluctant to make immigration into a political issue, but on a constituency and back-bench level, critical voices were raised. Several MPs from constituencies with a high concentration of migrants were hard-pressed for service delivery and found themselves caught between newcomer and indigenous' demands. By the mid-1950s, pressures on the Cabinet for stricter controls had grown significantly while opposition to immigration had also started to gain momentum. Although the campaign for further restrictions received significant attention in the aftermath of the 1958 riots in Nottingham and Notting Hill, immigration did not become a major issue in the subsequent general election (Layton-Henry, 1980). It did, however, contribute to strengthen the faction that advocated for more restrictive regulations since the 'race riots' had transformed immigration from a regional to a national issue (Hansen, 2000). Although the debates in parliament were fierce, with pro- and anti-factions being present in both parties, the Conservative rationale for further limitations was that Britain was in danger of becoming 'overcrowded'. Labour was initially opposed to a new legislation since, in their opinion, it would be a betrayal of the Commonwealth as well as a policy that condoned racist views (Geddes, 2003). Similarly, the more progressive wing of the Conservative party saw further tightening of entry controls as legitimising racial discrimination, while the policy's strongest supporters could be found among the 'self-made Conservatives// ... //with popular authoritarian views' (Layton-Henry, 1980: 57). But a shift in the overall discourse was beginning to emerge. By the early 1960s, the acute need for labour had largely been met and the necessity to impose further controls was also beginning to resonate with the views of the public. An additional prompt was the changing composition of the migrants themselves with the Indian subcontinent gradually replacing the West Indies as the main source of newcomers (Gibney and Hansen, 2005). A key feature of the Commonwealth Immigrants Act 1962 was that the distinction between British citizens and its colonies, and those who held passports from independent Commonwealth countries, was clarified. Controls were consequently imposed on all Commonwealth migrants *except* for those who had been born in Britain, held British passports issued by the British government or were included in the passport of a person allowed entry under these two criteria (MacDonald and Blake, 1995). The act further reduced numbers by instituting a work permit system. This divided all future Commonwealth migration into three tiers: (1) migrants with pre-arranged employment, (2) those with special skills in short supply, and (3) everyone else (but with preferential treatment for war veterans).

However, several interest groups, and the pro-Commonwealth lobby in Parliament, had pushed for the act to include possibilities for family reunification, especially for wives ('dependents') and children under 16. This drastic change was implemented on short notice and without the approval of the affected New Commonwealth governments. Although the act aimed to reduce flows, it did in fact serve to stimulate further secondary migration. An additional feature of the 1962 act was how British citizens, living in the newly independent commonwealth countries, were exempt from these controls if they held a British passport. This unexpected 'bonus' applied primarily to the white settlers in East Africa but would also come to affect a large number of Asians living in Kenya and Uganda.

Although Labour had initially been critical to these changes, there was also a significant level of intra-party disagreement on the issue of control. The party's GAL wing considered further restrictions to go against key ideals of internationalism and racial tolerance, and further saw the Commonwealth as an important tool for future interstate cooperation. The SI wing, on the other hand, was keener to impose more restrictions since they wanted to avoid any further tensions to develop between the indigenous and the new – *ethnic* – working class. However, Labour very quickly adopted a similar view to that of the Conservatives when it realised that marginal seats could be at stake (Smith, 2008). Although a pro-Labour swing took place at the national level, the Conservatives made significant gains on the constituency level when pursuing a harsh anti-immigration campaign (Geddes, 2003). By the mid-1960s, immigration had developed into a key concern for Labour, such that it was identified to be a potential vote loser. When elected in 1964, the Labour government decided to regain control over the 'issue' and did not only renew the act but also tightened entry controls.[3]

In the post-act period, political attention would thus shift away from 'immigration' and onto 'integration' since the idea that immigration had to be firmly controlled was becoming the consensus view. The Labour government had worked hard to remove the 'issue' as a potential source of internal division by accepting Conservative proposals to amend the Race Relations Bill. The then home secretary, Roy Jenkins, had been the driving force behind the new and more encompassing Race Relations Act, which came into effect in 1968. The new act would also cover discrimination in the labour and financial service sectors. But the expectation that immigration had become a settled issue was, however, short-lived. A successive series of independence strives and the 'Africanisation' policies that were introduced in Kenya and Uganda sparked new migratory waves. Although the 1962 Act should have prevented the East African Asians from entering, Hansen (1999) suggests that this was in fact made possible because their passports were issued by the high commission rather than by the colonial administration. Their rapid exodus, and coupled with Enoch Powell's 'rivers of blood' speech, would thus reignite the debate. This unexpected, and arguably unwanted, situation once again brought up the close relationship between 'immigration' and 'citizenship'. It was also realised that the act had, in effect, penalised white settlers when restricting the entry for Commonwealth citizens. The Labour government was also starting to feel the electoral, as well as Conservative, pressures to reform the act. The outcome was the Commonwealth Immigrants Act 1968, which was proposed, debated and passed in just three days. The act introduced further restrictions and with the East African Asians in mind established that unless (1) born in Britain or (2) with at least one parent or grandparent being born, adopted, naturalised or registered in Britain as a citizen of Britain or its colonies, entry was subject to immigration control (Solomos, 2003). But the act also introduced a non-statutory voucher scheme, which allowed heads of households, in possession of a British passport, to settle with their dependents. Although the scheme aimed at bringing down numbers, the primary and secondary flows did in fact continue, which was largely made possible because of this clause. The act did therefore pose additional – electoral – problems for Labour. A fear of losing votes was twinned with an equal amount of anxiety of also losing the 'ethnic vote', which the party had previously been the main beneficiary of (Thorpe, 1997).

Yet, these reforms did almost immediately encounter some unexpected consequences. A substantial number of the Kenyan Asians found themselves being sent back and forth since no country would in effect recognise them as 'their' citizens (Hussain, 2001). Although the Conservatives had not opposed the bill as such, there was nevertheless significant disagreement within the party. The bill went against a pledge that had been made by the previous Conservative government, that the Asian community's right to enter Britain would be respected should Kenya adopt hostile policies (Hansen and King, 2000), and further splintering was to follow when the Race Relations Bill was proposed in April 1968. Critical voices were also raised regarding the lack of rights for those refused entry, and regarding the absence of an appeals procedure. As a response, the Labour government introduced the 1969 Immigration Appeals Act, which allowed appeals to be made against the immigration authorities. Powell's re-emphasis on the immigration 'issue', his subsequent departure to the Ulster Unionists and the discussions surrounding the acts came with further electoral implications. First, it mobilised the ethnic vote in Labour's favour and contributed to a higher turnout among these groups. Second, it tied immigration more closely to the Conservatives in the view of the public. (Layton-Henry, 1980).

There were nevertheless some unresolved issues with the 1968 Act. In particular, these concerned the question of who 'belonged' since it was still difficult to determine who was returnable to Britain and who was not. More importantly, the existing immigration regulations were also a matter of confusion since two sets of controls were in place: one for aliens and one for British subjects and Commonwealth citizens (Dummett, 2005). In the subsequent general election, the Conservatives campaigned to end large-scale immigration, and the 1971 Immigration Act was presented as the key measure to achieve this aim. However, the act also contained a provision, which established the right for already-settled migrants to be joined by their immediate family and which, in effect, counteracted its aims. But the act's main contribution was that it made no distinction between Commonwealth and non-Commonwealth migrants, and how it further clarified the concept of 'substantial connection' so as to more obviously separate those who had the right to settle from those who did not.

Although Powell had called for even stricter measures to end all family reunification and to further encourage repatriation, the Heath administration strongly resisted. Such a position was made possible due to the bipartisan agreement that emphasised how immigration should be controlled and limited while integration was to be strongly encouraged (Hansen and King, 2000). The 1971 Act introduced the definition of 'patriality', which stressed the ancestral and territorial aspect of belonging. The act also gave persons with a British-born grandparent privileged access to entry. It furthermore allowed Britain to practise a racialised policy by 'stealth' (Freeman, 2006) since the act excluded almost all (non-European) New Commonwealth migration while admitting most of the (European) Old Commonwealth migrants. As such, it effectively tore down the last remaining barrier between British and Commonwealth citizens when putting the latter on par with all other types of migrants in terms of entry restrictions. Although Powell's claims were not formally adhered to, the act did nevertheless contain several elements that can be interpreted as being distinctly 'Powellian'. The employment voucher scheme was, for example, replaced by a system of work permits, which did not give the primary migrant or his/her dependents the right to settle permanently. The act also included the possibility of financial provision for voluntary repatriation (Layton-Henry, 1980). The bipartisan consensus had a remarkable longevity and managed to survive the Ugandan Asian crisis in 1973, the rise of the National Front as well as Margaret Thatcher's 'swamped by people of a different culture' speech in the late 1970s.

When Powell withdrew from political life in the mid-1970s, a political vacuum emerged. As such, the support for the National Front increased, but it also meant a shift in emphasis towards issues of 'race relations' as well as further attempts to (re)capture the ethnic vote. These changes resonated particularly well with the Conservative party, which had set up special constituency units to target the West Indian and Asian communities. Labour, on the other hand, was still experiencing some conflicting sentiments towards the resident migrants. On the one hand, there was the party's pro-migration wing, and on the other, there was the Trade Union Congress. While the unions had already been in favour of free movement by the time of the 1961 Commonwealth Immigrants Act, and had denounced the 1971 Act for being racially discriminatory, they had, in principle, also accepted the stricter controls that were proposed (Freeman, 2006). Nevertheless, both parties continued to converge, with Labour's Green Paper (1975) being virtually identical to the Conservatives' 1972 proposal on nationality (Dummett, 2005). With immigration (once again) falling off the electoral radar screen, attention (once again) turned to integration and the Race Relations Act 1976 was passed without much Labour opposition.

With Thatcher's entry, the Powelling sentiments had resurfaced. Although tapping into populist concerns over the 'forgotten' (white) working-class, the Conservatives had simultaneously recognised the need for a more liberal line on race so as to appeal to the Black vote (Messina, 1985). The Conservative's move towards a more nationalist rhetoric was in an attempt to mediate the consequences of a neo-liberal reform agenda while protecting British national sentiments (Boswell, 2003). Appearing 'tough on immigration' would coincide with the gradual decline of support for the National Front, and the immigration 'issue' reached full circle when it, once again, became strongly associated with the party.

In order to deal with the perceived 'dangers' of the already-settled ethnic communities, the Conservatives tightened the 1971 Act and also set out to prevent any future flows of dependents and marriage partners (Gordon, 1985; see also Kicinger, 2004). An additional goal was to deal with some of the inherent contradictions that the citizenship legislation still contained. Although the various acts had effectively brought down most of the primary numbers, resident subjects were still in possession of several rights that were associated with a British citizenship. These included voting, standing for parliament, working in public service and serving in the armed forces. Since discrimination in favour of citizens of a sovereign state was acceptable under international law, the way to resolve this unwanted situation was to construct a narrower definition of nationality (Layton-Henry, 1994). These changes were introduced in the 1981 Nationality Act. This piece of legislation served to rationalise British citizenship, and gave nationals the automatic right to take up residence. A new definition was thus created by dividing the overarching category of 'Citizen of the United Kingdom and Commonwealth' into three subcategories: British citizen, British Dependent Territories citizen and British Overseas citizen. These distinctions further strengthened the racial connotations of previous divisions when disguising them within the overall framework of 'British citizenship' (MacDonald and Blake, 1995). These changes only marginally managed to bring down the number of migrants but they nevertheless (re)emphasised that Conservative policies were more effective than those of the previous Labour government. Again, the stated aim was to create and maintain healthy race relations through the halting of further immigration. By the mid-1980s, policies had become more coherent while support for the National Front had been undercut by the Conservative's emphasis to continue with further restrictions. Additional changes in 1988 meant that the right for primary (male) migrants (settled before 1973) to bring their families was repelled. The British Nationality Act 1981 substantially diluted the *ius soli* principle in favour of *ius sanguinis*, rationalised the post-war nationality laws and further legitimised the 1962–1980 waves of restriction. The act thus removed any ambiguities in the nationality and immigration legislation. As such, it marked the 'final word' in the debate on post-war colonial migration, and in a similar vein to what was happening in other West European countries, the discussion headed in the direction of asylum seekers and refugees (Haste, 2006). These questions came to dominate political discourses up until early 2000s when labour migration made a comeback.

The Netherlands (the EU)

The degree of politicisation has been comparatively weak and an issue of low priority for both the electorate and for the political elites. To speak of a distinct *EU* dimension of conflict, from the post-war period through to the early 1990s, is therefore somewhat of an exaggeration. However, beneath these elite agreements, and the 'permissive consensus' that prevailed, a few items still managed to develop into (relative) sources of conflict.

Prior to signing the Treaty of Rome, the concept of a federated, or integrated, Europe was met with some reservation, and subsequent

Dutch governments came to resist several variations of these French-led plans. However, these early hesitations were soon superseded by strong, pro-integrationist stances. And much like in Belgium these positions were put forward under a banner of 'of national interest', and where the economic benefits of increased supranational cooperation were frequently stressed. The elites' generally pro-EC/EU positions were similarly reflected (or at least not challenged) by an equally high level of public support. A variety of explanations have been put forward for this backing, and range from those referencing particular socio-geographic factors to the purely economic. As such, 'Europe' developed into an issue of sustained low saliency during the national elections, and rarely garnered much attention from the mainstream parties. Indeed, any resistance or antipathy has been virtually non-existent, and neither the radical left or right parties, which would later develop such stances, were sufficiently focused or organised on the issue (Kriesi, 2007).

Although Eichenberg and Dalton (1993) refer to the Dutch as traditional supporters of international organisations, Hylarides (2001) suggests this to be a more recent phenomenon. For the first half of the twentieth century, the Netherlands adopted a stance of principled neutrality. This position was partly based on a Calvinist worldview but also on a crude national self-interest since Germany could not protect Dutch maritime interests and the British would not be able to support their territorial integrity. Neutrality was further manifested in the position taken up during World War I, and for the belated membership in the League of Nations. However, the failure to uphold such a position, especially following the German invasion in 1940, marked the end of this policy. By the mid-1940s, Dutch governments began pursuing a variety of agreements, especially with Belgium and Luxembourg, which would later result in the establishment of a free-trade zone between these three states. Yet, Hylarides also notes how these agreements had been produced with an overarching aim of improving international *cooperation* rather than *integration* as such. Indeed, these had been scaled back from earlier, more ambitious, proposals due to Dutch worries about how a more integrationist outcome was anticipated to have negative implications for the domestic economy.

After the Schuman Declaration, which proposed further cooperation in the coal and steel sectors, the successive Dutch governments started to become more welcoming. The expected – *economic* – benefits were however tempered by concerns over how much such agreements would impact on national sovereignty. These objections were later addressed through Dutch proposals that requested a European Council of Ministers that was to link national governments to the high authority proposed by Schuman. Although resisting the proposed plans for a European Defence Community (EDC), Dutch governments eventually began to support these plans (although in the end, the EDC was voted down by the French Assembly, making the Dutch position moot). The events surrounding the Suez crisis marked the final transition from 'wavering support' to a 'fully-fledged, pro-integrationist' position. Since many European states were constrained by the strenuous Soviet–US relations, the only way to contest a diminishing (national) influence in international affairs was to invest heavily in an increasingly integrated Europe. The ratification of the Treaty of Rome signalled the official end to this brief – and comparatively mild – Euro-hesitant period. By the 1960s, clear preferences were expressed that strongly supported the development of supranational institutions as well as the 'Community model' more broadly (Harmsen, 2004).

A continuous theme running through the Dutch party politics of the EU was how membership, cooperation and integration were all framed within a discourse relating to the national interest. Membership was often portrayed as a matter of economic advantage as well as contributing to the country's leverage in the international arena. Regarding the former, especially, these benefits were linked to the creation of a free trade zone and the ECSC but also to how the Netherlands was a net recipient of community funds (Harmsen, 2004). Since maritime and trade issues were of long-standing importance, the identified economic 'bonuses' fitted nicely within broader historical and foreign policy frameworks. As one of the continent's smaller states, supporting a distinctly European project further corresponded to ideas that saw supra-national institutions and cross-national cooperation as crucial for increasing the country's influence (Eichenberg and Dalton, 1993).

These positive *elite* views were also echoed in the attitudes of the Dutch electorate. Public opinion has consistently been on the more Euroenthusiastic side, with approval rates being among the highest of any member state (possibly only rivalled by Belgium). The proportion considering Europe to be 'a good thing' has generally hovered around the 70% mark (Harmsen, 2004). When support for the EC/EU generally went down across Europe following the economic woes of the 1970s, the Dutch continued to be one of its strongest supporters (Eichenberg and Dalton, 1993; Anderson and Kaltenthaler, 1996). By the same token, any significant (party) opposition remained pretty much non-existent up until the 1990s, and the three main Eurosceptic parties – PS (on the left), Lijst Pim Fortuyn (LPF) and Partij voor de Vrijheid (PVV) (on the right) – had yet to mobilise and attract sufficient electoral clout to be serious contenders. The former, corresponding to a typology of party motivated by concerns over labour market integration (Hooghe, 2007), had yet to materialise in its current format and did not win a parliamentary seat until 1994. Its predecessors, the Communist Party, had equally not posted any significant gains in either local or national elections during the 1980s, while LPF and PVV were not in existence prior to 1990.

The Netherlands (immigration)

When studying the Dutch 'politics of immigration', two features stand out: first, a rapid transformation into one of the vanguard countries for recognising *ethnic diversity* in public policy-making (Entzinger, 2003; Lucassen and Penninx, 1997; Kymlicka, 1995), and, second, a distinctively *Dutch* understanding and approach to these 'multicultural' policies (Vasta, 2007; Statham et al., 2005; Spiecker and Steutel, 2001). This context-specific interpretation is particularly important since the adopted policies did not emerge in response to the increasing and changing patterns of migration. Instead, certain pre-existing institutions – the *pillars* – were adapted and applied to this 'new' environment, creating what has arguably been a unique model of migrant integration (Duyvendak and Scholten, 2012; Vermeulen and Penninx, 2000).

Most interestingly, perhaps, is the broad consensus that prevailed between the political elites (Thränhardt, 2009). Penninx, for example, emphasises how ethnicity was 'systematically depoliticized by removing it from the political agenda and defining it as a (pseudo-)scientific or administrative problem' (2005: 40). As such, immigration was quite clearly steered towards the corporatist realms of the Dutch Scientific Council for Government Policy (WRR) (Scholten, 2009). This further meant that the political parties most often did not play a significant role in driving neither the immigration nor integration debates. Nor did they tend to emphasise the issue/s due to a virtual agreement of not letting the PRR parties play the migration card (Penninx, 2005). This deliberate exclusion managed to persist up until the end of the 1980s. The behaviour of the Dutch parties has thus been in line with the Belgian and Swedish experiences, that is, the political mainstream will aim for consensus and attempt to remove the immigration 'issue' from the electoral agenda as much as possible (Freeman, 1995). Yet, given that all of this was happening during a period of increasing partisan de-alignment, and a self-conscious re-evaluation of the Dutch party system (Wolinetz, 1988), the success of this 'cordon sanitaire' is all the more puzzling. Although the famous 'Ethnic Minority' (EM) policy has been re-evaluated in recent years – either as a policy 'failure' (Koopmans, 2010) or for not being *that* multicultural after all (Entzinger, 2003) – it nevertheless represents the enduring viability of a consensual model for decision-making (but see also Pellikaan et al., 2007). During the implementation stages in 1979, for example, the ruling VVD/CDA coalition appointed a minister from the *opposition* party, PvdA, to oversee the coordination process (Penninx, 2005).

The relatively late start in recognising the – de facto – state of migrant affairs was pre-empted by a national narrative that emphasised emi-, rather than immi-, -gration, and one which drew inspiration from historical trends as well as from the more immediate post-war departures to 'the New World' (Entzinger, 1985; Lucassen and Penninx, 1997). These understandings would later affect the framing of public policies and how they came to relate to 'ethnic minorities' rather than to 'immigrants' per se. Coupled with an expectation that the labour migrants would eventually return home, it was not until the late 1970s that the WRR recognised 'immigration' as a distinct policy area in its reports (Geddes, 2003). Since Dutch society was already structured around a series of 'minorities' – either ethno-religious (e.g. the French Huguenots and European Jews) or secular/confessional (Catholic, Protestant and Humanist communities) – the necessary *institutional* conditions were already in place to facilitate the 'pillarisation of immigration' along the lines of what the WRR had recommended.

The 'pillars' had traditionally been responsible for providing cradle-to-grave services to their members. However, they also went beyond the role of being a pure welfare provider when simultaneously organising other 'services' such as media outlets, civil society organisations and participation through workers' unions and parties. Indeed, these building blocks served as the basis for the Dutch corporatist system, which enabled further coordination across the different segments of society (Geddes, 2003; Lijphart, 1975). Although this pillarisation was crucial in shaping the pursued policies, its declining relevance would have important implications for the series of policy shifts that took place from the late 1980s onwards (Scholten, 2012).

The Dutch migratory experience can be divided into four relatively discreet periods: first, an initial out-flux of administrators, settlers and natives from the former colonies; second, a labour migration phase that dominated the 1950s and 1960s but which gradually diminished by the mid-1970s; third, a distinct shift towards asylum seeker and refugee migration in the 1980s; and, finally, a continuous wave of intra-EU migration. In effect since the Treaty of Rome, these EC/EU citizens were able to work and live in the Netherlands with few restrictions to their movement and employment arrangements. Unlike the other categories, however, these migrants were often more temporary in nature, and tended to be excluded from the 'ethnic minorities' model (Hollifield, 1992; Geddes, 2000; 2003).

As in Britain, the early post-war flows originated from the (former) colonies (Surinam, the Dutch East Indies (Indonesia) and the Dutch Antilles) but also included repatriated colonists. Many of these were able to claim Dutch citizenship through the myriad of individual policies that were in place, at least for an initial period of time. These flows did not trigger an immediate need for a nationality policy per se since they shared a modicum of familiarity with the Dutch language and culture, which thus distinguished their position from the latter flows of labour migrants and asylum seekers. Following a brief recession in the 1950s, the economy grew fast enough to necessitate a programme of sponsored labour migration. The efforts of Dutch industry, facilitated by several bilateral agreements, resulted in the inflow of 'temporary' guest workers from the Mediterranean basin, particularly from Turkey and Morocco (Entzinger, 1985; Odmalm, 2005).

Asylum applications picked up again by the mid-1980s. However, it wasn't until the 1990s that it developed into an 'issue' since the main policy concerns connected to the lower levels of integration of the *previous* migrant groups (Penninx, 2005). These policies were regulated under the Geneva Convention, which stipulated the terms and conditions for refugee status. The Dutch state had often recognised additional claims on humanitarian grounds, or where it was untenable for a person to be returned to their country of origin (Geddes, 2003), although – as became more apparent in the 1990s – decisions on these cases were often slow to be decided, as well as appealed upon (Penninx, 2005). What had started out as a relatively friendly gesture towards – *political* – refugees had by the late 1980s become a policy that was 'humane, but austere' (Geddes, 2003: 112), or what Penninx (2005) describes as a 'sober', welcome with only a minimum of housing and welfare provided for and with no access to the education or labour markets (see further Toshkov and de Haan, 2013; Hatton, 2009).

When the multiculturally orientated policies were finally introduced in 1979, they came in the form of an 'Ethnic Minorities' agenda rather than one that related to 'immigration' and/or 'integration' specifically.

And rather than covering all migrants, they targeted those identified to be 'problematic', in one way or another, for Dutch society and who suffered inequalities in their access to housing, education and/or on the labour market. A number of migrants, including the repatriated (white) colonialists and the intra-EU migrants, were essentially excluded from these measures (Entzinger, 1985), leaving the Moluccans, Surinamese, Turkish and Moroccans as the key target groups. Although these policies aimed to stimulate further integration, their very existence was said to have a 'minoritising' effect (Geddes, 2003), since the groups in question were often categorised as a foreign 'other' outside of the Dutch 'imagined community' (Anderson, 1983).

The groundwork for WRR's input had already been laid in 1976 by the Advisory Committee on Research Related to Minorities (ACORM), but the latter committee was located in the Ministry of Culture, Recreation and Social Work and as such had relatively little influence (Penninx, 2005). The WRR's conclusions and recommendations were conversely adopted almost verbatim by the Dutch government and formed the backbone for the EM policies of 1980, 1981 and 1983. Crucially, the EM Report called for cross-departmental coordination and implementation, resulting in a comparatively large group of players being involved in the immigrant-related policies.

The WRR's report thus called for a pluralistic approach to integration that was to be rooted in the existing 'pillar' structure and the politics of accommodation. It further contained three key aims: equality in law, equality in opportunity and emancipation (Geddes, 2003). The EM policy also suggested speedier access to local voting rights, and a clear pathway to citizenship. It furthermore aimed to end direct, and indirect, discrimination in housing, education, employment and health, and to create opportunities for participation proportional to the ethnic group's size. In this respect the Dutch approach has been similar to the race relations legislation that was pursued in Britain (Geddes, 2003). Finally, the report also called for emancipation. This was characteristically done through extensive funding of an *ethnic* civil society (Vermeulen and van Heelsum, 2009), by catering for mother tongue education and by subsidising religious organisations. Maintaining and strengthening the minority identity was conceptualised not only as a matter of equality but also as a source of strength for the Dutch society *as a whole* (Vermeulen and Penninx, 2000). This gave the 'ethnic' organisations a key role to play in the policy formulation and implementation stages.

A public recognition of the poor integration results led to the request of second report (Penninx, 2005). Released in 1989, it provided a strong critique of earlier policies. Most pointedly, the main objection was that there was too much emphasis on 'multiculturalism'. Rather than stimulating further integration, the report argued how these policies could in fact consolidate prevailing inequalities on the labour market and in the educational sector (Geddes, 2003). Although the report did not have the same immediate impact as its counterpart in 1979 had had, it nevertheless preceded and framed the later, more substantial, changes that would take place in the 1990s (Scholten, 2010).

Sweden (the EU)

Alongside Britain, Sweden has been classified as 'one of the outposts of Euroscepticism' (Archer, 2000: 87; see also Harmsen, 2005; Sitter, 2001; 2002; Taggart and Szczerbiak, 2002; Gstöhl, 2002; Ringmar, 1998; Miljan, 1977), a title she held up until to the end of the Cold War. A combination of factors has been put forward to explain this particular position. For much of the post-war period, it related to a desire of remaining as a neutral actor on the world stage. To be part of any type of supra-national organisation was thus out of the question (Ringmar, 1998). This 'non-membership' consensus cut across party lines as well as ideological affiliations. Although parts of the centre-right, most notably M and FP, did not exclude the idea of *eventually* joining, the question of neutrality was so well engrained that any discussion of membership was largely absent in the political conversations. Saliency levels were consequently low and remained as such all the way from Erlander's 'Metall-speech' in 1961 through the (bilateral) free trade agreement of the early 1970s up until the late-1980s when the *political* integration of the EC/EU became a more tangible reality (Widfeldt, 1996; Manners and Sorensen, 2007).

There have been further similarities with the British case. Regarding trade, for example, belonging to the free trade 'Seven', as opposed to the Community 'Six', was considered to be enough. And since there was also a strong belief in Sweden's post-war success story, it meant few incentives, or needs, to join for *economic* reasons (Bjurner, 2003). And even though SAP had managed to maintain Erlander's earlier position – that membership was incompatible with Sweden's goal of neutrality – the party had become increasingly split over time. The pro-faction recognised the economic benefits that membership could bring to a small, export-oriented country, and how being on the inside would provide further opportunities to push for key social democratic values beyond that of the national border (Lawler, 1997). But others saw membership as challenging the very foundations of Sweden's national identity, that is, 'the people's home' with full employment, universal welfare provision and a centralised wage-bargaining system. Becoming a member would not only have implications for the long-standing policy of non-participation in alliances during peacetime allowing for neutrality during wartime but also be likely to jeopardise the successful 'Swedish model' as such (Gstöhl, 2002).

The idea that the Union could erode these *Social Democratic* achievements was also firmly rooted among certain elements of the trade unions. Those with a predominantly national focus, for example, the Municipal Workers' Union, had argued against membership, whereas those that were more export orientated, for example, the Metal Workers' Union, tended to be more positive. A running argument for the latter was how numerous Swedish firms had already begun to establish themselves on the internal market. This situation was said to make it economically impossible for Sweden to remain as an outsider (Bieler, 2002).

For V, in particular, 'Euro-opposition ha[d] been a key note' since the 1950s (Christensen, 1996: 533), and the EC/EU – as well as the European Free Trade Association (EFTA) – was seen as instrumental in the creation of a more capitalist Europe. While the party was keen to promote free(r) trade on a *global* level, joining a distinctly *regional* scheme was not associated with any obvious socialist outcomes. The tension between rejecting (regional) economic and military integration while strongly supporting (international) cooperation consequently put the party in a rather peculiar position (Sitter, 2001). Yet, the EFTA affiliation had already meant significant trade with the member states, and moving towards the single market was anticipated to generate a further positive impact on Sweden's economic capabilities. The end of the Cold War pointed to how maintaining neutrality was becoming increasingly irrelevant, and coupled with the economic crisis that was on the horizon, the question of whether to join or not was becoming difficult to avoid. Although SAP was just as worried about how membership would affect Sweden's self-determination, V had very clearly identified national autonomy as being the first casualty. The expectation was that the EC/EU would get involved in certain domestic affairs – the state's retail monopoly on alcohol especially (Miles, 2001) – but also that membership was likely to bring further negative effects on welfare provision, gender equality and employment conditions (Gould, 1999). The concerns over holding on to national sovereignty, and the need to maximise parliamentary scrutiny of the associated directives, were not just limited to the parties on the left but were also issues that were raised *across* the political spectrum. To adopt a hard-line position, and emphasise the threat that supranational integration presented to the welfare state, was a stance that appealed to the disappointed SAP voter (Blomqvist and Green-Pedersen, 2004) but was also a strategy that could facilitate V's reinvention following the collapse of communism (Raunio, 2007). The party's emphasis on retaining national control was later echoed in the Euro-referendum campaign of 2003 when V was one of the strongest opponents to the common currency (Jonung, 2004). MP overlapped with V on issues of internationalism, especially regarding further cooperation on environmental issues, and was equally adverse to membership albeit for different reasons. Their central concerns related to issues of democratic governance and control. Joining was considered as likely to undermine national strives for further grass-roots participation and could also run the risk of increasing the militarisation of Europe (Jahn and Storsved, 1995; Raunio, 2007).

These weak (SAP) to strongly expressed Euroscpetic views (V, MP) provide a sharp contrast to the more (over)enthusiastic positions of the centre-right. M and FP were particularly keen to join, and the latter had been especially vocal about the benefits that the single currency and further enlargement would bring. Both parties had remained unconvinced by the official standpoint that membership was incompatible with neutrality (Widfeldt, 1996). Although CP was in principle partial to the idea of a Swedish membership, it was also hesitant towards the EMU and would not take a firm stand until the terms of accession were known (Kite, 2006). In that sense, they constitute the only centre-right party in Sweden that can be labelled as Eurosceptic (Raunio, 2007). This ambivalence traces back to the early 1960s when the party was strongly opposed to membership and raised similar objections to that of SAP. And more so than their bourgeois' partners, CP was also subject to the newly developed cleavage that pitted a pro-membership centre (the party elites) against an anti-membership periphery (the grass roots and the farm owners). By the early 1990s, however, the Federation of Swedish farmers had come to recognise the economic benefits of joining and would come to serve as the catalyst for CP's shift to a more Eurofriendly position (Batory and Sitter, 2004).

But the application era was also characterised by a rising level of public scepticism, which very much ran counter to the increasingly pro-EU position of the political elites (Lindahl and Naurin, 2005; Johansson and Raunio, 2001). Therefore, the EU 'issue' not only split the party system into pro/anti-factions but also constituted a significant headache for the parties themselves when they had to negotiate with the rank-and-file over which direction to take.

Sweden (immigration)

In contrast to the linear trajectories and confrontational approaches found among the other countries in this book, change *and* consensus have come to characterise the party politics of immigration in Sweden. Although legislation has gone through a series of shifts, with liberal approaches following more restrictive ones (and vice versa), these changes were often not preceded nor followed by any significant degree of party conflict. The corporatist arrangements are said to explain this remarkable level of cross-party agreement but also help us to understand why immigration has rarely been a politicised issue (see e.g. Boréus, 2006; Lindvall and Rothstein, 2006; Dahlström, 2004; Rydgren, 2004; Schall, 2004; Hammar, 1999; Brandorf et al., 1996).

Following a longer period of emigration, inward pressures had started to build up in connection to World War II. Although Sweden remained as a neutral actor, certain moral obligations still prevailed and borders were kept open, particularly towards the neighbouring states. However, the Swedish approach was somewhat contradictory which would become apparent when it engaged with the German Jews. When most of the non-Jewish migrants were admitted due to political persecution, to seek admission on the basis of racial claims was not seen as reason enough. This meant that a considerable number of claimants were denied entrance. However, this restrictive approach was soon reversed, and in 1941, practically anyone who applied was granted asylum (Widgren, 1982).

A comparative advantage developed in the post-war period since the industrial sector had remained virtually intact, and coupled with low birth rates and a swift economic expansion, the demand for labour grew rapidly. These factors further contributed to reinforce the shift towards a state of net immigration (Ekberg, 1999). But in contrast to many of the other receiving countries in Western Europe, Sweden was not able to draw on a colonial heritage for this workforce. Therefore, a treaty was signed in 1947 with Italy, Hungary and Austria for which labour recruitment was the main objective. The effects were however modest, and a second agreement was subsequently signed in 1954 between the Nordic countries. This aimed to facilitate labour mobility and resulted in a large influx of primarily Finnish migrants. Sweden also initiated a series of bi-lateral agreements with several Mediterranean countries, but when Germany and Switzerland employed an explicit guest worker system, such a scheme was never (fully) realised. Direct recruitment nevertheless occurred, but labour migration was not planned on a short-term basis, and these migrants were by and large viewed as potential settlers rather than as filling particular gaps in the labour market (Soininen, 1999; Soysal, 1998; Hammar, 1985).

For approximately 13 years (ca. 1955–1968), the approach reversed back to the policies that had characterised the early twentieth century. This 'golden age' of migration was facilitated by a series of institutional reforms that abolished visa requirements and further consolidated the Nordic labour market. These changes meant that potential labourers were allowed to spend up to three months looking for work and were only subject to a minimum amount of immigration control. The changes also impacted on the migratory patterns, which went from being collectively organised to being more spontaneous and dependent on networks and chain migration.

The political reasoning at the time was that labour migration made economic sense, and that it was beneficial, if not crucial, for industry and economic growth. Despite the entry controls being minimal, certain checks were still carried out in the form of a national evaluation process, which aimed to establish whether an existing – *Nordic* – labour pool was available or not. This put the trade unions in a remarkably strong position when deciding on this demand (see further Bucken-Knapp, 2009). The unions also identified some unexpected consequences from the increase in numbers and, in particular, from their spontaneous nature. Relaxing the entry requirements had also meant that many migrants found themselves without having secured either a job, a place of residence and/or a valid residence permit *prior* to migrating. Since to combat social exclusion was a key feature of 'the Swedish model', SAP and the trade unions saw it as imperative to promote citizenship, equal membership and full participation for the foreign labour force *as well* (Cousins, 1998). But this would not be possible unless numbers came down and immigration was significantly regulated. Otherwise, it was feared, exploitation and wage dumping would be likely outcomes.

As Sweden was about to enter into a recession by the mid-1960s, the unions – both blue and white collar – started to become more critical of the existing policies. During a consultation meeting in 1966, which included union representatives, the Labour Market Board and the Ministry for the Interior, the government eventually went with the position of the former two. A number of restrictions were proposed and later complemented by directives on seasonal labour as well. It is worth noting that neither of these regulations were debated in parliament, and they were also passed without much conflict or opposition (Spång, 2008; Ring, 1995). The formal end to this 'liberal period' thus came in 1968 when work visas – prior to entry – were re-introduced. This moved the migration management away from the market forces and back into the political realm. The social partners were now to jointly consult with the Labour Market Board on the demand for any future foreign recruitment. In practice, the numbers tended to depend on the availability of jobs but also on the state's ability to supply adequate housing, education and health care for these newcomers. The 1968 decision also stipulated that the domestic labour reserve had to be exhausted *prior* to foreign recruitment becoming an option (Ekberg, 2004).

While there was a cross-party consensus to halt the unregulated flow of labour, the opinions of the trade unions and of the employer federations were beginning to diverge. The former had pushed for a cap on numbers, primarily due to the social problems associated with a lack of work permits and job opportunities, while the latter had been in favour of keeping borders open since this would provide employers with a larger source of workers to draw upon. The composition of the migrants themselves had also started to change and was also increasing (Borevi, 2002). By the mid-1960s, yearly net migration averaged 28,000 and was dominated by South Europeans, whereas the levels of intra-Nordic migration were on the decline. Although the race angle was downplayed in the official evaluations that were made, Lundh and Ohlsson (1994) suggest that decreasing numbers was also an important measure to prevent any potential ethnic tension on the labour market as well as in the society at large.

The unions' worry that migrants did not have access to similar living and labour market conditions as the native population became the official motivation for the 1968 Governmental Bill (see also Belavusau, 2008). The bill emphasised how this mismatch was a concern for the pursued goal of equality, and linked the need for further controls to the desire of not creating a new *ethnic* underclass. The 1968 decision thus marked the beginning of the end to Sweden's labour migration era. After numbers peaked in 1969/1970, the official stop came in 1972 but in effect came to an end a year later following the oil crisis. This stop came to have a profound effect on the composition of migrants for the next 35 years. From this point onwards, four avenues of entry remained.

First, Nordic citizens were exempt from any mobility restrictions (and from 1995 onwards, this free movement applied to *all* EU citizens as well). Second, a very limited form of labour migration still existed but primarily applied to the highly skilled. The remaining routes – asylum and family reunification – would thus become the main points of entry up until 2008 when the laws regulating non-EU labour migration were reformed (SOU, 2006: 87). These changes not only diversified but also increased the stock of migrants, from predominantly European (between 1945 and 1973) to increasingly non-European (post-1973), from 1% (1940) to 15% of the total population (2011) (see further Entorf and Minoiu, 2005; Ekberg, 1999).

Despite Sweden's reputation for having a 'high international profile focusing on solidarity with the Third World [and where a] generous refugee policy was part of this solidarity' (Abiri, 2000: 13; Schuster, 2000), asylum did not feature prominently in the 1968 bill. Instead, the government simply noted that Sweden was bound by international conventions, and that the Aliens Act of 1954 already confirmed the right to asylum unless very strong reasons existed to the contrary. This meant that Sweden's commitment to refugees went beyond that of what the Geneva Convention stipulated (Spång, 2008). However, the rationale for granting asylum had so far relied on custom and praxis, and the government also noted that there was a need to formally codify these into law. This led to the investigative committee that was set up in 1975 and which subsequently made some suggestions to parliament for a legislative change. Again, these suggestions were not subject to any significant controversy and were passed with a broad parliamentary majority. Abiri (2000) further points to how this generosity was, by and large, possible due to the relatively small number of applications that were made (approximately 4,000–6,000 per year from 1972 to 1985) and were as such not overly expensive to uphold.

The critical juncture came at the end of the decade when applications rose suddenly, from ca. 20,000 (1988) to 30,000 (1999). This rapid increase, coupled with a party concern over the potential mass exodus from Eastern Europe, prompted the SAP government, and supported by M, to suggest a change to the prevailing legislation – the so-called 'Lucia-decision'. This change was enabled due to the design of the Aliens Act itself, which provided a certain degree of flexibility in re-defining who qualified as an asylum seeker (and who did not). The 'new' definition meant that only those covered under the Geneva convention, or those who had a very strong need for protection, would be considered as 'refugees'. Sustained worries about the increase in East European applications generated further revisions to the refugee categories and resulted in yet another proposition, which was again supported by the opposition. However, following the Lucia decision, a new cleavage had developed, and one that challenged the SAP – M consensus. Although CP considered the changes to be justified, FP, MP and V were all critical, partly because of the substantive changes that were proposed, and partly because of the lack of any preceding discussion in parliament. The early 1990s saw a further increase in anti-immigrant, and especially anti-asylum, sentiments among the Swedish population. In the spring of 1991, a new governmental bill (Prop. 1990/1991:195), based on the Commission Report on Refugee and Immigration Policy (SOU, 1991: 1), was proposed. The bill followed the path that had been set by the 'Lucia-decision', but it also narrowed the definition of asylum and introduced the concept of 'temporary protection'. The bill was supported by M and would most likely have been passed had it not been presented too close to the 1991 election. In the midst of this troublesome situation, a new party – *New Democracy* – entered the political scene. The party operated on the fringes of the radical right and used a mix of populist and xenophobic rhetoric, which brought the immigration 'issue' away from the consultation committees and back into the political spotlight. However, this did not mean that the political mainstream tried to co-opt or even outdo the new challenger. Instead, the response was one of disregard resulting in the survival of the cross-party consensus, at least for the time being (Dahlström and Sundell, 2012; Dahlström, and Esaiasson, 2011; Green-Pedersen and Krogstrup, 2008; Boréus, 2006; Dahlström, 2004).

4
'Pulled' or 'Pushed'? Increased Ideological Uncertainty on the EU and Immigration 'Issues'

The preceding chapter points to some variation across the four cases but also identifies some interesting similarities. The EU has been a particularly troublesome issue for the two key players in Britain, whereas in Belgium and the Netherlands it has only been the source of mild concern. Sweden, on the other hand, falls somewhere in between. Parts of the centre-left have struggled to accommodate a variety of views while the centre-right has not only been more enthusiastic but has also found the EU to be a much easier policy area to deal with. The degree of conflict and indecisiveness that has surrounded immigration shows a similar pattern, and has been much more of an 'issue' for the British parties than it has been for the remaining ones. Previous research had tended to explain these differences by emphasising certain context-specific factors (e.g. the instigator roles played by Belgium and the Netherlands, the British and Swedish 'exceptions', particular migration histories), or the changing geo-political and socio-economic climates (e.g. adapting to decolonisation, increased mobility and labour market demands) or by referencing particular foreign policy dilemmas (e.g. how to remain as a neutral actor on the world stage or how to manage the transition from 'colonial power' to 'member of the Commonwealth'). Yet, cutting across the specifics are questions of sovereignty (the EU) and equality (immigration), which appear to have been just as important for parties on the left as they have been for those on the right. This suggests that we may have to look elsewhere for an explanation of these unexpected similarities and counterintuitive positions, and that we may also have to place a greater emphasis on the ideological turmoil that parties go through when competing on such 'atypical' issues.

Whether the party-political conflict takes place along single, dual or multiple dimensions has come to characterise much of the political science debate (see e.g. Jahn, 2010; van der Brug and van Spanje,

2009; Enyedi, 2008; Kriesi et al., 2006; Kitschelt and McGann, 1995), but whether any multidimensionality *impacts* on party competition and strategies has often received less scholarly attention. This lack of attention is puzzling since a plurality of cleavages is likely to be challenging for parties when they decide on how to frame their position(s) on the two 'issues' (Money, 1999). What is argued herein is that multiple dimensions, and multiple positions, can give rise to a set of conflicting ideological 'pulls' (Odmalm, 2011), especially so when parties compete on cleavage elusive questions such as the EU and immigration. Often, however, these tensions tend to remain dormant and be less obstructive, but once the two 'issues' develop into a societal problems, parties will usually react to these cues (Green-Pedersen and Krogstrup, 2008). But once politicised, the FM/GAL and SI/TAN parties should experience *less* ideological tension than what their counterparts in the FM/TAN and SI/GAL categories should do. The latter pairings, on the other hand, are likely to be subject to a greater degree of strain and uncertainty since their views on the appropriate role of the state will come into conflict. Parties in the FM/GAL and SI/TAN categories may still experience some form of tension, or hesitation at least, but these ideological 'pulls' should be less challenging since their views on the state show greater congruence (Figure 4.1).

As Table 4.1 shows, the SI/GAL 'pull' appears more often in the four cases and applies to 42% of the parties studied. This combination suggests that parties are torn between particular understandings of how the EU/immigration will impact on 'their' society and where

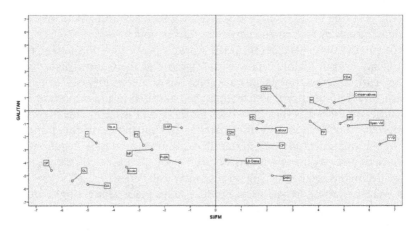

Figure 4.1   Average Manifesto Positions (1991–2010)

Table 4.1   Type of ideological 'pull' (grouped by country)

SI/GAL	FM/TAN	SI/TAN	FM/GAL
		N/A	
BELGIUM	**BELGIUM**		**BELGIUM**
GA (-5; -5.7)	CD&V (2.7: 0.3)		MR (4.8; -1)
Ecolo (-3.5; -4.3)			Open Vld (5.2; -1.2)
Sp.a (-3.5; -2.2)	**BRITAIN**		CDH (0.5; -2.2)
PS (-2.8; -2.7)	Conservatives		
	(4.6; 0.6)		**BRITAIN**
THE NETHERLANDS			Labour (1.6; -1.4)
SP (-6.4; -4.6)	**THE NETHERLANDS**		Lib Dems (0.4; -3.8)
GL (-5.6; -5.4)	CDA (4; 2)		
PvdA (-1.4; -4)			**THE NETHERLANDS**
	SWEDEN		VVD (6.4; -2.6)
SWEDEN	M (4.3; 0.2)		D'66 (2.2; -5)
V (-4.7; -2.5)			
MP (-2.5; -3)			**SWEDEN**
SAP (-1.3; -1.3)			KD (1.8; -0.8)
			FP (3.7; -0.8)
			CP (1.7; -2.7)

the emphasise is to be placed. Is the EU primarily a 'capitalist club' (SI), or an opportunity to deal with borderless and mutual problems (GAL)? And should entry policies be made more restrictive because of the anticipated, and largely negative, impact that immigration has on 'the economy' (SI), or should they be liberalised due to a 'no borders' and/or solidarity rhetoric (GAL)? The FM/TAN combination, on the other hand, 'only' applies to 17% of the parties. But they will equally have to negotiate the positive *economic* effects that the EU/immigration may bring (FM) versus how they will adversely impact on, for example, sovereignty, national identity and/or social cohesion (TAN).

And while the SI/TAN (0%) and FM/GAL parties (42%) could still experience some internal conflict, it should not be as pronounced as it is for the others since the degree of dimensional compatibility is higher.

SI/GAL parties

Of the four SI/GAL parties in Belgium, GA scores significantly higher on both dimensions (SI: -5; GAL: -5.7). In fact, the party 'out-lefts' its equivalents in both Wallonia and Sweden but is on par with the Dutch Greens. Yet the interview data suggest a fairly middle-of-the-road position on SI issues[1] but one that is also coupled with an unclear understanding of the party's GAL stance.[2] And somewhat surprisingly, given how the party has been in a governing position, GA does not appear to have moved beyond a purely environmental focus nor diversified its agenda[3] (Deschouwer, 2009; Müller-Rommel, 2002).

In accordance with what Chapter 3 has established, the interviewee also confirmed the party's 'EU: Positive' stance.[4] But the opposing ideological streams have however meant that GA has grown into a 'critical type of euro enthusiast', especially should these 'pulls' concern the role of the EU:

> [W]e worry sometimes, particularly when Europe is dominated by right-wing parties, and when everything is driven by an economic logic. This means that environmental issues, which we think that the EU should prioritise, are not high up on the agenda.
>
> (GA 1)

Lacking a broader issue agenda would also suggest that any consistent positioning on immigration could be difficult to attain. The MP, somewhat counterintuitively, refers to economic nationalism and the increased pressures on welfare expenditure that immigration *as well as* the regional divide give rise to:

> You can join your family *only* [original emphasis] if there are financial guarantees so that you won't become a burden to our social security system//...//today it is about economic nationalism, and the southern part [of Belgium] is abusing the system, they are not contributing to it. So we don't want any solidarity with them//...//.
>
> (GA 2)

Yet, this position presents a stark contrast to GA's views on asylum, which appears to be less about safe-guarding welfare and more about protecting the individual.[5] Its sister party in the south – Ecolo – does, however, adopt a more traditional Green discourse, and the interviewee makes reference to a number of GAL issues when describing the party.[6] But unlike their Swedish (and to a certain extent also their Dutch) counterparts, the Ecolo representative was prepared to acknowledge the 'old' left-right scale and where the party fits in. The interviewee further emphasised how a more regulated economy would also have positive spin-off effects on the environment:

> It's been a long-term discussion within the party, should we describe ourselves as being part of this framework or not? In the end, and for now at least, we describe ourselves as being left-wing//...//[i]t is

basically the economic system that has to be changed, the ways of production and consumption need more of a steer because they so profoundly impact on the ecological system. So I would say that the economy is pretty central to our approach at the moment.

(Ecolo 1)

The manifesto calculations (SI: −3.5; GAL: −4.3) would thus suggest a better fit with how the Ecolo MP characterises their party compared to how the GA representative described theirs. Although expressing an equally positive view on the European project – '[w]e've always wanted "more" Europe, and we've always been very much in favour of the EU' – the party has been just as hesitant towards the EU's current direction, and the MP stressed the need for a stronger *political*, rather than a stronger *economic*, union.[7]

But where the Flemish Greens identified a link between immigration's adverse effects on welfare and the social security system, the Walloon Greens were keener to emphasise a human rights and social justice discourse:

[I]t is a topic that can be approached from a social justice perspective as well. Asylum seekers without papers, e.g., there is no social justice for them, and that's something we strive for. Since we define ourselves as being a 'left-wing' party, it's pretty logical that that's the position we should take as well// ... //we also support the legalisation of people who are here without papers. We are not saying that we shouldn't have any rules at all but the thing is that there has been a lack of policing on this issue for decades. So you have all these people who have been here for more than 10 years, they have a family here; they have children here and we think that it is part of the state's responsibility to say 'OK you have kids and after 10 years here, you should be legalised'. So this is something we aim for, and we are the only party in Belgium that believes that that is the right thing to do.

(Ecolo 1)

Deschower suggests PS to be 'very strongly based on the traditional labour movement and on the socialist trade union' (2009: 78), whereas on the Flemish side the distance between SP.a and the unions not only has been greater but the party has also been more pragmatic regarding its views on state-market relations. This has further meant that PS has tended to be more sceptical towards any reforms that could signal an acceptance of 'the market', which, conversely, Sp.a has been more prone to embrace. This description does, however, run counter to the positions that are established here. Although both parties are clearly on 'the left', Sp.a has a higher SI score (−3.5) than PS does (−2.8). On the GAL dimension, however, the relationship is the inverse (Sp.a: −2.2; PS: −2.7). The Sp.a representatives corroborated these estimates but also stressed the party's centrist character,[8] and how it sees the state as having an 'obligation to protect people who might be the victims of the totally free market' (Sp.a 1). This emphasis on restraining 'the market' had gained further momentum following the economic crisis:

> [N]ot for nothing, the left parties have been leading the way in terms of how we should aim to limit the bankers and what they are doing. For example, the Commission of the Banking Association has always said that we cannot hamper with the Belgium banks since this would disadvantage them when they compete with all the other European banks, but on the other hand 'total economic freedom' does exaggerate things and does create huge problems.
>
> (Sp.a 1)

Although the Sp.a interviewees recognised that the 'left' tag may not be as relevant anymore as it once was, they also stated that the party had been ambivalent regarding *who* the market could benefit the most.[9] The GAL position, on the other hand, was associated with more clarity.[10]

While the PS representatives stressed the need for a well-functioning and properly run 'welfare state'[11], their interpretation of 'being on the left' had predominantly meant a focus on rights,[12] and improving access to particular services.[13] In contrast to what Deschouwer writes, then, these quotes suggest PS to be closer to a fairly standard – *Social Democratic* – vision where the market exists but is regulated,[14] and where strengthening equality[15] is a key goal. However, their solid manifesto positions would suggest the two parties to be likely to experience an equal degree of ideological strain on the EU and immigration 'issues'.

But once the EU becomes part of the equation, Sp.a appears to evolve into a completely different type of party. On the one hand, the interviewees identified the potential risk of the EU interfering too much in Belgium's domestic affairs[16], but, at the same time, some clear *economic* benefits were also recognised. This suggests a rather FM/TAN take on the party's relationship with the EU:

> [Membership] is vitally important for us as a relatively small country in the middle of Europe. So in economic terms we depend quite a

lot on our neighbouring countries and so on. It is crucial for our industries and for the service sector that trade is made possible and that it is made easier.

(Sp.a 1)

These conflicting positions have also been accompanied by an increased uncertainty as to how the party was to rank its issue priorities. Should the main effort be to counteract an increasing 'rightist agenda which emphasises economic freedoms'? Or should the party be championing further enlargement, which could then strengthen a sense of solidarity and common direction?

> We have always believed that the more members there are, the more solidarity we would have and the stronger Europe would be//...//but we also need to tackle other issues that have emerged because of the direction that the economic policies have taken, youth employment is an obvious one.
>
> (Sp.a 1)

The PS data suggest an equally lenient view as that of the two Green parties. But this view is also coupled with an uneasiness regarding the development that the EU has witnessed over time:

> [W]e are very pro-EU, of course we are, but we are also not too keen on the emphasis that has increasingly been placed on economics//...//the European model is first of all a social model. And we think that it's really important that these principles are maintained.
>
> (PS 1)

> [W]e are becoming increasingly critical of the policies that the EU has been following over the past fifteen to twenty years. We do believe that these are not balanced. They emphasise the role of competition too much. The EU should first and foremost be concerned with social rights.
>
> (PS 2)

The quotes certainly suggest a degree of tension, but for PS these 'pulls' are not limited to perceiving the EU as a 'capitalist club' versus being a source of international cooperation. The identified strains do instead appear to be about the 'proper' role of the EU.

For Sp.a, immigration has raised some rather fundamental questions relating to equality[17] but has also tapped into questions of solidarity and how this is to be achieved in an era of increased mobility.[18] These concerns were not just limited to certain tricky asylum cases[19] but have also applied to the 'less problematic' labour migration category.[20] But the tensions described suggest a stronger strain between the GAL and TAN factions of the party than between the anticipated SI and GAL wings.

For PS, on the other hand, immigration has come to moderate its SI stance, and thereby served to move it closer to an FM position. Yet the party's GAL position has simultaneously become reinforced. As such, this would go against what the manifesto analysis has assumed to be the case. PS's stance on 'labour migration',[21] for example, echoes that of parties in the FM/GAL category. The interviewees, however, did not qualify the party's position by limiting it to migrants in possession of *particular skills*, or who were considered to be in high demand.[22] The *global* economic disparities were further identified to be the prime causes for this increased mobility, and a situation which was also said to justify raising the levels of economic aid,[23] but the MPs also rejected the notion of halting further entry due to any negative impact that immigration would have on the *domestic* economy.[24] They also used a distinct GAL discourse when emphasising the 'worker' – rather than the 'national' – identity,[25] and how taking on migrants was an important act of solidarity.[26] But at the same time, increasing the supply of (undocumented) labour was said to put downward pressure on wages.[27]

The Dutch SP displays equally strong SI (−6.4) and GAL (−4.6) profiles, and are even farther to the 'left' than their Swedish counterparts V. Yet, the way in which the interviewees characterised the party's ideological positions suggests SP to be less 'extreme'[28] than what the manifesto analysis had anticipated (but see also Weakliem, 1991; Irwin and Thomassen, 1975). In contrast to V, however, the SP representatives emphasised how the party's GAL position also encompassed a particularly liberal stance on issues of abortion and euthanasia.[29] SP's ideological positions were clearly reflected in how the party has come to view a Dutch membership of the EU:

We are relatively vocal about the current problems that we have [in the EU]. These are primarily caused by the neo-liberal policies that have been pursued, and we feel very strongly about these changes. But it is also about the lack of transparency and democratic procedures that the EU suffers from. This has ultimately lead to a project that is not supported by the Dutch people.

(SP 1)

While it was anticipated that SP would be subjected to a significant degree of ideological tension, the quote suggests a relative ease with how the party has been able to combine two (fairly typical) SI and GAL objections to the EU. Yet, at the same time, another interviewee expresses some equally typical, but TAN-related, objections:

> [M]ost parties are willing to hand over more power and more sovereignty to the European Union, and we do definitely not want that. And that is a huge difference between us and them. Then, of course, there is the PVV. They think that the Netherlands should leave the EU but we do not share their position.
>
> (SP 2)

As one of the most leftist parties in this book, the ideological combination that SP displays would also suggest a strong antipathy towards labour migration. This sentiment should, however, be coupled with an equally strong but liberal approach to asylum seekers and refugees. This was partly confirmed by the interview data. Yet, one MP's understanding of 'asylum' points not only to a strong GAL approach to this category but also to how the party has conflated 'labour', 'bogus' and 'genuine' asylum claimants into one – nebulous – grouping that have sought a safe haven in the Netherlands.[30] These counterintuitive issue positions suggest that SP has more in common with those parties that would fall into the SI/TAN category. This situation was further accentuated by neither interviewee making any references to 'solidarity', 'the environment' or 'internationalism'.

The GL representative characterises their party in a similar vein to that of the Belgian Greens, that is, as one which 'combin[es] left-wing with green, and ecological politics' (GL 1). But for GL, being on the 'left' is understood in an almost exclusive GAL terminology.[31] This has further meant that the party's SI/FM placement has been associated with more uncertainty:

> We are a Dutch but also a European party with a social democratic background, so we believe in the regulated economy// ... //but we also emphasise individual rights more than [the social democratic parties] do. We are very much into social security, also for those who are not 50, white and male// ... //We're not against flexible or short-term work contracts as such, but we want them to work.
>
> (GL 1)

The interview data would thus support the party's GAL position (−5.4), whereas its SI location (−5.6) appears to be exaggerated. The manifesto statements on, for example, labour market regulation, or taxes, do not fully correspond with the interviewee's understanding of where the party is positioned.[32] These limited forms of ideological tension have also contributed to make GL's relationship with the EU a lot more complex than how it has been for its equivalents in Belgium:

> We are a pro-European party, one of the few that remain actually. Apart from D'66, the others are less enthusiastic right now. But not everything that Europe does is good//...//Its raison d'être, so to speak, was to resolve issues that were difficult for countries to deal with on their own, environmental problems especially, but also economic ones. And these issues can only be overcome through countries co-operating but then it evolved into being about how to facilitate for capitalist multi-nationals to co-operate. And, oddly enough, it then started to move in an anti-globalisation direction//...//we would like that the EU focuses more on social rights and on improving the environment because that's where it can make a real difference (GL 1)

Any similar uncertainties relating to immigration, however, do not appear to be present. To the contrary, in fact, the interviewee describes a remarkably 'open borders' approach to a variety of migrant categories:

> These policies are too restrictive, and the government has also tried to limit the right to have your spouse joining you from abroad. We don't like the idea of making it harder for asylum seekers to stay here, or the policies that make it more difficult for unskilled migrants to get work permits. We say, it's your choice who you marry and that spouses should be together, it's a human right. We're an aging society as well, so we actually need more migrant workers to come here//...//
>
> (GL 1)

The SI score (−1.4) for PvdA echoes that of their Swedish counterparts (SAP), but the party has got a higher GAL position (−4) than they do. The latter calculation would thus mirror the 'new left' space that has become fairly well established in Dutch politics over the past decades (De Graaf et al., 2001; Weakliem, 1991; Kriesi and van Praag, 1987), and one that has come to be occupied by a majority of the mainstream parties (with the exception of CDA). This would anticipate that PvdA will also experience significant strains between the two ideological dimensions. While the party's 'old' and 'new' left stances were confirmed,[33] the interviewees also acknowledged how the political landscape had changed. In a similar vein to their British and (to some of their) Belgian equivalents, this has meant that PvdA has gradually come to accept 'the market' but also that the party has had to deal with the declining relevance of the 'old' cleavage.[34] PvdA had therefore come to shift its focus towards some of these 'new' issues[35] and has adopted a particularly 'new left' stance on a variety of such questions.[36] While the first development is in line with what the other 'Social Democratic' parties in this book identified as the key political change in recent times, the second and third appear to be almost unique for the Dutch context (see also Green-Pedersen, 2001). The interviewees further acknowledged the overall state of flux that the Dutch party system was in (Mair, 1989), but they also highlighted how PvdA's origins in the labour movement were (still) very much present. This history had continued to be an important influence on the issues that the party has chosen to emphasise, and how these 'old' questions (still) tended to top their electoral agenda.[37] But the changing ideological and political landscapes have also impacted on the party's relationship with the EU:

It is a lot more ambiguous today than it used to be, then it was 'You want to join? Great!' We are not only more cautious but also a lot more critical these days. Should Turkey be able to join? I think they should but only subject to some very strict criteria. Should we give more money to Greece, Portugal and Spain? Not sure.

(PvdA 1)

Because of the EU, these people are allowed to work here, and they are taking jobs from 'our' workers.

(PvdA 2)

Remaining as a member is a given because we have always been a very European focused party. It has brought us wealth; welfare; stability and security. But we are also a net contributor to the EU's budget and don't get very much in return.

(PvdA 3)

The interview data also suggest how the GAL/TAN dimension has come to be the main source of framing on the immigration 'issue'. The 'mistake' made previously was how PvdA had often stressed the economic impact of immigration at the expense of its more socio-cultural implications.[38] But in contrast to the Swedish SI/GAL parties, who tended to emphasise 'rights' and 'a robust asylum procedure' but shy away from any references to 'duties' and 'labour migration', their Dutch equivalents were keener to emphasise the importance of *both*.[39] These differences offer a distinct contrast between the two cases. On the one hand, PvdA has come to adopt a remarkably *liberal* position on labour migration, especially of the less 'problematic' skilled variety.[40] Yet, on the other hand, the party's views on 'asylum' and 'family reunification' have rather unexpectedly pushed it towards the TAN sphere. This further suggests a tension to have emerged between the GAL and TAN wings of the party[41] (which, by and large, is absent in the Swedish case). The interview material has thus established a very different type of party than that that was predicted through the manifesto analysis. Even though the party representatives confirmed the overall SI/GAL classification, the immigration 'issue' has quite clearly pushed PvdA towards the FM/TAN category (see further Benoit and Laver, 2007; Budge et al., 2001). However, since any 'new' tensions were not identified, this would suggest that a more uni-dimensional – *GAL/TAN* – interpretation has come to dominate the Dutch conversation on immigration.

The estimated SI profiles for the Swedish parties (V: −4.7; SAP: −1.3) were also confirmed through the interviews. Although both parties reported to not be opposed to the 'market forces'[42] as such, their key concerns nevertheless related to the extent of privatisation[43] (Blomqvist, 2004; Pontusson, 1988), where V has often come to adopt the more interventionist position.[44] Although MP scores comparatively higher (−2.5), they portrayed a less clear ideological position.[45] While the interviewees endorsed the calculated GAL profiles[46] (V: −2.5; MP: −3; SAP: −1.3), they also identified a tension between 'the individual' and 'the collective'. The struggles that V and SAP have faced in terms of how to justify state intervention in one sphere but not in the other[47] had further come to affect their involvement with the EU as well with the immigration 'issues'.

V's relationship with the former had developed into a rather complicated one. Although the party's view of the EU is predominantly negative, with a withdrawal clause still being present in their party programme,[48] the interviewees also recognised how the EU had become 'a reality and [that] we have to go in and get our hands dirty in this process. And we do this with some enthusiasm actually, in the European as well as the Swedish parliaments.' (V3). The party has also been troubled by its overall goal of leaving the EU while simultaneously having to accept the outcome of the 1994 referendum.[49] V's objections thus dovetail with where it is ideologically located. The EU was not only perceived to be 'set up according to the needs of capital' but was also considered to suffer from some 'major democratic deficits//...//as more and more decisions are not taken at the national level anymore.' (V2). Yet, the party had also found it difficult to define what type of issue the EU 'issue' was and, more importantly, what it should be:

> [I]t's not just one issue. And that's the problem. On the one hand, it relates to the treaties and how much power the EU should have. Then the EU becomes very important because it's about democracy. But it affects all sorts of other issues as well and transcends several political levels//...//.
>
> (V3)

> [W]e want to have policies and regulations that apply to all member states e.g. on labour market protection or common rules for social securities, but we don't want this to happen 'over our heads'. It's difficult to say which one is more important though.
>
> (V 1)

Although MP started out as one of the main Eurosceptic parties in Swedish politics (Taggart, 1998), it has undertaken a remarkable journey since then and, if not fully embraced, then at least come to accept some of the benefits that interstate cooperation can bring. But a tension was indeed acknowledged:

> The EU has always been a source of ideological conflict for us. If we want to deal with environmental issues then this has to be done multi-laterally, and the EU is a great tool for doing this. But we are also deeply critical towards it from a democratic perspective.
>
> (MP 2)

Yet, it was not primarily due to the 'pull' between the party's SI and GAL positions but rather due to an intra-dimensional strain between different GAL views of the EU.

At the same time, these ideological parameters were also considered to be largely redundant for how the party chose to define itself[50], but as the above quote suggests, the GAL/TAN dimension has at least caused some internal conflict for the party. Somewhat surprisingly, however, any similar tensions regarding immigration were by and large absent.

This had further meant that there were few *internal* objections to the decision of aligning the party with the Alliance for the labour migration reforms that took place in 2008[51]:

> We managed to push through that failed asylum seekers would be able use this channel as long as they already had a job here. They could therefore stay as a labour migrant. So we agreed with the Alliance on that issue. Where we agreed with the Left was in terms of how the asylum policies had been applied too harshly. But then they didn't want any changes to the labour migration regulations whereas the Alliance did and that's why we went with them.
>
> (MP 1)

For SAP, the EU appears to have provoked an almost existentialist type of crisis.[52] This further meant that the party and its membership base have not only been out of synch but also been split into several groupings and smaller factions. Although the party elite have tended to be pro-EU, SAP had also had to deal with having a leading Eurosceptic in the upper ranks of the party and having to fight off continuous prompts to change the official party line:

> [O]ur leading MEP candidate, Marita Ulvskog, is the party's main Eurosceptic. Her position resonated very well in parts of the country, e.g. in the north, but less so in the Stockholm area. It has been a strategic dilemma for us over the past twenty years. [The party leadership] has, by and large, always been pro-EU but they are not necessarily representative of the party as such, or of our members or of the typical Social Democratic voter. The Euroscpetics have done a good job here but there are not that many of them and they don't tend to hold any key positions. So they have had a difficult time convincing anyone higher up about this.
>
> (SAP 1)

There was again a degree of uncertainty as to what type of 'threat' that the EU would constitute. In part, it related to a fear of the Union becoming a 'super market' and 'interfere in areas which SAP would not want to open up to the market' (SAP 1). Yet, some concerns were also raised about how the EU was beginning to develop into a 'super-power' and 'that Nazi-Germany [would] rise again in tandem with a somewhat racist element [in the party] that feared some of the other member states, especially the Catholic ones, and how religion could receive more influence in public life' (SAP 1). The interviewee's assessment thus connects to some strong SI *as well as* GAL objections relating to what the European project could evolve into. While these hesitations would correspond to what the manifesto analysis has anticipated to be the case, another representative pointed to how the party's opposing ideological positions had resulted in very clear strains between the two wings:

> [The] internationalist wing has been very keen on the EU because it could solve all these international questions but then you had a section which was very much focused on the smaller picture, on the everyday life of the trade unions; on the workers in the public sector etc. They didn't care too much about whether the private sector would benefit from the EU. These wings have embraced and not embraced the EU in different ways over time. And this divide was there from the beginning, from the time when the application was submitted up until today. But in the last election [2006] it felt like the two sides had reconciled a bit, possibly because we had such a prominent Eurosceptic as the first name [in the EP election].
>
> (SAP 3)

Similarly, when the two ideological streams are transposed to the key categories of newcomers (asylum seekers and labour migrants), this dilemma of 'labour market protectionism'[53] versus 'no borders'/'international solidarity'[54] was clearly identified, as exemplified by the following quote:

> Persson's position was indicative of the problems [we] have had when trying to juggle the need for low-paid migrant labour and the interests of the native workforce// ... //Refugees were not considered to push down salaries in the same way// ... //because they are kept outside of the labour market for so long.
>
> (SAP 1)

FM/TAN parties

CD&V has the lowest FM score (2.7) but a TAN position (0.3) that is otherwise fairly typical for the parties in this category. As a party based on Christian principles, it has traditionally focused on social issues[55] and sought to occupy the space in between 'socialism' and 'capitalism'. The party has, however, gradually come to moderate some of its more value-conservative traits that characterised its early incarnation (Deschouwer,

2009; Lucardie et al., 1994; Irving, 1979). The party's mediator position, between the 'old' left and right, and how CD&V has often put forward 'values' as their top electoral priority were readily acknowledged by the interviewees, but they also stressed the need for consensus building and the party's role in further linking the different segments of the Belgian society together[56] (see further Sinardet, 2010). But the interview material also suggests a fairly 'middle-of-the-road' position regarding state-market relations. As such, this stance would go against the position established through the manifesto analysis:

> [S]tate intervention is sometimes necessary, especially when markets cannot fill the needs of society. It's particularly important for us that every individual, every human being, gets the chance to develop. We cannot just assume that everyone has an equal ability or power to do so. The liberals, e.g., think that individuals are always strong enough. We say that you can only really reach your full potential when you interact with other people. So for us this view means that civil society also has an important role to play here.
>
> (CD&V 1)

While the interviewees emphasised how the party tended to be associated with the 'family',[57] conscious efforts had also been made to modernise this image and move away from the narrow focus on 'traditional family structures'. Yet, this progressive strive had simultaneously been counterpointed by a strong emphasis on the need for a common – *Flemish* – identity.[58] These neutralising positions would thus shed some light on CD&V's weak-to-centrist TAN-profile.

The interviewees do yet again portray a fairly typical – *Belgian* – position on the EU.[59] A number of historical, economic and social reasons were identified as being important contributors to this particularly enthusiastic position:

> [W]e helped to build the EU in the first place so it has been with us from the start. It is difficult to imagine Belgium and the EU as not being together// ... //I think that is the European way of doing things, to stress the social calling as well as the economic benefits.
>
> (CD&V 2)

But like the other Belgian parties, this strong – 'EU: Positive' – position had become moderated over time. The function of the Union and how its full potential could best be achieved were identified as key sources for this change in attitude:

Europe needs to develop its own identity. We don't want to focus too much on enlargement, we should instead talk about how to deepen the Union//...//we want to streamline the decision-making procedures so that we can reach better and quicker decisions, and also be able to react properly to the various global developments that are taking place, to what happens in Russia or China e.g. We want to create a solid block of countries that can work together as one. Europe is too dependent on all the nationalist positions today, and we would therefore like to realise the targets called 2020. This means that we are fully aware of the fact that we have to delegate much more power to Europe.

(CD&V 1)

The above quote suggests a mixed bag of views, and one which does not lend itself to any obvious fit with either dimension. On the one hand, the party's FM position is emphasised when the quote points to how the EU needs to become more effective ('streamline decision-making procedures'), yet enlargement, for example, is not primarily associated with an expanding market base but with the EU becoming unmanageable ('we should instead talk about deepening the Union'). Yet, on the other hand, the party's TAN stance appears to be pushed towards the adjacent sphere when the interviewee stressed the need for the EU to 'develop its own identity' and be less reliant on nationalist sentiments in the member states ('too dependent on all the individual nationalist positions.')

The spatial configuration that CD&V displays would also suggest a degree of strain on the immigration 'issue', but the interview data suggest a fairly pragmatic approach, and one which is very much in line with what Martiniello (2003) has characterised the Belgian approach to be like:

[I]f they can be a part of our society, and if society can bear the cost of absorbing these newcomers//...//then that fits with our vision. But if they can't and if society can't do this, then that becomes a problem and it would be so regardless of what type of migrant they are

(CD&V 1)

It is a very practical position that we have. E.g. our Prime Minister, Yves Leterme, went down to Serbia and Macedonia recently and he told people that they shouldn't come here//...//we have a fair policy, I think, but nowadays we stress that it has to be correct as well. People shouldn't come here thinking that they are entitled to asylum when they don't have a case. It's less about changing the policies as such and more about the execution of the existing rules.

(CD&V 2)

The Conservative Party has the highest FM score (4.6) in this category but an equally moderate to centrist TAN profile (0.6) as their Belgian and Swedish counterparts. The party is thus expected to be 'pulled' by these opposing ideological positions, but as it also functions in an FPTP system, any prevailing tensions may very well be trumped by this systemic effect. The FM calculation was readily acknowledged by the interviewees.[60] However, they also pointed to significant difficulties in assessing where 'the party' stands alluding to ideological inconsistencies between party leaders, the party and its membership base and between different ministerial posts[61], which would echo the idea of the Conservative's being ideology-free pragmatists (Bale, 2010). Conversely, the estimated TAN position seemed to correspond better with how the interviewees' understood the party's ideological trajectory to have developed, especially following Cameron's modernisation push (Ellison, 2011). But while certain features – particularly those relating to the party's views on alternative lifestyles[62] and defence[63] – had become moderated, others, for example, loci of decision-making, had been reinforced.[64] This process had, in turn, given rise to additional uncertainties over party identity and where it was heading.[65]

The interviewees further confirmed the troubled relationship that the Conservative Party has had with the EU. One MP, for example, highlighted the fractious impact that the 'issue' has had on the party:

The party is very prickly and very Eurosceptic. A lot of the members would instinctively not acknowledge anything that the EU has done or could do, and have no sympathy for why it's there in the first place. The party has become genuinely Eurosceptic, both in terms of our involvement and what our role should be in the Union. A good chunk of the party are also openly Eurohostile but there is also a tiny, tiny section that is more Europragmatic, not over the top enthusiastic but they recognise that there are some positive aspects of being 'in'.

(Cons 1)

These intra-party divisions had in turn generated several, often disparate, voices competing for attention.[66] While the interviewees acknowledged some *economic* benefits of belonging to the common market, they also pointed to how said market was not *free* enough:

[T]he free market aspect of the EU is something that we find very positive, however, the free market, as the EU sees it, still has a number of laws and regulations determining how it should work. It recognises uniformity but does not recognise trust in an individual legislation to get it right.

(Cons 3)

Europe is not the free trade heaven that people thought it would be, it has become incredibly protectionist.

(Cons 7)

[W]hile we are in favour of a freer market, we are not necessarily in favour of 'the free market' as it currently is.

(Cons 9)

Yet, the predominant view that emerged through the data was not how the EU's protectionist streaks could be reconciled with how it would serve to free up the market. The main 'hostility' instead connected to very fundamental fears of how Britain was increasingly ceding sovereignty and becoming part of a 'United States of Europe':

Sovereignty covers a lot issues// ... //the idea that they want to create a common foreign policy is just preposterous.

(Cons 2)

It's the loss of sovereignty. What's going on at the European level is gradually taking away the ability of Westminster to govern our country. A recent example of this was the gauntlet thrown down against the European courts. The court said that it was a breach of human rights to not allow prisoners to vote// ... //I think that this gradual withdrawal of sovereignty has really put some people off, me included, and I have seen obvious signs of moving towards this 'United States of Europe'-idea.

(Cons 9)

As expected, then, the interview material reveals a deeply divided party, but it also suggests how these divisions have not primarily been the result of any conflicting *ideological* 'pulls' that the party experienced. Instead, the main source of disunity appeared to be how the party was to merge these different degrees of hostility into one coherent position.[67]

Although the potential strains that arise from the EU appeared to be less problematic for the party, immigration has more obviously brought these tensions to the fore. Labour migration, for example, was acknowledged as being economically beneficial but was also considered to be overwhelming,[68] particularly following enlargement in 2004, and had acted as a disincentive for dealing with issues of domestic unemployment.[69] The immigration 'issue' also appeared to reinforce certain pre-existing TAN traits, especially of the nationalist kind,[70] when pushing the party towards a more welfare-state chauvinist position.[71] These conflicting views had equally come to affect the party's relationship with asylum seekers and refugees. Although the welcoming of people that had fled from persecution was considered to be part of a 'British tradition',[72] these categories were also associated with concerns over fairness[73] and with the erosion of national sovereignty.[74] And while 'numbers' were indeed identified as a key policy concern, it was not obvious what type of issue(s) they would constitute, or what strategy that the party should adopt to deal with this challenge. As one MP put it:

> [We] need to control numbers and be seen to be able to do this [but] do you want to send out an image that you are going to be hostile or nasty towards migrants?
>
> (Cons. 6)

The difficulties regarding what frame to adopt and how the party was to balance these opposing ideological streams had consequently meant that the Conservative's got it electorally 'wrong' on several occasions[75] (see also Charteris-Black, 2006).

CDA's FM score (4), on the other hand, is on par with the Conservatives and M but higher than that of CD&V. The party's TAN position (2), however, is the highest of all the parties in this category. Although their ideology rests on similar (Christian) foundations as that of CD&V and KD (Tromp, 1989), the Dutch interviewees were more readily inclined to acknowledge the close link between religion and politics.[76] But in contrast to a majority of the parties covered in this book, the CDA representatives made fewer references to a conflict between 'the state' and 'the market', and instead emphasised how their main foci was on 'society' and on 'social issues'.[77] The references made to being a centrist[78] to centre-right party[79] would thus partly confirm CDA's TAN location but do less obviously establish the party's FM position (see further Timmermans, and Breeman, 2012; van Kersbergen, 1994). The former location was echoed in the party's stance(s) on particular 'freedom' issues such as abortion[80], euthanasia[81] and drugs[82], but the interviewees also hesitated to refer to the CDA's position as one that was distinctly 'leftist' or 'rightist'. Although the party's market-oriented approach was readily acknowledged and would as such suggest a relative ease with identifying where CDA is located on the 'old' left-right divide,[83] the GAL/TAN dimension and where the party was located therein were – somewhat paradoxically – associated with less clarity.[84] But with solid, yet contradictory, positions, one would therefore expect a significant degree of tension across the EU *and* migration boards.

In a similar vein to the Belgian parties, the CDA representatives expressed a firm 'EU: Positive' position[85] but this stance was equally coupled with a hesitation towards the direction that the Union was heading in. Again, the EU appears to distort the positions that the manifesto analysis has established. The interviewees emphasised certain GAL-type benefits that come with cooperation – 'the EU provides opportunities to do things together like combating diseases and infections. These problems don't stop at the border' – but they also raised some TAN-related concerns over the EU's increasing powers – 'we have a very specific system of health insurance here which we try to protect from being taken over by Europe' (CDA 1) – and relating to enlargement – 'Turkey is a tricky one because of Islam. Some parts of the party are worried that Islam will have a greater degree of influence over Dutch society if Turkey joins' (CDA 3). The party's long-standing and Euroenthusiastic position had thus evolved into something that is closer to a 'Eurorealist' stance (CDA 2), and one that further resembled the position taken up by some of the more *Europragmatic* MPs in the British Conservative Party. Yet, the anticipated ideological tension has not been obvious even though some minor strains appeared to have emerged between particular GAL and TAN interpretations of the *function* of the EU.

Although CDA and PvdA are placed in different ideological spheres, the interview data with the former reveal some rather similar attitudes to that of the latter regarding *skilled* labour migration[86]. This could suggest that the manifesto analysis is likely to have underestimated the ideological transformation that PvdA has gone through over the past decades. Yet, it could also point to a significant degree of (mainstream) party consensus on the issue of 'skilled migration', which in effect has come to neutralise any ideological tensions experienced. Their diametrically opposed GAL/TAN positions would also suggest some very different views on, for example, 'asylum' but, again, the data reveal some puzzling similarities. While stressing how CDA has often sided with the more vulnerable groups in society, which would include the 'real' refugees[87] as well, it was also emphasised how the party had come to adopt a more hard-line approach on immigration – *in general*[88] – and particularly on those wanting to come to the Netherlands for family reasons.[89] The interviewees also expressed some hesitation towards the increased religious diversity of the Dutch society and especially should this plurality of faiths clash with certain fundamental *Dutch* ideals.[90]

M underwent a major transformation in time for the 2006 election and modified their views on, especially, taxation and 'the Swedish model' (Widfeldt, 2007). However, the calculated score would nevertheless place them firmly on the FM side (4.3). Questions relating to state/market relations appeared to have been comparatively easier for the party to deal with[91], but their weak TAN position (0.2) suggests that non-economic issues could be more challenging.[92] While the party's 'liberal-conservative' tag indicates a clear *ideological* steer on 'state-individual' relations,[93] the same tag could also involve a more complicated relationship regarding where to set the *limit* for some of these freedoms, and also be indicative of the challenges involved when the party negotiates, for example, alternative lifestyles versus traditional values[94] or national security versus personal integrity.[95] As with the CD&V and CDA, the M representatives also added some further qualifications to their, predominately, Euroenthusiastic position:

> Carl Bildt's position was always that we were 'The party for Europe' and this view carried on with Bo Lundgren as well but since Reinfeldt took over the party has started to become a tiny bit more critical. But I should really emphasise the 'tiny bit' here. We are still extremely positive but the critical voices have started to receive more attention, especially when it comes to how the EU works, e.g. supporting agriculture and the extent of its powers.
>
> (M 1)

In contrast to the other FM/TAN parties, however, M's slight uneasiness had not tapped into any concerns over losing sovereignty. Instead, and quite clearly so, it was linked to the party's FM stance and M's more general aversion to any further regulations of the market – 'we don't have a problem with the EU as an economic project but they want to introduce some unnecessary taxes and regulate things a bit more than what we would like' (M 1). And while the expressed views on labour migration:

> [i]f a company says, 'We need these Indian technicians' then they are probably right.
>
> (M 2)

would correspond to where the party is located on the SI/FM dimension, the asylum category has appeared to consolidate certain TAN characteristics, especially those relating to 'authoritarianism'[96], but this dimensional reinforcement had simultaneously been counterpointed by a strong GAL understanding of mobility, as per the following statement:

> [W]e think that people should be able to move and settle wherever they want.
>
> (M 1)

FM/GAL parties

Most of the parties in this category come with clear FM and GAL profiles. Therefore, they are not expected to experience any significant degree of 'pull' on either the EU or immigration 'issues'.

Given their history of economic liberalism, secularism and belonging to the 'Liberal/Social Liberal Party Family', the calculations that are made broadly correspond to where one would anticipate MR (Walloonia) and Open Vld (Flanders) to be located (Deschouwer, 2009; Dandoy, 2009). These mirror parties also show a greater degree of positional congruence than what the GA/Ecolo and Sp.a/PS pairings do. Where MR has an FM score of 4.8, Open Vld's is 5.2. And where the former's GAL position is −1, the latter averages −1.2. The solid position that MR exhibits on the 'old' cleavage was also acknowledged by the interviewee who alluded to party preferences for privatisation and how the state should (primarily) act as a referee in the market.[97] Although the views on state/market relations appeared to be relatively straightforward and unproblematic, the GAL/TAN dimension had been associated with a higher level of uncertainty:

> There is no party doctrine [on these issues]. Every single member and every single parliamentarian has the right to promote the ideas he wants to, and we have complete freedom when it comes to voting on ethical issues. However, we do sometimes find it difficult to agree on questions that are not about the economy. We have Catholics, Protestants, Muslims, Jews, and we have agnostics and atheists. So we have 'everybody' in the party which then means that there's usually a lot of debate but there is no party doctrine on what to think, unless freedom of thought or conscience can be labelled as such.
>
> (MR 1)

The above quote could thus point to an overestimation of the party's GAL position and that MR should also, in fact, be likely to experience some degree of tension. But the way in which the interviewee characterises MR's relationship with the EU suggests the two positions to be working together harmoniously:

> We are very pro-EU, like everyone else here, and we think that the EU is the only way forward// ... //we favour a strong European Parliament// ... //we think that the time has come to consolidate the Lisbon Treaty// ... //to promote [our] social goals you have to have a strong economy, and a growing one too, which means that the EU is the obvious answer.
>
> (MR 1)

Rather surprisingly, therefore, when MR's position on immigration is described, it suggests a very different type of party, and one that has more in common with those falling into the SI/TAN category. On the one hand, the MP expressed a desire for a Canadian-style point system to be introduced since the current state of 'wild immigration' meant that non-qualified people had gravitated towards Belgium, yet 'we have no jobs [for them]'. But on the other hand, a rather hard-line approach to asylum was also portrayed:

> [W]e don't want to have all the economic refugees of the world [here]// ... //we do believe that those who don't qualify should be sent home.
>
> (MR 1)

For Open VLD, their 'old' politics identity[98] was associated with a greater sense of clarity than the 'new' one[99] was. And like its Walloon sister party, some equally positive views on the European project[100] were also expressed. Yet, the dimensional uncertainty could help to explain the somewhat counterintuitive statements that were made as well. The interviewees not only emphasised a desire for *widening* the democratic gap but also that they would like to see the EU to develop further as a social *and* military power:

> [W]e think that more political and more military power is good for Europe. And we are in favour of giving the EU more authority on some topics where it currently does not have it, on social regulations and justice e.g.
>
> (Open VLD 2)

In contrast to MR, however, the party's stance on immigration was more consistent with their classification of being an FM/GAL-type party:

On this topic [immigration and asylum], I think everyone agrees that Belgium should be a country which is good to live in for as many people as possible// ... //but we've always said that people should be responsible for their own 'happiness'. And if they get the chance, then that's what they should do// ... //we don't want a society where everyone can do whatever they want to or where they get money from the government whenever they ask for it.

(Open VLD 1)

Our position is that immigration, overall, is a good thing. And that we do need migrants because parts of our economy needs them. So they can be very beneficial for our society but, of course, as one country we cannot solve all the poverty in the world. This means that we do have to have some form of selection criteria and mechanisms that regulate entry.

(Open VLD 2)

The Labour Party went through a significant ideological transformation, starting in the early 1990s and culminating in the landslide victory of New Labour in 1997 (Heath et al., 2001). These changes meant that the party had, if not embraced, then at least come to acknowledge the beneficial role that the market forces[101] could have. As such, the party has gradually moved towards an FM position but one that has been combined with a strong emphasis on social justice[102] (Glyn and Wood, 2001). Again, there should not be any significant strains due to the congruence between the FM (1.6) and GAL (−1.4) positions.

This ideological makeover was clearly identified by the interviewees who suggested the key changes to be Labour's views on state ownership[103], labour market structure[104] and taxation.[105] These changes had subsequently come to place the party in the same sphere as the Conservatives. The party's GAL position,[106] conversely, was deemed to have remained relatively intact and would as such place it closer to the Lib Dems.

Yet, the EU 'issue' had proved to be (almost) as divisive as it has been for the Conservatives, but for Labour the struggle involved reconciling its clearly opposing SI and GAL positions. The early views of the EU being a 'capitalist plot', and how it was 'all about big business and profits', began to change in the late 1980s as the Union was moving towards a 'social' rather than 'capitalist' Europe (Lab 3). These changes in attitude and perception had come about since Labour 'at least [had] the pretence of being more internationalist [than the Conservatives were]', and how the party was 'never comfortably Eurosceptic' (Lab 3). But Labour had also realised how the EU could be an opportunity to implement certain Social Democratic goals (e.g. increasing levels of employment and labour market protection), and by using the supra-national arena, these goals could be achieved domestically as well as beyond. But this gradual acceptance had also come with an increased level of tension in terms of what the *role* of the Union should be:

> [F]or the Blairites, the EU was part of a liberal philosophy, you know, the various freedoms it would offer for capital, labour, services and so on. And these needed to be supported of course but we said, 'You still need the welfare state'. That's why we thought that the European social model was such a good idea, and we fought very hard for that.
>
> (Lab 3)

On immigration, however, the interviewees reference a similar set of tensions to those expressed by the Conservatives. Labour migration was, on the one hand, acknowledged to benefit the overall economy[107], but raised questions about labour market[108] and welfare state protectionism,[109] on the other hand. These statements would suggest that the party's FM/GAL score might not accurately reflect some of the SI – as well as TAN – remains left over from its previous incarnation. Equally, asylum seeker migration had often subjected the party to further internal divisions between ideological commitments, and negotiating how social justice would be applied and to whom.[110] The interviewees further highlighted the difficulties involved when Labour had attempted to combine FM as well as SI approaches to immigration.[111]

For the Lib Dems, the degree of strain could in fact be *greater* due to their weak FM (0.4) but strong GAL profiles (−3.8). Although the former position was confirmed by the interviewees,[112] they also characterised the party as being 'centre-left'.[113] At the same time, the Lib Dems had been torn between key liberal-democratic instincts of being market friendly as well as being welfare state friendly[114], which suggests similar types of challenges as those faced by SAP (see also Russell and Fieldhouse, 2005; Bennie et al., 1994). While the party's 'old' position points to a degree of strain between its FM and SI wings, their 'new' position appeared to be more grounded, especially regarding personal freedoms,[115] decision-making procedures[116] and nationalism.[117] The overall classification that is made elsewhere of the Lib Dems being a fairly 'EU: Positive' party (Baker et al., 1999) was confirmed through the interviews. In contrast to Labour and the Conservatives, however, the interviewees made a clear connection between 'ideology' and 'issue' position:

A distinguishing feature of being a liberal, and being a Liberal Democrat, is internationalism, and European co-operation goes very well with this.

(Lib Dems 5)

Like a majority of the pro-EU parties in this book, the Lib Dems' representatives raised some (minor) objections regarding the direction that the European Union was heading in. Again, these concerned the balance between national versus supranational competencies, and how much EU intervention that was considered to be justified.[118] These concerns had, in turn, given rise to some *intra-dimensional* tension between the SI and FM factions of the party:

It has sometimes meant some rather odd positions by some MPs. They don't mind the EU intervening on issues, like work place discrimination, but they do mind when it comes to labour market regulation. What's the difference? Why is it appropriate in one but not the other?

(Lib Dems 5)

Although the party's ambivalent position on state-market[119] relations would also anticipate an equally hesitant approach to labour migration, the interview material does in fact suggest the opposite.[120] The MPs describe how the FM orientation[121] has often come to supersede any prevailing SI objections[122] the party has had. The clear GAL position was furthermore reflected in its views on asylum where solidarity had been a prime guiding light.[123]

VVD displays the highest FM score in this category (6.4), while their GAL position (−2.6) puts them in fourth place after D'66, the Lib Dems and CP. In contrast to the other Dutch parties, however, the VVD representatives explicitly rejected the use of the 'centre' prefix and would instead emphasise 'right-wing' when characterising their party.[124] But for VVD, this term was linked to an almost libertarian understanding of their 'old'[125] and 'new' positions.[126] While the former dovetails with the positions of CP, M and the Conservatives, the latter appears to be a rather unique stance for a party with a parliamentary representation. Although VVD had initially been hesitant towards the EU, this sentiment was soon trumped by a remarkably frank FM description of how '[the Netherlands] could earn a lot of money from Europe', and the party's position thus shifted to one which was 'very pro-European and very pro-integration' (VVD 2). Yet, this prolonged enthusiasm had in recent years given way to a more Belgian-style, 'Eurorealist' position which emphasised to 'put a hold on too much Europe and that not too many things are handled by Brussels' (VVD 2). While the other VVD representatives would corroborate this view, they also raised a mix of FM and TAN objections regarding the *direction* the EU has been moving in:

> VVD has always been in favour of membership. Even after the referendum we still were. But we want the EU to stick to its core 'duties', that is, the internal market; the economic sphere and safety issues. So we don't want to have too much EU in all the other areas where the member states can do it better.
>
> (VVD 1)

> [W]e think that membership has brought us a lot of benefits and that we should continue to be part of the Euro. But on the other hand, we also think there should be less Europe. Because they interfere too much, on too many topics and in too many areas//...//The EU has become too big in terms of what it does, it should do less and it should do it better.
>
> (VVD 3)

Yet, despite VVD's 'outlier' status, their attitudes on (skilled) labour[127] migration[128] and asylum[129] were in line with those expressed by the other Dutch parties (except for SP).

D'66, conversely, has the lowest FM score[130] of the Dutch parties (2.2) but one that is otherwise an average placement for the FM/GAL category. This is partly explained by how D'66 has gradually come to emphasise its *social-*, rather than its *liberal-*, affiliation, and partly due to the party's anti-establishment origins (Tromp, 1989). This further meant that the GAL/TAN dimension has become much more closely linked to their party identity[131] than it has for most of the other parties. As such, the high average score of −5 is a reasonably accurate reflection of where the party is located, given its 'new' politics origins. But the interviewee also stressed D'66's *centrist* character, and how this was the result of a particular ideological journey that had taken place in recent decades:

> And after we moved to the left we had a period of moving to the right. And then we said, 'We are just a party of social and liberal ideas'. Social used to be associated with the left, and liberal with the right. But we're social-liberal and not conservative at all. We are at the centre of the political spectrum.
>
> (D'66 1)

The anticipated harmony between ideological positions was also reflected in the party's relationships with the EU *and* immigration. The interviewee pointed to how the party has had an 'international way of looking at the world', which, in turn, had meant a resistance to any form of isolationism and to how D'66 had adopted a liberal approach to a variety of migrant categories:

> We are the most pro-European party in the Netherlands. We always have been but it has not always been easy to be this enthusiastic. Some things can of course be done better but we don't believe that we should get out of Europe; change the fundamentals or give more power to the nations. If we are to compete with China or the United States, then you can't do that alone or as a small country. We believe that we need to make use of the big internal market to able to do this. So we are pro-European, very pro-European in fact. A lot of the other parties are much more careful when it comes to working together in Europe.
>
> (D'66 1)

> It should be easier to come here, not just for those who really need help but also for those who really want to work, or get an education or just to find an adventure.
>
> (D'66 1)

But like PvdA the party had also come to recognise the need for a more realistic view on the immigration 'issue', and how it would need to pay more attention to 'the overall picture and get a broader view of the problem, rather than just saying "It's good for society and the economy to have open borders." ' (D'66 1).

KD has a lower FM score (1.8) than FP does, but their GAL positions (−0.8) are the same. This could indicate some degree of tension between the two ideological strands, but what the interviewees suggest is how the key strain has been between the GAL and TAN wings of the party.[132] They also pointed to how the party's FM instincts[133] had occasionally clashed with 'reality', especially in the aftermath of the recent economic downturn.[134]

The party's 'EU: Positive' position was justified in a similar way to that of their Belgian and Dutch equivalents, and the interviewees also raised similar objections

> We have been very EU friendly, and this partly relates to the type of party that we are. The EU was set up by Christian Democrats and that has come to influence our positive view. We also like the idea

that the EU is based on co-operation which, as a party, we strongly believe in. So it has been very positive from the start but there has also been a fraction that has been more sceptic but they have never been particularly influential nor have they won any of the voting rounds on EU issues.

(KD 1)

The EU is a very KD project, but the way it works now, especially on issues of subsidiarity, could be improved. So when we occasionally debate it, it's primarily about the EU's democratic nature rather than about its economic aspects.

(KD 2)

Although 'democratic deficit' versus 'further co-operation' was identi-fied as a potential divider, there was also the realisation that 'the EU is here to stay and that it would be very difficult for Sweden to not be part of it' (KD 1). These minor strains stemming from the party's low GAL score could thus explain why the interviewees identified 'how much the EU should be able to influence us and what type of influence we actually have over the decision-making process' (KD 1) to be key 'issues' for the party. However, these tensions did not appear to have affected the party's positions on either labour[135] or asylum seeker migration.[136] While the FM/GAL classification would tally with how the party has positioned itself on immigration, the EU appeared to give rise to some (minor) ideological tension.

Much like their British and Dutch sister parties, FP has had to balance social- and market-liberal tendencies,[137] where the emphasis on either strand had tended to shift over time.[138] While the party's FM traits (3.7) were easily identified by the interviewees, they also pointed to a 'pull' in the SI – as well as TAN – direction due to FP's social-liberal roots.[139] These strains had however not caused much intra-party fragmentation, nor any major disagreements, but had rather served to reignite dor-mant ideological discussions of where the party should be heading, and what type of party it should be.[140] Yet, the GAL position's (−0.8) relative proximity to the centre ground had occasionally come to juxtapose[141] the classic-[142], social-[143] and market-liberal wings,[144] and especially so should the discussion concern particular 'freedom' issues (smoking and alcohol consumption[145] most obviously but also in relation to 'newer' issues like file sharing[146]). An identified challenge was how the term 'lib-eral' had been subject to concept stretching when frequently adopted and used by different MPs in the party, regardless of which ideological 'team' they were affiliated to.[147] The increasing state of intra-party flux could equally mean that there should be a greater level of uncertainty, as well as ideological strain, regarding how FP has engaged with the two 'issues'. Although the party's overall position on the EU suggests an almost unfeasible level of enthusiasm[148] – and one that is possibly only rivalled by their Dutch counterparts, D'66 – some minor points were nevertheless raised. These reservations did, however, correspond to the party's solid FM position, whereas any GAL/TAN-style objections were largely absent:

> We don't discuss membership at all really but there are several things with the EU that can work better, and some things that can be more efficient. But it's not a 'critical' position in any way, we really like the basic idea of working and trading together and that's something that we are very much in favour of.
>
> (FP 1)

The party's view on immigration,[149] particularly of the labour variety, was similarly in line with its FM/GAL classification. The interviewees pointed to how FP had always been keen on a 'more market' approach in this process,[150] a position that furthermore corresponded to the overall stance that the Alliance has come to adopt. Asylum had largely remained a non-issue, although family reunification was said to be an increasing source of conflict, especially since FP entered into a governing position in 2006.[151]

CP had also made an ideological re-orientation[152], but unlike M (in particular), they have moved further in the FM direction.[153] Although the party shares similar social-liberal origins to that of FP,[154] it has increasingly come to emphasise 'the individual' and 'the free market' while still aiming to retain the party's previous focus on 'green issues'. As such, the manifesto calculations (FM: 1.7; GAL: −2.7) correspond to where the interviewees considered the party to be heading, but the estimated FM score likely underplays the significant shift that has taken place over the past decades. The firm grounding in the FM/GAL dimensions[155] was, as expected, echoed in the party's views on the EU as well as on immigration. Although CP was initially sceptical to a Swedish membership, and had been remarkably split during the referendum campaign, the ideological journey that the party has undertaken since meant that it has come to embrace almost every aspect of 'Europe'[156]:

> One aspect is as a project for peace, you just have to look at the developments that have taken place in, say, Portugal and Greece to

understand how important the EU is. Another one is that there is more unity and more economic opportunities in Europe today. It has become so much easier to trade with the other European countries today than how it used to be. What's lacking is the common currency.

(CP 4)

This positional change was also clearly linked back to the party's dimensional relocation, from the SI/GAL to the FM/GAL category:

It's a consequence of our ideological 'reinvention'. If you are pro-freedom; pro-trade and pro-openness towards the rest of the world, then you can't say no to, or be hesitant towards, an EU membership, or even to the EU as such. If you want a better environment, then you can't say no to cooperation or to a common climate policy either. There is basically more logic to our 'Yes'-position today.

(CP 1)

And as their coalition partners, labour migration[157] was perceived to be a largely unproblematic issue, and a question that is best left up to the employers, rather than the state, to decide[158] upon. But at the same time, the rapid *ideological* transformation meant that the membership base was not always able to keep the same pace as that of the party elites.[159] It was also expected that CP should be less conflicted regarding asylum seeker migration. While the interviewees emphasised how the party had a sustained commitment to the treaties that Sweden had signed up for,[160] they also described an intra-party shift[161] taking place where immigration – *in general* – was something that should be facilitated rather than be constrained.[162]

The empirical data (see Tables 4.2 and 4.3) would thus suggest mixed support for the proposed hypotheses, which, to recapitulate, were the following:

H1. Parties with SI/GAL or FM/TAN combinations are *more* likely to experience conflicting ideological 'pulls' on the EU/immigration.
H2. Parties with FM/GAL or SI/TAN combinations are conversely *less* likely to experience such strains.
H3. Parties in FPTP systems are *less* likely to experience *any* 'pulls' (SI/GAL *or* FM/TAN) compared to parties in PR systems.

The SI/GAL parties have been more likely to experience an ideological tension on immigration (30% of the cases) than they have been on the EU (20%), compared to 25% (immigration) and 0% (the EU) for the FM/TAN category (H1). It is worth noting, however, that GA and SAP

Table 4.2   EU (confirmed cases in bold)

Parties *likely* to experience conflicting 'pulls' (party/party family)	Parties *less* likely to experience conflicting 'pulls' (party/party family)
SI/GAL **BE/FL: GA (Green)** BE/WA: Ecolo (Greens) BE/WA: Sp.a (Socialist/Social democratic) BE/FL: PS (Socialist/Social democratic) NL: SP (Socialist/Social democratic) NL: GL (Green) NL: PvdA (Socialist/Social democratic) SWE: V (Socialist/Social democratic) **SWE: SAP (Socialist/Social democratic)** SWE: MP (Green) **FM/TAN** BE/FL: CD&V (Religious/Christian democratic) GB: Conservatives (Conservative) NL: CDA (Religious/Christian democratic) SWE: M (Conservative)	FM/GAL BE/WA: MR (Liberal/Social liberal) **BE/FL: Open Vld (Liberal/Social liberal)** BE/WA CDH (Religious/Christian democratic)* GB: Labour (Socialist/Social democratic) **GB: Lib Dems (Liberal/Social liberal)** NL: VVD (Liberal/Social liberal) **NL: D'66 (Liberal/Social liberal)** SWE: KD (Religious/Christian democratic) **SWE: FP (Liberal/Social liberal)** **SWE: CP (Liberal/Social liberal)**

Notes: (H1) SI/GAL parties experiencing conflicting ideological 'pulls': 2/10 = 20%.
(H1) FM/TAN parties experiencing conflicting ideological 'pulls': 0/4 = 0%.
(H2) FM/GAL parties *not* experiencing conflicting ideological 'pulls': 6/10 = 60%.
(H2) SI/TAN parties *not* experiencing conflicting ideological 'pulls': N/A
(H3) Parties in FPTP system *not* experiencing conflicting ideological 'pulls': 2/3 = 66%.
(H3) Parties in PR system experiencing conflicting ideological 'pulls': 2/21 = 9.5%.
*No interview data.

appeared to be just as conflicted on both areas, whereas for V, the key source of strain emerged in relation to immigration. Equally, the sole-confirmed party in the FM/TAN category (Conservatives) has been more likely to be 'pulled' on immigration than it has on the EU (H1).

Most of the FM/GAL parties (60%) reported to not have experienced any significant strains on either the EU or immigration. Yet, it was surprising to find that the latter 'issue' had *still* given rise to a substantial degree of internal turmoil for some of these parties (MR, Labour and VVD in particular) (H2). And the number of parties that – regardless of combination – reported an *intra*-dimensional conflict to be present has been just as surprising, and not something that was fully anticipated based on the manifesto analysis. It was also assumed that the institutional effects stemming from the FPTP system would be likely to

Table 4.3 Immigration (confirmed cases in bold)

Parties *likely* to experience conflicting 'pulls' (party/party family)	Parties *less likely* to experience conflicting 'pulls' (party/party family)
SI/GAL	FM/GAL
BE/FL: GA (Green)	BE/WA: MR (Liberal/Social
BE/WA: Ecolo (Green)	liberal)
BE/WA: Sp.a (Socialist/Social	**BE/FL: Open Vld (Liberal/Social**
democratic) BE/FL: PS	**liberal)**
(Socialist/Social	BE/WA CDH (Religious/Christian
democratic)	democratic)*
NL: SP (Socialist/Social democratic)	GB: Labour (Socialist/Social
NL: GL (Green)	democratic)
NL: PvdA (Socialist/Social	**GB: Lib Dems** (Liberal/Social liberal)
democratic)	NL: VVD (Liberal/Social liberal)
SWE: V (Socialist/Social	**NL: D'66 (Liberal/Social liberal)**
democratic)	**SWE: KD (Religious/Christian**
SWE: SAP (Socialist/Social	**democratic)**
democratic)	**SWE: FP (Liberal/Social liberal)**
SWE: MP (Green)	**SWE: CP (Liberal/Social liberal)**
FM/TAN	
BE/FL: CD&V (Religious/Christian	
democratic)	
GB: Conservatives (Conservative)	
NL: CDA (Religious/Christian	
democratic)	
SWE: M (Conservative)	

Notes: (H1) SI/GAL parties experiencing conflicting ideological 'pulls': 3/10 = 30%.
(H1) FM/TAN parties experiencing conflicting ideological 'pulls': 1/4 = 25%.
(H2) FM/GAL parties *not* experiencing conflicting ideological 'pulls': 6/10 = 60%.
(H2) SI/TAN parties *not* experiencing conflicting ideological 'pulls': N/A.
(H3) Parties in FPTP system *not* experiencing conflicting ideological 'pulls': 1/3 = 33%.
(H3) Parties in PR system experiencing conflicting ideological 'pulls': 5/21 = 24%.
*No interview data.

trump any prevailing 'pulls', which, conversely, should have been more pronounced in the PR systems. This has only been confirmed for the Lib Dems, however (on the EU and immigration). The Labour *and* Conservative MPs, on the other hand, reported such strains to be very much present – on both issues for the former, and on immigration for the latter. The counterintuitive number of parties in the PR systems that did *not* experience any of these 'pulls' was equally puzzling (H3). The next chapter digs deeper into the effects that these strains will have and pays special attention to whether they have resulted in a higher frequency of ownership claims being made in their respective party manifestos.

5
The Changing Modes of Party Competition (1991–2010)

The West European party systems and the role of ideology do indeed appear to have changed. As explored in the preceding chapter, both 'issues' have been problematic for parts of the mainstream to engage with, especially so when the political space is characterised by a plurality of cleavages and should parties also have conflicting views on the role and remit of the state. Although some of the parties (particularly of the liberal and post-material type) seem to be more ideologically in tune, others (particularly of the social democratic/socialist and conservative type) have found the opposing streams more difficult to handle. But at the same time, immigration appears to cause a greater degree of internal tension than the EU has done. A reasonable expectation would thus be that the more ideological strain that parties experience, the more likely they are to focus on (re)claiming ownership rather than risking to accentuate these tensions by negotiating what type of choice that they will offer to the electorate. Yet, this may not be the only reason for why parties rarely seem to offer any alternatives on these questions. Should parties' issue positions converge, then it will also make electoral 'sense' to emphasise competence and their track record of delivery instead (Green, 2007; Green-Pedersen, 2007; Petrocik, 1996). And the effects of an FPTP system may equally prompt parties to frame their positions in ownership – rather than choice – discourses (Green and Hobolt, 2008). This chapter will further explore these ideas by setting out the following hypotheses:

H4. Parties subject to conflicting ideological 'pulls' are more likely to use ownership discourses than parties that are not.

H5. When issue positions converge, parties frame their stances in 'Ownership' discourses.

H6. When they diverge, positions are framed in 'Choice' discourses.

H7. Parties in FPTP systems are more likely to engage in ownership struggles than parties in PR dittos.

What the manifesto analyses reveal is partly what was expected to be the case, yet it also highlights some interesting anomalies. The Belgian parties have most obviously corresponded to the Euroenthusiastic positions sketched out in chapters 3 and 4, whereas the equally enthusiastic stances in the Dutch case have not been fully evidenced. The British data have also confirmed the development that has taken place since the late 1980s. While both Labour and the Conservative Party have predominantly taken up opposing stances ('EU: Positive' in the former, and 'EU: Negative' in the latter), the Lib Dems' position has been somewhat less enthusiastic than anticipated. The Swedish parties, on the other hand, display a pattern that largely maps on to the positional divisions discussed earlier and one which has also been confirmed through the interview material (Tables 5.1–5.5).

Manifesto positions (EU): Negative $(-7/-1)$ – positive $(1/7)$

Table 5.1   Belgium – Flanders

	1991	1995	1999	2003	2007	2010
GA	0	0	0	2	4	1
Sp.a.	0	2	2	2	0	2
CD&V	3	5	2	2	2	4
Open Vld	4	1	1	1	4	2

Table 5.2   Belgium – Wallonia

	1991	1995	1999	2003	2007	2010
PS	1	1	2	2	3	1
Ecolo	3	0	4	2	2	2
CDH	2	2	1	3	2	1
MR	2	0	0	3	4	4

Table 5.3 Britain

	1992	1997	2001	2005	2010
Lab.	4	4	4	4	2
Lib. Dems	3	3	4	3	5
Con.	0	−2	−3	−3	−3

Table 5.4 The Netherlands

	1994	1998	2002	2006	2010
SP	−2	−5	−3	−1	−1
GL	−2	0	3	2	3
PvdA	0	4	1	2	3
D'66	3	1	4	3	4
VVD	1	2	1	5	2
CDA	5	3	3	1	3

Table 5.5 Sweden

	1991	1994	1998	2002	2006	2010
MP	−3	−3	−2	−3	−3	−3
V	−2	−4	−4	−4	−4	0
SAP	1	2	3	3	1	2
CP	−1	−1	−2	0	2	4
FP	3	3	1	3	2	4
KD	1	1	0	1	0	1
M	3	3	1	2	2	6

But it is on the immigration 'issue' that we find the most unexpected outcomes. The Belgian parties were assumed to congregate somewhere along the 'Restrictive' continuum, yet the Flemish positions have tended to fall on both sides of the divide. A similar discrepancy also applies to the Walloon parties but with the difference that their positions can predominantly be found in the 'Liberal' policies sphere. The Dutch manifestos suggest no obvious pattern since a majority of the parties alternate between liberal and restrictive positions from one election to the next. The notable exceptions are GL and PvdA. The former is the only party to consistently have occupied the same sphere ('Liberal') across the studied period, whereas the latter is the sole party to be placed at the midway point (and during four elections as well). The British and Swedish parties correspond better to where one would expect their positions to be. In the former, it involves a clear cleavage between the restrictive Labour and Conservative positions versus the liberal, Lib Dem stances. In the latter, there is evidence of a positional convergence in the 'Liberal' policies sphere (Tables 5.6–5.10).

Manifesto positions (immigration): Liberal (–7/–1) – restrictive (1/7)

Table 5.6   Belgium – Flanders

	1991	1995	1999	2003	2007	2010
GA	−1	−1	−2	−3	−4	−1
Sp.a.	0	0	0	0	−1	1
CD&V	3	−1	0	−1	2	1
Open Vld	2	2	0	3	1	1

Table 5.7   Belgium – Wallonia

	1991	1995	1999	2003	2007	2010
PS	0	2	−2	−5	−5	−5
Ecolo	−2	0	−4	−4	−6	−6
CDH	0	0	0	0	−3	−1
MR	1	2	0	0	0	0

Table 5.8   Britain

	1992	1997	2001	2005	2010
Lab.	1	1	−4	1	2
Lib. Dems	−2	−2	−4	−3	−2
Con.	2	1	0	1	1

Table 5.9   The Netherlands

	1994	1998	2002	2006	2010
SP	2	−1	−1	1	1
GL	−2	−4	−3	−6	−5
PvdA	0	−3	0	0	0

D'66	−2	−2	1	−1	−2
VVD	2	1	5	−1	2
CDA	1	−2	2	−1	1

Table 5.10   Sweden

	1991	1994	1998	2002	2006	2010
MP	0	0	0	−1	−1	−2
V	−1	0	−2	−1	0	−1
SAP	−1	0	0	−2	−1	−1
CP	−2	0	0	0	−1	−2
FP	−1	−1	−1	−3	−1	−2
KD	−1	0	0	−1	0	−4
M	−1	0	−1	−2	−2	−2

The calculations made for the EU further suggest that 'Choice' should be the main mode of framing (57.8%, 78/135), followed by 'Ownership' (31.1%, 42/135) and 'Neither Ownership nor Choice' (11.1%, 15/135) (see Table 5.11).

Table 5.11   Manifesto positions and expected modes of competition: EU (1991–2010)

	E1	E2	E3	E4	E5	E6
	1991	1995	1999	2003	2007	2010
GA	0 (Noc)	0 (Noc)	0 (Noc)	2 (O)	4 (O)	1 (O)
S.pa	0 (Noc)	2 (O)	2 (O)	2 (O)	0 (Noc)	2 (O)
CD&V	3 (O)	5 (O)	2 (O)	2 (O)	2 (O)	4 (O)
Open Vld	4 (O)	1 (O)	1 (O)	1 (O)	4 (O)	2 (O)
PS	1 (O)	1 (O)	2 (O)	2 (O)	3 (O)	1 (O)
Ecolo	3 (O)	0 (Noc)	4 (O)	2 (O)	2 (O)	2 (O)
CDH	2 (O)	2 (O)	1 (O)	3 (O)	2 (O)	1 (O)
MR	2 (O)	0 (Noc)	0 (Noc)	3 (O)	4 (O)	4 (O)
	1992	1997	2001	2005	2010	
Lab.	4 (O)	4 (C)	4 (C)	4 (C)	2 (C)	
Lib Dems	3 (O)	3 (C)	4 (C)	3 (C)	5 (C)	
Cons.	0 (Noc)	−2 (C)	−3 (C)	−3 (C)	−3 (C)	
	1994	1998	2002	2006	2010	
SP	−2 (C)	−5 (C)	−3 (C)	−1 (C)	−1 (C)	
GL	−2 (C)	0 (Noc)	3 (C)	2 (C)	3 (C)	
PvdA	0 (Noc)	4 (C)	1 (C)	2 (C)	3 (C)	

Table 5.11 (Continued)

	E1	E2	E3	E4	E5	E6
D'66	3 (C)	1 (C)	4 (C)	3 (C)	4 (C)	
VVD	1 (C)	2 (C)	1 (C)	5 (C)	2 (C)	
CDA	5 (C)	3 (C)	3 (C)	1 (C)	3 (C)	
	1991	1994	1998	2002	2006	2010
MP	−3 (C)	−3 (C)	−2 (C)	−3 (C)	−3 (C)	−3 (C)
V	−2 (C)	−4 (C)	−4 (C)	−4 (C)	−4 (C)	0 (Noc)
SAP	1 (C)	2 (C)	3 (C)	3 (C)	1 (C)	2 (C)
CP	−1 (C)	−1 (C)	−2 (C)	0 (Noc)	2 (C)	4 (C)
FP	3 (C)	3 (C)	1 (C)	3 (C)	2 (C)	4 (C)
KD	1 (C)	1 (C)	0 (Noc)	1 (C)	0 (Noc)	1 (C)
M	3 (C)	3 (C)	1 (C)	2 (C)	2 (C)	6 (C)

Note: O = Ownership; C = Choice; Noc = Neither Ownership nor Choice.

On immigration, the situation is slightly different (see Table 5.12). The predicted number of 'Choice' framings drop to 42.2% (57/135), whereas for 'Ownership' it increases marginally to 31.9% (43/135). The 'Neither Ownership nor Choice' category does conversely go up to 25.9% (35/135).

Table 5.12 Manifesto positions and expected modes of competition: immigration (1991–2010)

	E1	E2	E3	E4	E5	E6
	1991	1995	1999	2003	2007	2010
GA	−1 (C)	−1 (C)	−2 (O)	−3 (C)	−4 (C)	−1 (C)
Sp.a	0 (Noc)	0 (Noc)	0 (Noc)	0 (Noc)	−1 (C)	1 (C)
CD&V	3 (C)	−1 (C)	0 (Noc)	−1 (C)	2 (C)	1 (C)
Open Vld	2 (C)	2 (C)	0 (Noc)	3 (C)	1 (C)	1 (C)
PS	0 (Noc)	2 (O)	−2 (O)	−5 (O)	−5 (O)	−5 (O)
Ecolo	−2 (C)	0 (Noc)	−4 (O)	−4 (O)	−6 (O)	−6 (O)
CDH	0 (Noc)	0 (Noc)	0 (Noc)	0 (Noc)	−3 (O)	−1 (O)
MR	1 (C)	2 (O)	0 (Noc)	0 (Noc)	0 (Noc)	0 (Noc)
	1992	1997	2001	2005	2010	
Lab.	1 (C)	1 (C)	−4 (O)	1 (C)	2 (C)	
Lib Dems	−2 (C)	−2 (C)	−4 (O)	−3 (C)	−2 (C)	
Cons.	2 (C)	1 (C)	0 (Noc)	1 (C)	1 (C)	
	1994	1998	2002	2006	2010	
SP	2 (C)	−1 (C)	−1 (C)	1 (C)	1 (C)	
GL	−2 (C)	−4 (C)	−3 (C)	−6 (C)	−5 (C)	
PvdA	0 (Noc)	−3 (C)	0 (Noc)	0 (Noc)	0 (Noc)	

D'66	−2 (C)	−2 (C)	1 (C)	−1 (C)	−2 (C)	
VVD	2 (C)	1 (C)	5 (C)	−1 (C)	2 (C)	
CDA	1 (C)	−2 (C)	2 (C)	−1 (C)	1 (C)	
	1991	**1994**	**1998**	**2002**	**2006**	**2010**
MP	0 (Noc)	0 (Noc)	0 (Noc)	−1 (O)	−1 (O)	−2 (O)
V	−1 (O)	0 (Noc)	−2 (O)	−1 (O)	0 (Noc)	−1 (O)
SAP	−1 (O)	0 (Noc)	0 (Noc)	−2 (O)	−1 (O)	−1 (O)
CP	−2 (O)	0 (Noc)	0 (Noc)	0 (Noc)	−1 (O)	−2 (O)
FP	−1 (O)	−1 (O)	−1 (O)	−3 (O)	−1 (O)	−2 (O)
KD	−1 (O)	0 (Noc)	0 (Noc)	−1 (O)	0 (Noc)	−4 (O)
M	−1 (O)	0 (Noc)	−1 (O)	−2 (O)	−2 (O)	−2 (O)

Note: O = Ownership; C = Choice; Noc = Neither Ownership nor Choice.

Disaggregating the cases reveals some interesting variations. 'Ownership' claims are anticipated to dominate the Belgian manifestos since a majority of the Flemish *and* Walloon parties are located in the same – *EU: Positive* – sphere. In the remaining cases, it will be the exception, however, and party rivalry should instead be characterised by the different sets of 'Choices' that parties offer. Although relatively fewer instances are identified, there should be more parties in Belgium that put forward 'Neither Ownership nor Choice' statements than there will be in Britain, the Netherlands and Sweden.

In terms of immigration, the predictions (do again) tell a different story. In Belgium, there is significant variation between the two regions. The Flemish parties display remarkably lower levels of 'Ownership' classifications than their Walloon counterparts. Equally low levels are also found in Britain and the Netherlands but with Sweden being a distinct outlier. In fact, Sweden and the Netherlands are each other's mirror opposites regarding the expected modes of competition ('Ownership' in the former, and 'Choice' in the latter). The anticipated number of 'Choice' offerings are relatively high in Flanders, Britain and the Netherlands, but with Wallonia and Sweden displaying fewer instances of this category. Where the two 'issues' diverge, however, is on the number of 'Neither Ownership nor Choice' classifications, and the immigration figures here are higher than they are for the EU. Having established the expected modes of competition, the next step is to link these predictions with how parties have *in fact* framed their stances. Tables 5.13 and 5.14 show the aggregate results per competition type and election, whereas Tables 5.15 and 5.16 break these results down by party, frequency and total number of elections.

Table 5.13   De facto modes of competition/EU (aggregate %)

	E1	E2	E3	E4	E5	E6
Ownership	88	83	92	87	70	87
Choice	71	70	63	79	71	67
Neither Ownership nor Choice	33	25	25	33	29	13

Table 5.14   De facto modes of competition/immigration (aggregate %)

	E1	E2	E3	E4	E5	E6
Ownership	79	67	58	79	83	80
Choice	50	33	17	50	75	53
Neither Ownership nor Choice	4	4	17	20	16	13

Table 5.15   Modes of competition: party/frequency/total nr of elections (EU)

	Ownership	Choice	Neither Ownership nor Choice
GA	4 (6)	5 (6)	3 (6)
Sp.a	4 (6)	4 (6)	1 (6)
CD&V	6 (6)	6 (6)	3 (6)
Open Vld	6 (6)	2 (6)	0 (6)
PS	6 (6)	1 (6)	2 (6)
Ecolo	5 (6)	2 (6)	1 (6)
CDH	5 (6)	6 (6)	0 (6)
MR	4 (6)	2 (6)	4 (6)
Lab.	5 (5)	2 (5)	2 (5)
Lib Dems	5 (5)	5 (5)	0 (5)
Cons.	5 (5)	2 (5)	1 (5)
SP	4 (5)	3 (5)	3 (5)
GL	5 (5)	5 (5)	3 (5)
PvdA	5 (5)	5 (5)	0 (5)
D'66	5 (5)	5 (5)	2 (5)
VVD	5 (5)	5 (5)	3 (5)
CDA	5 (5)	5 (5)	2 (5)
MP	4 (6)	6 (6)	0 (6)
V	4 (6)	5 (6)	0 (6)
SAP	3 (6)	3 (6)	4 (6)
CP	4 (6)	3 (6)	2 (6)
FP	6 (6)	5 (6)	0 (6)
KD	5 (6)	2 (6)	0 (6)
M	4 (6)	6 (6)	1 (6)

Table 5.16 Modes of competition: party/frequency/total nr of elections (immigration)

	Ownership	Choice	Neither Ownership nor Choice
GA	6 (6)	5 (6)	1 (6)
Sp.a	3 (6)	0 (6)	0 (6)
CD&V	5 (6)	5 (6)	1 (6)
Open Vld	5 (6)	1 (6)	0 (6)
PS	6 (6)	3 (6)	1 (6)
Ecolo	5 (6)	3 (6)	2 (6)
CDH	5 (6)	1 (6)	0 (6)
MR	5 (6)	1 (6)	2 (6)
Lab.	5 (5)	0 (6)	1 (5)
Lib Dems	5 (5)	1 (5)	1 (5)
Cons.	5 (5)	0 (5)	3 (5)
SP	5 (5)	3 (5)	1 (5)
GL	5 (5)	4 (5)	0 (5)
PvdA	5 (5)	4 (5)	1 (5)
D'66	4 (5)	4 (5)	0 (5)
VVD	5 (5)	3 (5)	1 (5)
CDA	5 (5)	2 (5)	0 (5)
MP	1 (6)	3 (6)	0 (6)
V	2 (6)	4 (6)	0 (6)
SAP	1 (6)	4 (6)	0 (6)
CP	1 (6)	2 (6)	1 (6)
FP	6 (6)	1 (6)	1 (6)
KD	1 (6)	3 (6)	0 (6)
M	4 (6)	5 (6)	0 (6)

The overall picture points to how 'Ownership' *and* 'Choice' have come to characterise electoral competition on the EU. Up to E5 the average confirmation ratio is 84% for the former and 70.8% for the latter. This relationship changes marginally in E6 (Ownership: 87%; Choice: 67%), although only the Belgian and Swedish parties are included.

The immigration figures, on the other hand, are remarkably different. Between E1 and E5, the average confirmation ratio for 'Ownership' is 73.2% compared to 45% for 'Choice'. And while the latter figure decreases between E5 and E6 (from 75% to 53%), the 'Ownership' scores not only remain higher but are also sustained (83% in E5, and 80% in E6). Conversely, the 'Neither Ownership nor Choice' scores for the EU average 29% (E1–E5) and 13% (E6), whereas for immigration the scores are 12.2% (E1–E5) and 13% (E6).

The calculations thus suggest a mismatch between the *anticipated* and the *actual* modes of competition. GA exhibits a slightly higher frequency of 'Choice' statements on the EU than Sp.a does, but Sp.a and CD&V have conversely put forward 'Ownership' and 'Choice' statements in equal measures. Open Vld, on the other hand, behaved more as expected and emphasised 'Ownership' more often than they do the other categories. GA was further assumed to adopt a 'Neither Ownership nor Choice' approach in the periods between E1 and E3 but such a strategy has only been confirmed for E3.[1] Simultaneously, however, the party has also opted for a distinct ownership approach.[2] But in E2, the manifesto data point to how a choice was in fact offered[3], whereas in E1 there was no mention of the EU at all. A similar scenario also applies to Sp.a. In E1, they not only put forward some rather basic statements regarding the role of the EU[4] but also framed their stance in 'Ownership'[5] *and* 'Choice'[6] discourses. And in E2, E4 and E6, the expected 'Ownership'[7] claims are also accompanied by 'Choice'[8] and 'Neither Ownership nor Choice'[9] statements.

The Walloon parties are not only more consistent but by and large also behave as predicted. 'Ownership'[10] claims are made more often than 'Choice' are but CDH puts forward more of the latter.[11] Yet, the number of times that the Belgian manifestos express rather basic, or non-committal, statements[12] is surprisingly high, given their tendency to congregate in the 'EU:Positive'-sphere. This would partly confirm the lack of issue politicisation that chapters 3 and 4 established but also highlights the strategic reasoning at play. While the overall issue consensus helps to explain the predominance of ownership-style discourses, parties may equally want to draw attention to particular *aspects* of the EU 'issue' that they are trying to claim ownership over, and be positively associated with, while downplaying others. Where PS, for example, stresses how the EU can function 'better' should it only adopt a new *economic model*:

> [T]he first challenge for the EU's economic recovery is to find a new model of stable and sustainable growth.
>
> (PS, 2010)

Ecolo emphasises the role that the EU must play as an *international actor*:

> While [the EU] continues to fulfil its original mission of peace//...//the demands//...//have increased beyond its level of development. The EU does not meet these new challenges.
>
> (Ecolo, 2007)

Converging issue positions appear to have stimulated a higher frequency of ownership-style language in the manifestos, but since this mode of competition has also applied across the party system, any dimensional 'pulls' or systemic effects seem to be less relevant than what was initially assumed (Hs.4, 5 and 7). And although H.6 does not apply, there are nevertheless instances when the Belgian parties have simultaneously put forward 'Ownership' *and* 'Choice' statements.

In Britain, competition was expected to be characterised by the set of choices that the respective parties offered. This tactic is however the exception and the Lib Dems is the only party to consistently have done so (H.6). Yet, their statements have also been coupled with an equal amount of ownership-style claims (H.7). Labour and the Conservatives have continuously acted against expectations, and their statements have contained a distinct ownership flavour during several elections (Hs.6 and 7). The calculations for E1 suggest ownership competition to have prevailed since both Labour and the Lib Dems are located in the same *EU: Positive* sphere (H.5), and since the Conservatives are placed at the midway point, they should conversely downplay or ignore the EU. In the remaining elections, competition should be geared towards 'Choice', given the *EU: Positive* (Labour, Lib Dems) and *EU: Negative* (Conservatives) positions that were adopted (H.6). Although the predictions for E1 are confirmed,[13] the Conservative manifesto also includes a number of strong ownership strives, for example, on the function of the Union:

We will continue to resist changes to the Treaty of Rome that would damage British business. We will redouble our efforts to reform the Common Agricultural Policy and will stoutly defend the interests of British farmers and consumers.

(Conservatives, 1992)

and on (further) integration:

We will resist Commission initiatives which run counter to the principle that issues should be dealt with on a national basis wherever possible. We will insist on more effective control over Community spending and will resist pressure to extend Community competence to new areas.

(Conservatives, 1992)

In the subsequent elections, the manifesto data suggest more mixed results. In E2 and E3, Labour makes clear ownership attempts,[14] whereas in E4 and E5 ownership claims[15], choice[16] and 'matter of fact' statements[17] run in parallel. The Conservatives have behaved in a similar fashion. Although a choice is indeed offered – for example, on 'the Euro' (E2[18]) and on a 'Common Defence/Foreign Policy' (E4[19]) – the main thrust is on communicating and portraying competence.[20] The Lib Dems also offer a 'Choice',[21] but their manifestos are equally characterised by distinct ownership discourses.[22] The British data would thus partially support Hs.5 and 6, whereas H.4 does not apply since the interview material has not confirmed the anticipated 'pull' for the Conservatives. The evidence for H.7, on the other hand, is very strong. All of the British manifestos contain a high number of statements that signal parties' intent to (re)claim ownership over the EU 'issue'.

In the Netherlands, SP has consistently fallen in the *EU: Negative* sphere, whereas the remaining parties (except for GL in E1) have been equally consistent when placed somewhere along the *EU: Positive* continuum. This suggests competition to be characterised by the different visions or outcomes that the Dutch parties intend to offer to the electorate (H.6). The manifesto data support these predictions. A majority of the parties that were anticipated to offer a 'Choice' have also done so.[23] But the number of times that 'Ownership' claims were also made have been just as frequent[24] (H.7). This tendency to push the party's 'Choice' position while simultaneously making 'Ownership' claims is a strategy that has applied virtually across the board. And even though PvdA and GL were also expected to put forward 'Neither Ownership nor Choice' claims (in E1 and E2 respectively), their manifestos have in fact been characterised by several statements stemming from *both* categories.[25] And like in Belgium, the number of 'Neither Ownership nor Choice' statements has been remarkably high,[26] especially so given where the parties are spatially located.

The Swedish centre-left parties have more frequently framed their positions as a matter of 'Ownership' *and* 'Choice',[27] whereas for the centre-right it has primarily been in terms of the former.[28] This runs contrary to what was expected to be the case, given their spatial locations, and because of the PR system that they compete in (Hs.6 and 7). But such an outcome also raises questions about how any ideological tension has come to affect their modes of electoral competition (H.4). For SAP, where the ideological strains have been most obviously present, attempts at claiming 'Ownership' are evidenced in three manifestos (E3[29], E4[30] and E6[31]), and for M and V, which conversely experienced less tension, it is evidenced four times (in E1–E3 and in E6,[32] and E2–E5[33], respectively). Yet, this type of framing has also been present among the

FM/GAL parties (H.4), which were *not* expected to behave accordingly (MP: E1–E3; E6[34]; CP: E1–E3; E6[35]; FP: E1–E6[36] and KD: E1–E4; E6[37]). And when the statements were assumed to be framed as 'Neither Ownership nor Choice', this has not been confirmed for either of the four parties that had a score of (0). Although this is explained by some manifestos not referencing the EU at all (V (in E6), CP (in E4) and KD (in E5)), the latter party quite clearly used an ownership lens in E3[38] (on 'Function of the EU').

The manifesto analyses had further anticipated a relatively even spread of strategies on the immigration 'issue'. But the de facto struggles suggest that ownership competition has clearly dominated in the respective elections. And this has been the case regardless of electoral system, degree (and type) of 'pull', or should parties be placed on different sides of the immigration coin.

The regional divide is once again present in the Belgian case (see further Deschouwer, 2013). Although the sole instance when a Flemish party (GA, E3) was expected to make ownership claims has been confirmed[39] (Hs.4 and 5), the empirical support regarding 'Choice' has been higher[40] (H.6). But this strategy is also likely to be coupled with a distinct ownership[41] approach as well. The 'Neither Ownership nor Choice' predictions have, conversely, not been supported. For Sp.a. and Open Vld, the results are explained by their manifestos not referencing the 'issue' at all (between E2 and E4 for the former, and in E3 for the latter). But in E1, Sp.a's language is distinctly ownership orientated,[42] which is also an approach that applies to CD&V in E3.[43]

In Wallonia, the number of predicted 'Ownership' claims has not only been higher but so has the confirmation ratio[44] (H.5). Equally, when these parties were expected to frame their positions as a matter of 'Choice' (Ecolo and MR in E1), it has only been partially confirmed (H.6). Although Ecolo utilised both 'Ownership' and 'Choice' discourses,[45] MR has instead adopted for an exclusively ownership-style approach.[46] The comparatively higher frequency of 'Neither Ownership nor Choice' claims is again explained by the lack of coverage (Ecolo in E2, CDH and MR in E3). But the latter two parties also acted against their expected behaviour when they emphasised ownership (CDH in E1[47] and E2[48]), when they coupled ownership claims with non-committal statements (MR in E4[49] and E5[50]) or when they have combined ownership with choice statements (MR in E6[51]).

The British parties have very consistently acted against their anticipated behaviour. While the data would support the 'Ownership'[52] and 'Neither Ownership nor Choice'[53] predictions that were made (E3), none of the 'Choice' predictions have been confirmed (Hs.5 and 6). The political conversation has instead – and quite clearly so – been steered towards parties trying to (re)claim ownership over the immigration 'issue'. The findings also suggest how such a strategy has been used to neutralise any ideological 'pull' that Labour and the Conservatives, in particular, experienced (H.4). Yet, at the same time there are also strong reasons to believe that the FPTP system has played a role here. Ownership claims are by far the preferred mode of framing and are present regardless of whether parties have been 'pulled' or not (H.7).[54]

Since the Dutch parties are placed in different policy spheres (with the exception of PvdA in E1, and between E3 and E5), they should thus be expected to emphasise the 'Choice' that they offer to the electorate. But this assumption has only been partially confirmed since *across the board* parties have tended to stress their 'Ownership' capabilities more often than the anticipated 'Choice' positions[55] (Hs.4, 6 and 7).

The Swedish parties, finally, were expected to emphasise 'Ownership' since they have predominantly come to occupy the same policy space (H5). However, the results suggest that 'Choice' has been the preferred mode of framing (H.7). The centre-left, in particular, has more frequently put forward such statements.[56] But when 'Ownership' claims are made, any perceived incompetence is not primarily attributed to individual parties, or to the incumbent government, but rather to a *state* failure of not having been able to deal appropriately with certain migrant categories.[57] This would arguably point to how the strong consensus culture that has surrounded the immigration 'issue' has become so entrenched and inseparable from the Swedish state's raison d'être that it has transcended the individual parties and party families. The centre-right parties, conversely, have more frequently engaged in ownership competition but also display significant variation between them. FP, in particular, has fully conformed to the predictions that were made and framed their position as a matter of competence, or in relation to the party's sustained commitment to the 'issue',[58] across all of the six elections. The statements put forward by CP and KD, on the other hand, have tended to emphasise 'Choice'[59] more often than they have 'Ownership'.[60] The behaviour of SAP and M is, however, puzzling. The former has *not* engaged in any significant ownership competition even though this type of behaviour was expected for spatial reasons and because of the conflicting 'pulls' that the party experienced[61]. Although M presents 'Ownership' discourses more often than SAP does, the high frequency of 'Choice' statements[62] that both parties offered suggests how the PR system may very well override any incentives that parties have had for competing over ownership (H.7). The 'Neither Owner-ship nor Choice' predictions have only been confirmed twice. This is again related to the relative lack of references made to the 'issue' in their respective manifestos (MP in E1 and E3, V in E2, SAP in E3, CP in E2–E4 and KD in E2–E3, E5).

The overall findings suggest the EU to have been an easier question for parties to engage with compared to immigration. This is evidenced by the even spread of tactics that the mainstream has opted for on the former but also by the predominance of 'Ownership' approaches that are present on the latter. While some of these outcomes are not entirely unexpected (in Belgium and Britain especially), it was surprising to find such a high frequency of statements that alluded to competence, or to a sustained commitment, on *both* issues (in the Netherlands and Sweden in particular). The degree of 'pull' and parties' (in)ability to come to terms with these strains would partly explain why the mainstream has often taken the safer *ownership* route rather than risking any adverse electoral outcomes by offering a *choice*. Yet, for a majority of the parties in this book, an intra-dimensional strain has also been present, and this finding would thus shed further light on the identified behaviour. But this tension has, somewhat surprisingly, been more prominent in relation to the EU than it has on immigration.

6
The Death of Ideology, or Ways of Dealing with an Increased State of Flux

The rationale for this book was to explore the changing nature of party competition in an era of increased ideological uncertainty and disconnect between parties and electorates. A key concern was to assess the relevance of parties' ideological placements – especially in multi-dimensional spaces – and whether opposing stances would generate any conflicting 'pulls' once the EU and immigration were factored in. By conducting a manifesto analysis, and by being sensitive to the institutional context that parties function in, some predictions were made regarding the type of party that should be more *and* less likely to experience such strains. A set of seven hypotheses were then explored by bringing in qualitative (semi-structured interviews with political elites) and quantitative data (quantifying manifesto statements). A secondary objective was to, more broadly, assess the alleged decline of 'visions' in contemporary European politics. That is, should the anticipated tensions *not* be recognised, or not be perceived as particularly problematic for the concerned parties, then this would allow for some more general conclusions to be made on the relationship between ideology, party behaviour and modes of competition.

The overall results point to several interesting – and sometimes counterintuitive – developments. First, ideology still matters to parties. But although it continues to be an important driver – for party identity, for the solutions offered and for the policy positions adopted – its relevance has not applied equally, or in the same way, across the four cases. The identified 'pulls' appear to be stronger within those parties where the class struggle has been, and to some extent still is, central to their party identity. Yet, the dilemma of how to balance more state intervention in one sphere with less intervention in the other has also been a tension that has characterised the broader SI/GAL category and one that was present *regardless* of context. For some of the parties in the FM/TAN category, on the other hand, any equivalent strains appeared to have been weaker.

When compared to the EU 'issue', immigration seems to be a much more difficult area for parties to engage with, and has therefore come to crystallise these tensions more often. At the same time, however, a majority of the interviewees also reported how their party had been subject to an inter-dimensional 'push'. This situation became apparent as the European project was said to gradually have moved away from its original purpose. That is, the dormant ideological tensions tended to (re)surface once the EU developed into more of a *political* union rather than being a distinctly *economic* one. The SI/GAL combination would again appear to be more troublesome for parties to negotiate than what the FM/TAN coupling has been. Although the FM/GAL parties may have found both areas easier to deal with, the EU had nevertheless come to affect their party *identity*. An additional set of tensions had thus emerged here as some of these parties had been trying to reconcile these *intra*-dimensional 'pulls'. Concerns over the 'proper' role of the Union, and should policies and directives interfere too much with state sovereignty, had occasionally pushed their positions closer to the FM/TAN category. But such an ideological transformation, or adjustment at least, has taken place within some of the SI/GAL parties as well. The difference being that once the EU/immigration was factored in, their issue positions had in fact become moderated rather than reinforced or pushed towards the adjacent dimension. A few of the 'Green' and 'Socialist' parties have, however, constituted an anomaly for the conducted study. The Belgian and Dutch ones, in particular, should have been more conflicted than what their MPs reported, yet this was only fully confirmed for GA. This is in itself a surprising finding. As a 'new left' party they should operate according to a different set of ideological parameters (similar to those of GL and MP), and any 'pulls' should be, if not redundant, than at least perceived to be less problematic for the party. While the interviews conducted with the 'Socialist' parties would confirm that some ideological tension was indeed present, this strain had tended to be *intra*- rather than *inter*-dimensional.

And, second, should ideology continue to matter, then it would appear to be just as important that parties also get the balance 'right'. The difficulties experienced by, especially, the SI/GAL parties, but also by those in the FM/TAN category, suggest that when parties have conflicting views on the role of the state, they are also conflicted on how to interpret the effect(s) of the EU and immigration. This may in turn make it difficult for them to internally negotiate and agree on what type of 'issue' the two issues constitute. However, the weak TAN scores for some of these parties raise further questions as to how any variability within each ideological pair matters for the strength of these 'pulls'. The Conservatives, CD&V and M may be spatially close to each other but the FM/TAN combination seemed to be much more problematic for the first party than it has been for the latter two. Varying levels of dimensional saliency could of course explain this, and would as such help us to understand the Swedish case (see e.g. Grendstad, 2003; Sundberg, 1999; Granberg and Holmberg, 1986). But it was less obvious why the Conservatives would be so much more troubled by multidimensionality and by the intra- and inter-dimensional 'pulls' than what CD&V has been. And this was even more puzzling considering how the party functions in an FPTP system (Raymond, 2011; Hopkins, 2009; Urwin, 1970). Should the Conservative Party thus be indicative of the tensions caused by this particular combination, then placement on the FM/TAN dimension alone may represent yet another source of strain as any 'modernisation' attempts will engage elites and rank-and-file members with different FM/TAN views, as well as with different issue positions and with different issue priorities. For those parties that managed to get the balance 'right', primarily through the combination of FM- and GAL positions, then any of the cross-cutting challenges that the EU and immigration can give rise to may be easier to deal with but should also be less divisive and less likely to cause any further intra-party fragmentation. But this, of course, presupposes that party elites and party members are willing and able to make the connection between their 'ideological' and their 'issue' position, and that there is also some form of consensus on the societal effects that the EU and immigration can and have had.

Finally, institutions also matter but appear to matter less than what was initially assumed. As the British data highlight, the FPTP system does indeed encourage broad programmatic appeals, which, in terms of the EU, has often trumped any prevailing ideological tensions, but the overall findings would nevertheless suggest how the studied parties have been subjected to some form of ideological strain. Especially so when they have conflicting views on the role and remit of the state (GA, Conservatives, V and SAP), and should any (re)balancing attempts not yet have filtered through (Labour). This further stresses the importance of getting the balance, at least partially, 'right' so as to be able to reconcile any of these internal ideological differences.

Little wonder, then, that when ideological uncertainty increases, it is also accompanied by an increasing amount of manifesto statements that try to evidence competence and an ability to deliver. At first glance this would correspond to what theories of 'issue ownership' would predict is likely to happen (Green, 2007; Green and Hobolt, 2008; Petrocik, 1996). However, most of the parties in this book have not only made 'ownership' claims when there has been a virtual convergence of positions. In fact, such claims have been present even when the assumption was such that parties should have framed their stances as a matter of 'Choice', and they were also evidenced when parties were assumed to offer very basic or non-committal statements. But as suggested in previous chapters, one should perhaps not be entirely taken aback by this development. The cross-cutting nature of both 'issues' has tended to make it very difficult for the political mainstream to decide on dimensional fit and societal impact and, subsequently, how they are to frame the potential 'Choice' that they are to offer. And should parties also get the balance 'wrong', then this may very well result in sustained, and arguably unwanted, attention from the electorate, from their mainstream competitors and from the populist radical right. To try and (re)claim ownership can therefore be a safe and convenient way for parties to get out of this rather unpleasant ideological bear trap, and especially so should the choice on offer border that of their more radical competitors.

Some of the results generated through this research have been in line with what the 'party competition' and 'institutions' literature have identified as key developments in the field (see e.g. Holian, 2004; Dalton and Wattenberg, 2000; Budge and Farlie, 1983). This is most obviously the case in Britain where ownership struggles have indeed come to dominate campaign discourses *even* when the manifestos were expected to offer a choice (in E2–E5 on the EU, and in E1–E2 and E4–E5 on immigration). Although Labour's and the Conservative's behaviours run in parallel with their office-seeking ambitions, attempts to claim – or at least challenge – ownership has also featured heavily in the primarily vote-seeking Liberal Democrats' manifestos. This further suggests how the centripetal forces of the British system (Sartori, 1976) are so strong that even when parties are 'pulled' by opposing ideological streams, when they are placed in different policy dimensions or when they have different electoral aims, they are still steered towards competing over ownership. But this mode of competition is not solely the domain of parties that happen to operate in an FPTP system. It has equally come to characterise competition in the more centrifugal PR systems, and parties have by and large opted for an ownership approach there as well. The findings would thus confirm the overall state of flux that West European party systems are said to be in (Mair, 1989; 2008). But they also point to how the changing political landscapes have meant that parties have had to adapt their strategies and tactics, very much in response to these challenges.

A few queries have however emerged over the course of writing this book, and they have only been dealt with in brief. One relates to the identified differences between the office- and vote-seeking parties. The former category has more obviously struggled when trying to (re)define their party's ideological identity, and have as such been much more likely to be 'pulled' between the two ideological dimensions. This could very well relate to the 'catch-all' approach that these parties are forced to adopt, which, conversely, tends to be less relevant for the smaller, and primarily vote-seeking, parties. This would in turn suggest that size, organisational culture and party structure also matter, and that these factors are likely to serve as additional sources of tension that need to be factored in. A second question concerns the regional divide that is present in Belgium. This split has not only served to pit the mirror parties against each other but has also given rise to some rather peculiar manifesto positions and party understandings of the two 'issues'. These have been particularly puzzling – even counterintuitive – in relation to the immigration 'issue', and did not seem to follow any obvious pattern or logic.

And, finally, the results have highlighted the need for political scientists to adopt a 'mixed methods' and a 'mixed modelling' approach when trying to make sense of the changing nature of party competition, in general as well as on specific issues. The manifesto analysis did enable certain predictions to be made but had these quantitative results not been supplemented by the qualitative data then the conclusions that were reached would only tell half the story. This discrepancy came to the fore when the figures suggested one type of party but the interview data would point to another. And since some manifestos contained very brief accounts or would lack statements that referred to the EU and/or immigration, it is likely that the 'true' position for some parties has been underestimated. These challenges thus echo some of the reservations that have been made elsewhere, regarding how useful – and *reliable* – manifestos are for the scholarly understanding of parties' ideological and issue positions (see e.g. Gemenis, 2012; Dinas and Gemenis, 2010; Walgrave and Nuytemans, 2009; Franzmann and Kaiser, 2006; Pelizzo, 2003) but they also highlight the ongoing methodological struggles that the comparative researcher faces.

Notes

2 Competing in Multidimensional Party Spaces

1. While a more orthodox approach would refer to this divide as a 'Socialist–Capitalist' one (see e.g. Clark and Lipset, 1991), the definition adopted here more accurately reflects the changing nature of this cleavage and how it has increasingly come to revolve around relative degrees of acceptance of 'the market' (Huber and Inglehart, 1995).
2. It should be noted that spatial theory contains a number of 'ifs' and if one or more of these assumptions are violated, the expected results tend to disappear (Grofman, 2004).
3. The manifestos were gathered from (1) http://www.polidoc.net, (2) by personal arrangement from Manifesto Research on Political Representation, Science Research Centre, Berlin (WBZ), (3) by personal arrangement from individual parties (Belgium), (4) http://www.rug.nl/bibliotheek/services/dnpp (the 2003 election has been omitted since the CDA and PvdA ran the same manifestos as they did in 2002), (5) http://www.politicsresources.net/area/uk/man.htm and (6) through the CD-ROM 'Swedish Election Manifestos, 1902–2002' (http://snd.gu.se/en/catalogue/search/manifestos). The manifestos for the 2006 and 2010 elections were downloaded from individual party websites.
4. This category includes any mentions not covered by the other categories.
5. For example, [Immigration (in general)] 'People from abroad make a positive contribution to British society'. (Labour, 2001) (–1); 'Do you know that 100,000 asylum-seekers have entered our country in the past seven years and that most of them have stayed illegally?' (MR, 1995) (+1); [Student Migration] 'America and China know how to lure the best students and scientists. These people must come and stay here!' (VVD, 2006); (–1); 'We want to encourage students to come to our universities and colleges, but our student visa system has become the biggest weakness in our border controls.' (Conservatives, 2010) (+1).
6. Despite several attempts, the research assistant was not able to carry out any interviews with representatives from CDH.

3 (Almost) Contesting the EU and Immigration (1945–1990)

1. The laws were subsequently tightened in 1993 and then again in 1994.
2. The Belgian Nationality Code was thus restructured along these lines in 1991.
3. Although these measures were also coupled with the Race Relations Act 1965, which outlawed discrimination in public places and incitement to racial hatred.

4   'Pulled' or 'Pushed'? Increased Ideological Uncertainty on the EU and Immigration 'Issues'

1. '//...//on economic issues, [we are] generally speaking a left-wing party//...//very much in favour of keeping social rights, e.g. pensions and housing benefits, spending on the vulnerable segments of society//...//[We are not] afraid to propose a new tax even, if we think that's necessary.' (GA 2)
2. 'I also think of [the party] as being very progressive and a bit alternative.' (GA 2).
3. 'It's an ecological party//...//whose core business is probably the environment.' (GA 2)
4. 'Apart from Vlaams Belang, no one is particularly critical of the European Union [in Belgium]//...//the bottom line is that we are all euro enthusiasts.' (GA 1)
5. 'We want to put human beings and their human rights at the centre of our reasoning. And the vulnerability of people too. Our position is also about protecting people. On asylum, for instance, the current discourse is all about letting as few people in as possible, whereas for us the main concern is that everyone who needs asylum should get it.' (GA 2)
6. 'Ecolo was founded by different associations, so you had feminists; Third World activists; anti-nuclear and pro-environmental movements etc. All these people didn't get any answers from the traditional parties, so they decided to create a new party that would defend all of these issues.' (Ecolo 1)
7. 'We want Europe to be a political power, which we don't think it is at the moment. The big, big fundamental issues that we are facing, e.g. the changing climate; the economic slowdown; the lack of social protection, these are all questions that Belgium, as a very small country, can't deal with on its own.' (Ecolo 1)
8. '[T]he only way to describe the party is that it's to the left. Not, so to speak, on the outskirts but more as a centre-left party.' (Sp.a 1)
9. 'We cannot be described as an old, left-wing party anymore. We are not against the market as a matter of principle and neither are we for extensive state intervention. We believe that the market forces can be useful and are necessary for furthering our goal of the good life for everyone. However the market often tends to favour the rich and the privileged, and often produces unjust outcomes for everyone else. Therefore, corrective state intervention is crucial.' (Sp.a 2)
10. '[W]e are definitely left-wing here, our values are the opposite of conservative. We believe that every individual has the right to live in accordance with his or her own values. Whether they are religious, libertarian or something in-between. The only restrictions are of a societal nature, every individual has to respect the rights of others and the rules that have been democratically decided upon by society.' (Sp.a 2)

    'Our party is different compared to the others//...//[we] stress democracy, human and social rights, both here and abroad.' (Sp.a1)
11. 'The key issue for us is to have a good social security system but the more important thing is to say that we want to live in a country where it is easy

to live. And by 'easy' we mean access to education, to justice, that we have a functioning healthcare system and a labour market that works. And those are very important issues for us to defend.' (PS 1)

'We are in favour of the welfare state basically. Its benefits, its health care, its pensions, and holidays as well actually. It's all part of the same concept for us.' (PS 3)

12. 'We are very much on the "left" but for us, "the left" means being in favour of rights' (PS 1)

13. 'We think that public education, transport and so on, should be free, or if not free than at least affordable to the largest possible number of people.' (PS 2)

14. '[I]t's very important to have these rights and to defend them//...//there should be a balance between the economic and the social systems.' (PS 1)

15. 'These economic and social issues need to be defended, the rights of foreign people or of the individual, and gender issues as well.' (PS 2)

16. '[I]t's absolutely certain that we are now following an agenda that is set by the European Commission, e.g. what the budget rules should be. This means that the European agenda is very much present and dictates the direction that they want us to go in.' (Sp.a 1)

17. 'We believe in openness and we welcome newcomers, but we also believe that rights and responsibilities work in tandem. Those who come here from elsewhere should be expected to make a contribution to society by learning the language, by working and by paying taxes' (Sp.a 2)

18. '[It] is an issue where the party has perhaps changed a little bit. We have always stressed solidarity because this is a key issue for us so it has certainly not been in our interest to have more and more people over because that makes this aim very difficult to achieve. But now, of course, we have the next generation, and more people are coming over and we are not able to treat them well. We can't provide them with a proper education and other services. In other words, we are not able to treat them correctly.' (Sp.a 1)

19. 'They said they were from Kosovo, and not from Albania, so they would have a greater chance of staying. Now 20 or so years later it became evident that these people had lied and that meant that the whole family was to be sent back to Albania. This was a very difficult decision to make because they were obviously fleeing from something, just not the 'right' thing, and not from the 'right' country.' (Sp.a 1)

20. '[A]s far as economic migration is concerned, well, the sky is maybe not the limit because we need to be able to treat these people correctly as well.' (Sp.a 1)

21. 'We have a problem of demography. And if we don't get young people coming here from other countries, then we'll have a problem with the social model of Europe.' (PS 1)

22. 'It's not only people with a certain level of education, or from certain labour categories. We have to accept immigration.' (PS 1)

23. 'We say "If we have immigration, it's because we are not doing enough for the south"//...//if we do more [for them], then that's the best way to regulate it.' (PS 1)

24. 'They say, 'Why should we do that? We are interested in some people, and they are the people that we want to have in Europe', and voila, problem

solved, 'but the others, they can stay over there'. We don't want to see immigration in that way// . . . //It's not a question of the economy and we don't want to say that we don't want any further immigration to Belgium.' (PS 1)

25. 'There are workers from several countries [here] but first of all they are "workers." ' (PS 2)

26. '[I]t's about showing international solidarity. And this means that it is really important to give this person the right to stay here, and that they have the same rights as the Belgian people have.' (PS 1)

27. '[W]e also know that they create competition so the regularisation of workers is very important because it keeps wage levels up.' (PS 2)

28. '[T]he differences between the rich and the poor, the importance of good unemployment schemes, the issue of a decent retirement age, these are the things that are important to us. And healthcare// . . . //[we have a] large stake in defending the welfare state, this means e.g. not increasing the retirement age or cutting unemployment benefits or the grants to students// . . . //' (SP 1)

29. '[W]e are more progressive on abortion and euthanasia [but] the Netherlands is also an outlier given the widespread support for these types of issues.' (SP 1)

30. '[S]trict but fair// . . . //asylum seekers that are persecuted for political or sexual or religious ideas and beliefs must find a safe haven [here]// . . . //But we are also strict toward those who seek economic benefit or opportunities and who want to come to the Netherlands for that.' (SP 1)

31. 'It would be wrong to say that we are 'left-wing trade unionists' for instance. Our position is more related to a form of liberalism. And it's an ethical one as well. We are very liberal in lots of ways, almost libertarian on things like abortion, euthanasia and gay marriage. Prostitution even.' (GL 1)

32. '[W]orking arrangements, e.g., that's something which we think should be more flexible. The Netherlands has been very old-fashioned in that respect and has a tax system that's based on the male bread-winner. And that system has to be changed so you can have a better work/life-balance, say with a 2–3 day working week. That's where the debate comes from.' (GL 1)

33. '[W]e're the party that stands up for equal rights, and for the equal distribution of income. Emancipation is very important as well because it helps people to make their own lives better// . . . //We are basically a left-wing party.' (PvdA 2)

34. 'In the 70s the party stressed the role of the state// . . . //and in the early 80s, our party platform was full of economic planning. And no employer could be seen on it. It was just about the state and about economic regulation.' (PvdA 1); 'At the same time we need innovation, so we can get more growth and more out of the economy, so we say "Ok, we need a social welfare system, but we also need the innovation and that the economy is sustainable and not a threat to the environment"// . . . //[I]t has to be sustainable, but it cannot be the case that the rich people get a good outfit and the poor people have to pay the price.' (PvdA 2); 'We say, "Well, we are not against it as such but we have to regulate it and we have to look at where, how and if the market is the best place to deal with it or not".' (PvdA 3)

35. '[I]n the 70s and 80s we opened up to new movements, environmental and women's groups e.g. which has continued up to today. And this was combined with a rather liberal attitude towards citizens' rights and being very critical towards too much governmental activity in spheres that should be, well, for the citizens, the whole privacy issue e.g.// ... //[the party became] very critical towards the paternalistic approach to governing.' (PvdA 1); '[On the left you have two choices] are you conservative or progressive left? And we are progressive left. In the beginning, we were more about maintaining what we had, so we were more conservative then. In the last 4–8 years we've started to move and become more progressive.' (PvdA 2)

36. 'But [deciding on the party platform] has changed, today the individual members can also vote. This means that about 75% of the divisions can vote, and 20% of those votes are from our individual members.' (PvdA 2); 'On things like medico-ethical stuff, gay marriage and abortion we are very progressive. There is hardly any difference between our party and, let's say, GL// ... //"[T]here are also direct discussions between the rank and file and the MPs. And sometimes when a motion is approved by the members at the congress, then we also have to take these discussions into account."' (PvdA 3)

37. 'Work and social security, followed by organisation of the public sector, e.g. medical care and education' (PvdA 1); 'You see that the economic crisis is huge and a lot of people are losing their jobs. So we have to fight to keep a good system of social welfare.' (PvdA 2); '[O]ur mantra is work, work, work. We've always had the aim to emancipate the people from the lower social classes, we want to enable their social mobility.' (PvdA 3)

38. '[I]t's not that the cultural dimension is not important. It is. I think we underestimated that for a long time and we had a very blue-eyed vision about immigrants coming and integrating here// ... //[w]e've left that view far behind today' (PvdA 1); 'For several years nothing happened and people wouldn't integrate properly. You got some money and that was it. And then we said "Well you have to do these courses and you have to understand the Dutch society as well"' (PvdA 2); 'But we also know that you cannot receive every single migrant. So we do have stricter immigration laws today than we had in the 80s and 90s. And that's all fine with us.' (PvdA 3)

39. '[Today] there's a lot more emphasis on people having rights but they also have duties. And some people say that duties come first, telling migrants that they should comply with Dutch values and rules. So [society] has changed and the party has changed as well.' (PvdA 1); 'Now we say, "If you want to come here, then you first have to do a course in your home country", a short course on the Netherlands, and you have to know something about the society that you are going to. When you come here you have to get your "Dutch license". A certificate in other words, you have to do an exam on the Dutch society and in the Dutch language. As a government we are now spending a lot of money to make that happen, and to help the people on those courses// ... //.' (PvdA 2)

   'All these guys who are, you know, in crime, all these little Moroccan boys who are fourteen-fifteen years old and that terrorize their neighbourhoods after six o'clock in the evening, we all agree that they should be addressed. And severely so one could say.' (PvdA 3); '[W]e want to be a knowledge intensive economy, so we need more skilled people coming here. If we can use those people and if they want to come here then they are welcome.' (PvdA 1)

40. 'Skilled migration is not a huge issue because everyone agrees, and everybody says "Yes we have to improve the arrangements for those skilled workers"' (PvdA 2)

41. 'It's not primarily about economics, the bigger issue is about the people already living here. The ones with mixed backgrounds e.g. The youth from these groups are, well, having trouble and causing trouble//...//[W]e are much stricter [today], and there is still much debate within the party. Some people say that we are way too strict and that we are focusing too much on the cultural side and not enough on the social and economic side.' (PvdA 1)

    'But now we are in a coalition again so things are beginning to change. We are still less open than we used to be but we are a lot more open than we were, say, four years ago//...//[n]ot all party members agree on that. So there is a lot of discussion about what to do and which direction to take.' (PvdA 2)

    'We are in favour of regulated migration but in a humane and just way. So we say that if you have people who are really fleeing from war and famine, then you should always be able to take these people into your country. But we also know that you cannot receive every single migrant//...//Integration issues are much more important than immigration issues are, although, of course, you can never fully separate them.' (PvdA 3)

42. 'We don't hold the opinion that the state should own *everything* [original emphasis] but it should be a key player and have extensive influence.' (V 1); '[O]ur policies combine ideas of the planned economy while at the same acknowledging that the market forces do sometimes work.' (SAP 4)

43. '[I]t should be democratically run institutions and not primarily private actors.' (V 1); '[T]he public sector//...//is important because it acts as a stimulant to the economy and creates jobs and redistributes societal resources as a way to deal with inequalities.' (V 2); '[I]n the late 1980s we moved towards the centre-right but this was also coupled with a very critical discussion regarding privatisation, maybe everything couldn't be solved by the market.' (SAP 2)

44. 'There's not really any area where we would welcome more private ownership.' (V4); '[E]mployers gain enormous power during times of high unemployment, it becomes a lot easier for [them] to push for their positions and they have a lot more say over the situation.' (V 3)

45. '[W]e believe very strongly in individual freedom even though we also believe that sometimes collective solutions are also necessary.' (MP 1); '[W]e don't fit on conventional Left-Right scales. We have decided to be part of Red bloc because we haven't been able to reach an agreement with the Blues' (MP 2)

46. '[We have a] very clear position on e.g. issues relating to personal freedom' (V 4); '[P]olitics is also about individual freedom, the environment

and feminism. The latter is especially important to the party' (V 1); 'We are very much a grassroots' party and they do have a lot of influence.' (MP 1); 'Above anything else, we see climate and environmental issues as fundamental for the survival of humankind' (MP 2); '[T]he key points are justice, solidarity and individual freedom' (SAP 4)

47. 'At the same time, we favour a personalised maternity and paternity insurance which is very much about state interference.' (V 4); '[I]t has been very difficult for us to combine freedom of choice with equality// ... //[W]e wanted was what best for mankind [so] we needed to have a extensive control over society and the individual.' (SAP 3); '[This dimension] is sometimes more problematic since it requires us to decide on things that are not obviously "social democratic" '. (SAP 4)

48. 'V is the most EU-critical party in parliament. There is still the decision that was taken at our party congress which says that we would rather see that Sweden left the Union.' (V3)

49. '[W]e accept the referendum and the decision to join that was taken back in 1994// ... //[a]t the same time, our party program says that we should strive for Sweden to leave the EU. I think this is somewhat of a contradiction.' (V 1)

50. 'Our ideology is not based on something that was written hundreds of years ago// ... //one has to have "common sense" as a starting point.' (MP 1); '[S]ometimes we are the new social liberal party, and sometimes we are the strong Green party and other times we are the party for solidarity.' (MP 2)

51. 'We have an "open borders"-approach// ... //this meant that we could co-operate with the Alliance on labour migration'. (MP 2)

52. 'The EU has been an open wound for us for quite some time now.' (SAP 3)

53. '[W]e don't like the idea that businesses can use labour migration as a tool to undermine the trade unions or as a way of undercutting salaries and to basically create a pool of cheap labour' (V 4); 'If you leave recruitment up to individual firms then there's so much that can go wrong.' (SAP 4)

54. '[I]t has been easier for the party to have a clear position on asylum and refugees because that has to do with certain values which are more compatible with who we are and where we stand.' (V 1); '[It is a] very fundamental act of solidarity and it is important that you actually help out here' (V 2); '[T]hese values have become rather well established in the party, that is, solidarity and openness towards those that have suffered but coupled with a hesitation towards labour migration.' (SAP 1)

55. 'Social questions are very important to us, family issues e.g., and we also want to have a decent system of social security and that we are able to take care of those people that are in a weaker position in society.' (CD&V 2)

56. '[W]e try to offer consensus, so our party is, and has been, closely affiliated with the peasants'; workers' and employers' movements. That's very important to us, we offer not just one topic or 'solution' but also a 'model' for society. (CD&V 1)

57. '[W]e are convinced that we are working for all kinds of families, the single households; the separated, and the newly composed ones but we also have a problem of matching this view with that of the voters and the general

public// . . . //they think 'family values' but we are also about trying to give some more practical and concrete advice to families. In general.' (CD&V 1); '[W]e see ourselves as the party for the family, but I don't think that's how people see us, they think of us as the party for a particular *type* [original emphasis] of family'. (CD&V 2)

58. 'We think that people realise themselves through being part of a group, and that you need some form of common basis to be able to do so. Identity is therefore linked to the cultural society that you belong to. For us this is the Flemish community and the Flemish identity that sticks the most. We are of course Belgian and Europeans as well but our strongest affiliation is with the Flemish people. And within our state structures we think that the Flemish community should have more competencies so we that we can take better care of our people.' (CD&V 1)

59. 'We are Euro-lovers. We always have been, and we think that it has done a lot for Europe and for Belgium as well' (CD&V 1); 'We've always been very strongly in favour of Europe. So for us the whole constitution thing, and being afraid of losing power, has never been an issue. And especially not for our party. Belgium is so small and we have always believed that we need to be part of a bigger entity.' (CD&V 2)

60. '[W]e are a centre-right party// . . . //favouring lower taxes, less state intervention, etc.' (Cons 2); 'Tax credits e.g., actually destroy incentives to work.' (Cons 4)

61. 'IDS was clearly Thatcherite-right; Howard was Authoritarian-Thatcherite-right, except in certain policy areas where he was, funnily enough, a bit of a social-liberal. Hague was seen to be on the Thatcherite-right// . . . //Defence policy is currently a lot more to the right than trade is// . . . //[W]hen pragmatism trumps dogmatism, that's where a lot of the confusion// . . . //comes from.' (Cons 3); 'The membership base is a lot more to the "right".' (Cons 6)

62. '[T]he new MPs are a lot more relaxed in their views on e.g. civil partnerships.' (Cons 2)

63. 'What's significant now is that the party has ring-fenced the NHS but not defence.' (Cons 1)

64. '[Cameron] talks about openness, transparency, democracy// . . . //but the way that he has run the Conservatives has been the complete opposite.' (Cons 2)

65. 'Where do *you* [Cameron; original emphasis] stand here?// . . . //You can't have a Left *and* [original emphasis] a Right-wing approach.' (Cons 3); '[T]he most extreme free marketeers tend to be the most authoritarian on social issues.' (Cons 4)

66. '[T]he EU now has the ability to dictate policy through various directives or to force Britain to go to Brussels to do certain things// . . . //[I]t seems like there are endless policy areas where the EU has jurisdiction rather than the national governments. It's also this idea that the EU is a club which we are paying a lot into but not necessarily getting that much back from.' (Cons 2)

'The majority thought that the EU was a good idea, "nothing nasty can happen unless we agree to it". What has changed today is that the enthusiasts are no longer as enthusiastic anymore because membership costs us a lot of money.' (Cons 7); 'There are so many differences between the member states today. You need to ask yourself, what is the purpose of the Union?' (Cons 8); 'I think they are appalled by how the political development is marching steadily towards the 'United States of Europe', that's the one war cry that the party unites around. They do *not* [original emphasis] want a political union. An economic union, fine, because that will hopefully create jobs and bring prosperity.' (Cons 9)

67. '"Decontamination" became a buzzword during the election and decontamination means not talking about Europe, at least not ad nausea like the party did before.' (Cons 1); 'The strategic position has been to downplay it since it gives unnecessary attention to UKIP.' (Cons 3); 'It's horrible, but having said that, what can I do? Nothing. I can't go to the party because they don't want to talk about it.' (Cons 7)

68. '[W]e got that unprecedented influx of people that the country wasn't really prepared for.' (Cons 2); 'You have to find somewhere for them to live, to go to school, to be treated, and that creates pressure.' (Cons 5); '[I]t's whether or not they manage to adapt which is the issue.' (Cons 6)

69. 'If you have 3 million unemployed then they can fill those positions.' (Cons 3); '[Y]ou don't need to import cheap labour in order to get the job done.' (Cons 5)

70. '[I]t's our history and our heritage//...//Immigration evokes those types of quite fundamental questions' (Cons 5); '[Y]ou go from a situation of being a predominantly "white" country and then finding that this is no longer the case.' (Cons 6)

71. '[W]hether or not you have a perception that public services are being allocated in an unfair way.' (Cons 4); '[P]riority was given to people who had just arrived.' (Cons 5)

72. '[W]e've always opened our doors to immigration, e.g., Jews fleeing the Nazis.' (Cons 5)

73. 'It's not about//...//ethnicity or race, it's about fairness.' (Cons 4); '[W]hat you have to pay out now, and what you get back later, that equation does not work out in the taxpayers' favour.' (Cons 5); 'They had traditionally been promised jobs, council accommodation, a relatively settled situation in other words but now they feel that people are taking this over.' (Cons 6)

74. '[O]ur ability to control immigration has gone down to zero.' (Cons 7); '[T]he issue of Human Rights makes it very difficult to deport illegal immigrants.' (Cons 5.)

75. 'Every time that tactic has been made explicit, it has not worked' (Cons 6).

76. 'Many of our voters are not religious and they don't go to church but they do believe that our Christian roots are important for the Dutch and European societies and that these roots should be well kept. That's the basis of our political thinking. We believe in a strict division between church and state. But we also believe that religion and politics are intertwined.' (CDA 3)

77. 'The way that people relate to each other lies at the core of society and we have to make the best out of people's social behaviour. Not so much that the state or the market 'should' organise it, it's rather how society itself should be able to organise it//...//Norms and values are important issues to us.' (CDA 2)

78. 'It's grounded in religious principles// . . . //which shape the discussions that we have within the party, how to approach and deal with issues. It is also a stable party, located in the middle.' (CDA 1); '// . . . //it's not based on any fundamentalist Christian ideas but rather on the more general values stemming from a Christian tradition.' (CDA 2)
79. 'We have always been seen as a centre party, but more centre-right than centre-left.' (CDA 2)
80. '[A]bortion should be the very last resort// . . . //if you look at these types of issues, we are maybe a little more to the right. A bit stricter perhaps.' (CDA 1)
81. 'How can we – as a society – discuss how to deal with these issues? Not just that you finish your life and that's it, problem solved.' (CDA 1); 'The CDA is pro-life and has strong opinions on medico-ethical issues, on medical euthanasia for example// . . . //' (CDA 3)
82. 'And that's not typical for the Netherlands, that's typical for *some* [original emphasis] parts of the Netherlands, for the big cities especially. So more and more people have started to think that we've gone too far. And that we have to find a new common *moral* [original emphasis] ground for how to cope in society.' (CDA 3)
83. 'In a coalition, we usually co-operate easier with VVD than with PvdA.' (CDA 1); '[D]uring the elections people often talk about VVD and us against PvdA and the D'66. So there is a 'left' and a 'right' in that sense.' (CDA 2); 'I think we are a bit more to the right than the left. We need to try and bring down the debt that we have so we have to make some quite serious and difficult decisions as to how this should be done. At the moment, I think that we push this more than the left does. On, e.g., health care we try to be more market oriented, reduce costs and raise the quality of health care etc.' (CDA 4)
84. '[I]f you look at our position on medico-ethical issues then you can't say that we are very right-wing, I see the liberals as being more right-wing than we are. But on medico-ethical questions, they are totally opposed to what we stand for. So I can't answer this, they are very difficult questions in comparison' (CDA 2); 'But it's not a left-right thing, because the liberals are thinking the other way around. They are on the financial economical side. They are more right-wing than we are.' (CDA 3)
85. 'It's in our genes as one of the EU's co-founding groups, so it would be odd for us to not be in favour of it as well.' (CDA 2); 'We are a very pro-Europe party.' (CDA 3)
86. 'Some migrants are highly qualified and therefore needed, but we also have some that we know will never be able to fully participate. The young married mothers from the centre of Morocco for example.' (CDA 2); '[W]e are very strict regarding people who don't have any intellectual luggage.' (CDA 3); 'We have a liberal approach towards people with skills and if they want to come here and work, then we want to make it easier for them to do so.' (CDA 4)
87. 'We say, "We should be strict on asylum", but nevertheless consider the situation of the very vulnerable// . . . //[W]e will always lean towards the position of the weak, of children and so on.' (CDA 2); '[W]e believe that you have to have an open door for the real refugees but that you also have

to have a closed door for the economic refugees. You know, the ones that just try their luck.' (CDA 3)

88. '[T]he bottom line is that we have to be strict on immigration – that's our starting point.' (CDA 1)

89. 'The people that want to set up a family here, or that want to marry some-one from abroad, they are for the most part uneducated and cause a lot of problems when they are here, those are the numbers that we need to bring down.' (CDA 4)

90. 'Everybody is equal but we have a problem with those people who do not live according to the norms and values of Western society. And then we come to the issue that there are people from different countries here and how we go about seeing them as Dutch citizens. The Netherlands is not one of those traditional melting pot societies.' (CDA 2); '[R]eligion is an important issue for us. But that also means that people have a right to freedom *from* religion. On the other hand we are also very harsh on the abuses of religion. For example, we've had some Imams who preached that homosexuals should be thrown off the highest tower in the Netherlands. So when it comes to violence in the name of religion, we are very harsh on that.' (CDA 4)

91. '[W]e do believe in market solutions to economic problems.' (M 3)

92. '[We've] not been very consistent when it comes to those non-economic types of questions// ... //They have provided us with, perhaps not an identity crisis, but definitely some challenges.' (M 3)

93. '[T]he individual should be able to decide more and the state should decide less, that's the essence of what the party is about.' (M 2)

94. '[They] were against it because they thought that marriage should follow the traditional religious traditions.' (M 2); '[A] majority of the party would not [characterise themselves as feminists].' (M 1)

95. '[W]e are a lot more in favour of CCTV and monitoring [today].' (M 1)

96. 'Clearer, more consistent and more demanding rules for those refugees who want to become permanent residents// ... //For the annual meeting we proposed a contract// ... //things like accepting fundamental democratic values, human and women's rights, etc.' (M 1)

97. 'We are only really prepared to accept a very minimal amount of state own-ership. We are quite liberal in that respect. We favour the strong market economy of course but there should still be some regulations. We are not against them as such but the key players should be private, and the state's role is to impose those types of regulations that prevent the abuse of power or any distortion of competition, things like that.' (MR 1)

98. 'As a liberal party there are certain questions that lie to the very core of who we are and what we stand for// ... //we don't want taxes to go up, they should stay low// ... //our party is about economic issues and social security, those types of things.' (Open VLD 1)

99. 'Although everyone in the party feels that these are the themes that res-onate well with people, we don't really have an obvious tradition to fall back on that would allow us to have a firm position on such questions. And we don't have enough people who are working on them either, not enough voices basically.' (Open VLD 1)

100. 'As we see it, the EU offers several opportunities for working together, it makes trade easier, it creates a bigger market, and then you get all those positive spin-off effects that come with free trade as well.' (Open VLD 1); 'European expansion has worked wonderfully well. It has never made us lose any wealth, but always generated more. It has enabled the other countries to grow to our level because the economic benefits are so great when you have a bigger market to sell your goods on. So I'm convinced that if we do that with Turkey as well, it would still work.' (Open VLD 2)

101. '[T]here is more consensus today// ... //but with the difference being that Labour is much more interventionist than the other parties are.' (Lab 2)

102. 'You can have growth and prosperity based on a capitalist system and you can sustain a base level of employee's rights// ... //[The Conservatives] think that you should just let the market rip and if the jobs go, then they will go and new opportunities will come out of this// ... //But we don't believe that.' (Lab 1); '[It's] primarily a party about social justice// ... //that comes from the perspective that we need to create a fairer society with more equal opportunities.' (Lab 2)

103. 'We used to advocate for the nationalisation of certain industries but that's no longer an important issue for us.' (Lab 2); '[D]ropping Clause 4 is really the key change here.' (Lab 3)

104. '[Y]ou have less protection if you are made unemployed// ... //But the rest of Europe has a consistently higher rate of unemployment than we do.' (Lab 1)

105. 'We chose to expand our labour market and to give people opportunities. How do we compensate for that? Well, we built in the tax credit system as a way to make it pay for people to work.' (Lab 1); 'By not increasing income tax as much as we could have done we also lost the image of being the party of high taxes.' (Lab 2)

106. '[We have] always been the small "L" liberal party on these questions// ... //social issues, women's rights, they are an important set of issues ... I'm trying to find an umbrella term to put them under ... lifestyle issues I guess ... people's attitudes towards difference in society.' (Lab 2)

107. 'We have a skills shortage and need certain workers to come here that are not available domestically.' (Lab 1); '[M]aximising economic growth and keeping inflation down were the major factors here. It was primarily a practical position rather than an ideological one.' (Lab 2) '[There] was a surprising degree of agreement between the trade unions and the federation of British employers on this issue.' (Lab 4)

108. '[They were] basically a set of economic tests in order to control numbers and to ensure a sense of fairness// ... //The controversy// ... //was about the effects of population growth and the pressure on our services that further migration would have.' (Lab 1); '[P]eople think that too many people have been let in// ... //e.g. where I live there is a lot of construction going on and if someone's son can't get a job on the site and then he sees a lot of Eastern Europeans working there then you can understand that.' (Lab 2); '[T]he unions were very concerned about how further immigration [from the new member states] would affect wage levels and workers' rights.' (Lab 3)

109. '[F]airness to those who seek asylum//...//was weighted against the competition over and pressure on resources and public services that the influx of people can and does generate in some communities.' (Lab 1)
110. 'To be fair to those that genuinely need the protection, then you have to protect the system.' (Lab 1); 'What happened around 2000 was that the Home Office started, for the first time in a very long time actually, to talk about an "immigration policy". I do not think that there was a real discussion about immigration policy prior to that.' (Lab 4)
111. 'The problem of "foreigners stealing our jobs" arises if you have different wage levels in one country and if people are then paid those levels if they are contracted to do work somewhere else where wages for the same type of work are actually higher.' (Lab 3); '[T]he phrase 'British jobs for British workers' implied that we are going to make it much more difficult for people to come here and work//...//What we are in control of is migration from outside the EU//...//It was a liberal approach but I think what happened was that the Home Office got the numbers completely wrong. They grossly underestimated the number of people who would come here.' (Lab 4)
112. 'I don't want the shops to be run by the state but I don't want private companies to run the railways either.' (Lib Dems 1); '[W]hat type of service are people getting and how can it best be provided? If it is best provided by a private actor, then that's the right answer. If it's provided best publicly, then that's the right answer.' (Lib Dems 2); '[W]e wanted to increase income tax – slightly – to allow for more spending on education//...//you need strong health and safety and employment protection policies but we also felt that some of the bureaucracy imposed on business was unnecessary.' (Lib Dems 3)
113. '[W]e are centre-left and we are liberal, those are the key things really.' (Lib Dems 2); '[It's] based on several key principles, individual liberty; social justice – and those go hand in hand – environmentalism and sustainability, internationalism. We are in essence a supranationalist party.' (Lib Dems 3)
114. 'The free marketeers dominate the party today but not exclusively, there are some people who are still more to the social side.' (Lib Dems 1); '[S]ome things are just *better* [original emphasis] when run publicly and some things are just *better* [original emphasis] run privately.' (Lib Dems 2); '[M]arket forces are "better" at solving economic issues than the state is but the difference is that we think that there should also be a strong safety net.' (Lib Dems 4); 'The publication of the "Orange Book" was very influential since it meant a clearer emphasis on economic mechanisms to solve economic problems//...//This type of thinking has gained ground but it's not universal in the party.' (Lib Dems 5)
115. '[T]he state should not interfere or have an opinion on this as long as it's between consenting adults//...//there are tensions and it's always a question of balance//...//civil liberties, identity cards, the environment, social justice, fairness, those are the things that voters think of first.' (Lib Dems 2); 'There is a strong argument for decriminalising cannabis//...//You can control it a lot better, you take away the necessity to be involved in crime and you can control the quality of the drug.' (Lib Dems 4)
116. 'We have a greater degree of flexibility in terms of disagreements within the party, a lot more so than the other two have.' (Lib Dems 1)

117. '[W]ho are the British? We are a bastard race and we must recognise that.' (Lib Dems 1); '[W]e find it hard to say "You are British and you are not"//...//immigration broadens and enriches "Britishness" for us.' (Lib Dems 4)
118. 'There's a lot of discussion [in the party] regarding balance, how much should the EU be able to intervene? Particularly in terms of some domestic policies, on the labour market e.g.' (Lib Dems 5)
119. 'Our commitment to free trade is the reason why we support Europe but free trade has to be genuinely free. And that also means fair trade. Not just within Europe but between Europe and the rest of world too.' (Lib Dems 5)
120. '[T]he British economy would suffer enormously if we didn't have migrant labour.' (Lib Dems 1); '[T]here is a mismatch between what the government wants and what the firms want.' (Lib Dems 4)
121. '[W]e regard immigration to be an overall positive thing//...//You widen the market and the economic base, it's basically a free market view that we have on migration.' (Lib Dems 4)
122. '[I]immigration should be commeasured with the economic need of the country and the public good//...//you need to make a fair assessment of how many people you need and with what type of skills that you need.' (Lib Dems 3)
123. '[I]t is civilised people's duty to look after people, from whatever country, who are fleeing genuine persecution and terror' (Lib Dems 3); '[W]e hold a lot of people in detention for a long time, over a year sometimes, and many of them are then released//...//you shouldn't hold someone for that long, particularly when we then often say that they are ok and can stay in the country.' (Lib Dem 2)
124. '[W]e're a right-wing party in economic terms. And I specifically mention that this is the 'correct' answer because in the Netherlands every party has a tendency to describe themselves as being a "centre" party. So a lot of people say that we are centre-right, and others say that we are centre-left. But most of the time, just to be clear, I leave out the word "centre"'. (VVD 1)
125. '[It's a] liberal party in the sense of being in favour of small government; and being in favour of freedom of choice on a variety of issues, for people as well as companies.' (VVD 1)
126. 'But [the 'old' position] is combined with a number of specific liberal issues [as well], which most of the time are considered to be 'left-wing' but I don't think they are particularly left-wing anymore. E.g. we were in favour of a euthanasia legislation; we were among the first parties to be pro-abortion, already in the 70s. On a lot of immaterial issues, we are a very liberal party.' (VVD 1)
127. '[W]e don't look at the background of people but we judge them according to what they can contribute and how they see their future here//...//skilled workers are "fine"'. (VVD 1)
128. '[W]e've always had three issues in mind. That is, pro-integration; reduce the high number of migrants – only allow entry for people that really have to find shelter here or that can contribute to our society, such as knowledge workers – and to stop discrimination in society' (VVD 1)

129. '[A]sylum seekers and their stories, they have to be investigated very, very carefully//...//[our] position hasn't changed, in 1992 all the other parties considered it to be a very, very right-wing position. But since then the centre-ground has shifted rightwards.' (VVD 1)

130. 'The party tended to focus on issues like giving money to people who needed it the most; proper healthcare and housing, those types of things. But in recent years we seem to be keener on reducing the level of national debt and that the budget needs to be balanced. And these are positions that have traditionally been associated with 'the right'.' (D'66 1)

131. '[W]e were set-up in 1966 with the aim of breaking the old political powers, especially those of the three big parties that decided on everything here. And we thought that we needed to have more people, not just groups, in politics and to show them that the power of the people is always bigger than thinking of people as 'groups'.' (D'66 1)

132. '[W]e push for traditional family values and the party is quite resistant towards change, e.g. same sex marriages. This has been a source of conflict because I think that as a political, rather than religious, party we shouldn't interfere with people's life choices//...//In other areas, we are probably more to the right, e.g. stricter alcohol regulations, many of our social welfare policies are very much geared towards extensive state intervention.' (KD 1); '[W]hen you make decisions under the influence of drugs or alcohol, then you are not capable of making the right decisions. That's when the state has to come in.' (KD 2)

133. '[E]veryone should be able to be self-sufficient because to work is better than taxing and spending as a means of supporting these people.' (KD 2)

134. '[With] the priorities that we need to make and with the limited resources that we have, will it then be possible to remove certain taxes because they are ideologically "right"? That's when ideology and "reality" come into conflict.' (KD 2)

135. 'We thought that a more flexible labour migration policy would be a great way to deal with global poverty.' (KD 1)

136. 'We believe in open borders, we don't like the idea of "Fortress Europe". Several of our members are engaged in churches and they have been very involved in the reception of refugees' (KD 1)

137. 'There is a degree of tension between the two strands [note: neo- and social liberalism]. I sometimes wish to see less interference by the state and more 'freedom from' but at the same time I want to have an even stronger safety net for those people that are *really* [original emphasis] vulnerable.' (FP 1); '[The party is] sceptical of too much state involvement but it's also a party that today falls in between the two blocs.' (FP 2)

138. '[W]e have switched a lot//...//[today] I think we are moving in a more market-liberal direction.' (FP 2)

139. '[H]owever, it has not been very liberal on certain issues, e.g. on alcohol, and it has also been quite interventionist in e.g. certain welfare sectors such as health care, education and childcare.' (FP 3)

140. 'Freedom of choice is very important for us//...//we then try to work with the issues that come up and ask ourselves "what's the right thing to do here?" or "what would the liberal position be?"' (FP 1); '[T]he liberal

ideology is quite well developed which is a strength for us// ...//we can always fall back on these ideas, "what would a liberal do here?" ' (FP 3)

141. '[I]t creates tension// ...//especially between the more authoritarian and the more libertarian groups in the party.' (FP 3)

142. '[W]e have moved towards the "classic liberal" position// ...//the social liberal strand used to be much stronger than it is now.' (FP 1)

143. '[T]hese tendencies are still there. That is, intervention, in an almost paternalistic fashion so as to prevent individuals from harming themselves and others.' (FP 3)

144. 'The party has been characterised by a belief in free trade and openness towards the rest of the world.' (FP 3)

145. 'On e.g. same-sex adoption or HBT-rights, we have a very strong tradition of freedom// ...//When it comes to drugs, however, it's a very different story. There we tend to be more restrictive because drugs and alcohol cause so much damage.' (FP 1); 'I don't think banning things is a particularly liberal thing to do. There are also so many non-discussions around, e.g. the ban on smoking.' (FP 2)

146. '[T]here are some questions – file sharing e.g. – which are a no-go area in terms of whether we should make them an election issue or not.' (FP 3)

147. '[T]here is always a lot of discussion between the social-liberal and the classic-liberal Liberals, e.g. "what is liberalism? What should it be?" Is it liberal to ban certain things if it is in the interest of the individual? Or is the ultimate goal complete freedom from any type of constraints?// ...//Everyone uses "liberalism" as a form of alibi to justify their own positions, so ideology is important in the debate but you change it around and use it in different ways.' (FP 2)

148. 'We are extremely positive towards the EU, as an idea and as a project as well as a trade facilitator. You'll have to look very hard to find a member who is negative towards it.' (FP 1); 'We are very enthusiastic about the EU// ...//it goes back to these ideas of free trade and we were always fighting with the "old" M about who was the most pro-EU party.' (FP 3)

149. '[W]e have a very positive view on immigration. But we also need it to "work" for Sweden and in Swedish society.' (FP 2); 'We are fundamentally very positive towards immigration and this view is based on the idea that in a liberal world, people should be able to live wherever they want. In practice, this is of course not always possible but that's our "compass" as it were.' (FP 3)

150. '[T]he party pushes for much more liberal policies, "you want to come here and work? Sure." ' (FP 2); 'The Alliance basically overruled [the trade unions] and said that it should be up to the employer to decide on who and how many that should come here.' (FP 3)

151. '[Our position is] not fixed and it's influenced by the number of asylum seekers that arrive from year to year// ...//and if we're in a governing position or not// ...//apart from the troubles we experienced with the FRA-law, [family reunification] has been the biggest schism in the party' (FP 2)

152. '[Since 2001] we have really gone deep into ideology and tried to become a party that is driven by ideas// . . .//our list of issues has also expanded' (CP 1); 'The "green" tag is very important for the party because of our long history of raising and campaigning on environmental questions. But it is equally important because liberal theory has never quite been able to deal with the "environmental issue" in a proper way.' (CP 2); '[A] liberal and a green party that caters for individual choice and a minimum level of social security. That's who we are and where we stand.' (CP 4)

153. '[T]his position encompasses a number of values that are to the "right", e.g. believing in oneself and that the individual is perfectly capable of doing things on her own without the constant prompting by the state.' (CP 1); '[O]ur roots are in promoting enterprise, the market economy and liberalism. Today we are a liberal and a bourgeois party but also one that has a strong commitment to "green" questions' (CP 3); '[T]his is quite straight forward actually; you can't have more individual choice through the socialist model of organising society// . . .//The key change was how we've quite clearly moved towards the economic right.' (CP 4)

154. '[W]e're also a social liberal party but then again, we do have a strong belief in the free market and in individual choice.' (CP 4)

155. 'What we are doing now is to broaden the party and talk about economic *and* [original emphasis] freedom issues// . . .//[Our] voters have historically been sceptical towards 'the state' and there has been a lot of emphasis on devolution and freedom// . . .//[W]e were more conservative in the past// . . .//semi-teetotal, emphasising morals and ethics and so forth. HBT-questions were non-existent, and we liked the 'Swedish way' and the established norms for doing things.' (CP 1); 'If you consider e.g. the idea of conservative family values, or the belief in a slow paced progress, then that's not part of the party's ideology.' (CP 2); 'You will not reach this "goal" of increased freedom if you do not also trust individuals to make the right choices for themselves.' (CP 4)

156. '[T]hese days we embrace the EU as a global actor, as an actor for peace, and as something that can create good internal relations and promote trade. What's left from the old days is the EMU "issue", which means that we still can't say that we are a "Yes to the EU" type of party.' (CP 1)

157. '[M]oving for labour purposes shouldn't be an issue in the first place, if people want to come here and work, why not? I don't see the problem with that.' (CP 1)

158. '[T]he employer, rather than the state, should have more say in who comes in. This was a sore point for the left.' (CP 1); '[I]f you get offered a job, why shouldn't you be allowed to move here and take it?' (CP 2); '[F]ree mobility is something good, and essential, for the market economy.' (CP 3); '[A]s a party, we have no problem at all with labour migration.' (CP 4)

159. '[It] has also meant that the party is slightly out of sync with its membership base.' (CP 1)

160. 'We are very much in favour of a generous policy here// . . .//our position is very much on the liberal side of the spectrum.' (CP 4)

161. '[W]e were a bit hesitant towards internationalism and we tended to embrace Sweden and the Swedish values// . . .//[T]he party has, both

nationally and in the manifestos, become a lot more positive towards immigration.' (CP 1)

162. 'If you look at our core values// . . .//then it becomes clear that we should also be in favour of cross-border trading, free mobility and the right to be who you want to be.' (CP 1); '[T]he goal was "free immigration" but that requires a completely different social security system and since we don't have that at the moment, then we can't have free immigration.' (CP 2); 'Sweden should take its share of responsibility when it comes to refugees.' (CP 3)

5   The Changing Modes of Party Competition (1991–2010)

1. 'Democratic reform is also an important condition for the anticipated enlargement eastwards.' (GA, 1999).
2. 'If the EU's political structures are to be ready for the 21st century, an extra boost of sober realism is necessary// . . .//[W]e must look at what the EU needs to do to increase its role in the international arena. This means short-term adjustments to the Treaty of Amsterdam. And resources provided for the extension of the EU// . . .//The Greens are convinced European federalists.' (GA, 1999)
3. 'For GA, the choice is clear. Many ecological and social problems require an approach at the European level. But this will only happen when there is a fully-fledged political Europe. The commission must be replaced by a true European government.' (GA, 1995).
4. 'For Sp.a, the European Community is at the heart of foreign policy' (Sp.a, 1991).
5. 'Deepening the European integration process is far from complete. In its commitment to a democratic and federal EU, Sp.a wants to expand two fundamental areas [cultural/fiscal policies]' (Sp.a, 1991).
6. 'Sp.a is not happy with the current state of Europe. It threatens to be an increasingly liberal project// . . .//[t]he social and fiscal aspects are increasingly lagging behind.' (Sp.a, 1991).
7. 'A single market also requires social convergence between the member states' (Sp.a, 1995); 'The EU must support social policies in the member states, rather than making it difficult for them.' (Sp.a, 2003).
8. '[M]ore Europe but also a different type of Europe. Not just free trade but also social and ecological rules. Not just a single currency// . . .//but also tax rules. Not only free competition but also regulations on industrial; environmental and science policy.' (S.pa, 1995); 'The Iraqi conflict is another example of where Europe should speak with a strong voice' (Sp.a, 2003); '[S]trategies for the future// . . .//should focus on expanding our European social model where the welfare of the people is key.' (S.pa, 2010).
9. 'Greater specialisation within a Common Defence and Security policy framework, and working through the opportunities provided by the Treaty of Lisbon.' (Sp.a, 2010).
10. For example, 'The EU must continue to develop a true Common Foreign and Security Policy based on the values of peace, progress and democracy.' (PS,

1995); 'We must implement a European socio-economic policy with momentum for growth.' (PS, 2007); 'Establish a Common Foreign and Security Policy.' (Ecolo. 1999); '[T]he Reform Treaty remains necessary to reinvigorate the European project and also allows for better implementation of policy priorities.' (Ecolo, 2007); 'The EU must take into account the concerns of its citizens//...//[a]t times, [the EU] can give the impression of becoming a technocracy or a privileged forum for just a few large nations.' (MR, 2003); 'Europe must again become a space of hope for Europeans, and especially for our country. We must revive the EU as a political project.' (MR, 2007).

11. For example, 'The European economy should be more supportive of labour and of the living standards of all European citizens.' (CDH, 1999); 'CDH is in favour of closer policy coordination so as to overcome the economic differences in growth, inflation and competitiveness that persist between the countries in the Euro area.' (CDH, 2007).

12. For example, 'Belgians have their hopes but they also have concerns about the state of the EU.' (PS, 2007); 'Democratic reform is also an important condition for the anticipated enlargement eastwards.' (GA, 1999); 'A seat for the EU on the UN security council' (CD&V, 2003); 'It is not very likely that the draft Treaty will lead governments to do that with which they do not agree.' (Ecolo, 1991); 'We all benefit from this [most recent] enlargement. The new members are taking advantage of our investment companies and the funding available for regional and social development.' (MR, 2007).

13. 'The Maastricht Treaty was a success both for Britain and for the rest of Europe. British proposals helped to shape the key provisions of the Treaty including those strengthening the enforcement of Community law, defence, subsidiarity and law and order. But Britain refused to accept the damaging Social Chapter//...//and it was excluded from the Maastricht Treaty.' (Conservatives, 1992)

'Isolation from Europe does not help anyone. So we chose to engage constructively in Europe, not to shout abuse from the sidelines//...//We will put democratically elected national governments in the driving seat of EU policy//...//Unemployment must be tackled by the European Community as a whole. We will use our influence in Europe to secure the necessary policies for co-ordinated growth; Labour will sign the European Charter of Local Self Government//...//When or if other members of the EC move to a monetary union with a single currency, we will take our own unfettered decision on whether to join. //...//We shall make the widening of the Community a priority//...//We shall seek to create conditions in which, at the appropriate time, the new democracies of Central and Eastern Europe can join the Community//...//We will opt in to the Social Chapter of the new European Treaty.' (Labour, 1992); 'We shall fail to get the best out of the European Community, because our leaders will continue to be afraid to tell us that shared success in the Community means sharing sovereignty too//...//Liberal Democrats will take decisive steps towards a fully integrated, federal and democratic European Community.' (Liberal Democrats, 1992).

14. 'Unlike the Conservatives, we see Europe as an opportunity//...//We hold to our promise: no membership of the single currency without the consent of the British people in a referendum.' (Labour, 1997); 'The Conservative

policy of opposing the enlargement of Europe in the Nice Treaty and their pledge to renegotiate the terms of Britain's EU membership is dangerous and ill thought-out. Standing up for Britain means fighting for Britain's interests in Europe, not leaving Europe – which threatens our national interest// ...//We will also insist that the Commission completes its internal reform programme// ...//We will keep the veto on vital matters of national sovereignty, such as tax and border controls// ...//Labour is pledged to do all it can to enable the first group of applicant countries to join in time to take part in the next European Parliamentary elections in 2004// ...//It is vital we ratify the Treaty of Nice which is essential to enlargement, Labour in government will do so.' (Labour, 2001)

15. 'We will put [the new Constitutional Treaty] to the British people in a referendum and campaign whole-heartedly for a "Yes" vote to keep Britain a leading nation in Europe.' (Labour, 2005); 'We are internationalists too: only co-operative global action – including a strong European Union – can tackle climate change and protect the world's precious environments// ...//In the next Parliament, we will use our leadership in the EU to push for a strengthening of Europe's 2020 emission reductions// ...// // ...//We will strengthen co-operation with our EU partners in fighting crime and international terrorism, and support practical European co-operation on defence, in partnership with NATO.' (Labour, 2010)

16. 'Bring closer EU membership for Turkey, the Balkans and Eastern Europe.' (Labour, 2005); 'We support the enlargement// ...//and believe that all Western Balkan states should open negotiations on EU accession by 2014// ...//Turkey's future membership is a key test of Europe's potential to become a bridge between religions and regions; there must be continued progress on its application to join the EU.' (Labour, 2010).

17. '[M]embership of the EU brings jobs, trade and prosperity; it boosts environmental standards, social protection and international clout.' (Labour, 2005).

18. 'If it cannot proceed safely, we believe it would be better for Europe to delay any introduction of a single currency rather than rush ahead to meet an artificial timetable// ...//We believe it is in our national interest to keep our options open to take a decision on a single currency when all the facts are before us. If a single currency is created, without sustainable convergence, a British Conservative government will not be part of it.' (Conservatives, 1997)

19. 'A Conservative Government will support European co-operation on defence but we strongly believe that such co-operation should take place within the framework of NATO.' (Conservatives, 2005).

20. For example, 'We will take whatever steps are necessary to keep our frontier controls. We will resist attempts to change the inter-governmental nature of co-operation in justice and home affairs. We will not accept the development of new legal rights that extend the concept of European citizenship.' (Conservatives, 1997); 'We intend to press for the single market to be completed and for competition laws to be stronger so that British businesses which play by the rules are not undercut by other companies that do not.' (Conservatives, 2001); 'We will ensure that Britain once again leads the fight for a deregulated Europe by negotiating the restoration of our opt-out from the Social Chapter.' (Conservatives, 2005); 'We will never allow

Britain to slide into a federal Europe//...//We will ensure that by law no future government can hand over areas of power to the EU or join the Euro without a referendum of the British people. We will work to bring back key powers over legal rights, criminal justice and social and employment legislation to the UK//...//The steady and unaccountable intrusion of the European Union into almost every aspect of our lives has gone too far. A Conservative government will negotiate for three specific guarantees – on the Charter of Fundamental Rights, on criminal justice, and on social and employment legislation – with our European partners to return powers that we believe should reside with the UK, not the EU.' (Conservatives, 2010)

21. For example, 'Our vision is of a European Union that is decentralised, democratic and diverse' (Lib Dems, 1997); 'Support a European Common Foreign and Security Policy that includes a significant defence capability consistent with our membership of NATO and other international institutions.' (Lib Dems,. 2001); 'Liberal Democrats believe that Britain should work to create the right economic conditions to join the euro (subject to a referendum) in order to safeguard investment in the UK and reduce the cost and risk of trade with the rest of Europe.' (Lib Dems, 2005); 'We believe that it is in Britain's long-term interest to be part of the Euro//...//[but] Britain should join the euro only if that decision were supported by the people of Britain in a referendum.' (Lib Dems, 2010).

22. 'We will give the House of Commons a more effective role in scrutinising European policy//...//As a first step, we will incorporate the European Convention on Human Rights into UK law so that it is enforceable by the courts in the UK.' (Lib Dems, 1997); 'We need to improve the quality of EU governance//...//This means ensuring that the principle of subsidiarity is fully respected.' (Lib Dems, 2001); 'But with enlargement to twenty-five member states, the EU needs reform to become more efficient and more accountable.' (Lib Dems, 2005); 'We will ensure that Britain maximises its influence through a strong and positive commitment. But just because Europe is essential, that doesn't mean the European Union is perfect. We will continue to campaign for improved accountability, efficiency and effectiveness//...//Liberal Democrats will work through the European Union to deliver a global deal on climate change//...//And we will put Britain at the heart of Europe//...//Push for a co-ordinated EU-wide asylum system to ensure that the responsibility is fairly shared between member states.' (Lib Dems, 2010)

23. For example, 'We are against further erosion of democracy through the transfer of sovereignty to the European Union' (SP, 1998); 'In the years following the adoption of the Maastricht Treaty, the emphasis should primarily be placed on extending EC membership' (GL, 1994); 'PvdA chooses an open, positive attitude towards European cooperation' (PvdA, 1998); 'D'66 supports the introduction of the Euro' (D'66, 1998); 'VVD wants the Netherlands to maintain its own identity in the EU' (VVD, 1994); 'CDA is a pro-European party. Our jobs, safety and environment do indeed depend on the EU.' (CDA, 2010).

24. For example, 'While the European Parliament is doing a decent job checking [the decrees from Brussels] it is by no means delivering since it lacks the

power to do so' (SP, 1994); 'GL has always been critical of "the Europe of the market"' (GL, 2006); 'PvdA is committed to a better Europe in a better world. We will use our influence in the Hague and Brussels to create a more social, innovative and sustainable Europe.' (PvdA, 2010); 'One thing is clear, the organisation of the Union must be reformed.' (D'66, 2002); 'Harmonisation of regulations at the European level is often ineffective and undesirable' (VVD, 1998); 'There will be more evaluation points in the accession process.' (CDA, 2006).

25. For example, 'The EU is still a very mixed order where inter-governmental and supranational styles of governance intermingle. The EU lacks a clear separation of powers//...//[and] there is duplication and overlap between the national and the European levels.' [ownership]; '[In] anticipating the economic convergence [between Eastern and Western Europe], a second rate membership could be created. That in itself is an example of the different speeds [of European integration]' [choice] (PvdA, 1994); '[T]he EMU is postponed until a minimum standard of social and environmental protection is established and until the opportunities are there to accept a European approach to tackle unemployment' [ownership]; 'The Netherlands should, where possible, work with likeminded groups //...//[and] strongly support the expansion and democratisation in European cooperation.' [choice] (GL, 1998).

26. For example, 'After two world wars and one Cold War there is peaceful cooperation today in almost all European countries.' (SP, 2006); 'Some people see the Euro as the final stage of integration' (GL, 2002); 'A Common Foreign and Security policy is slowly but surely forming.' (D'66, 1998); 'The Netherlands benefits from the EU in terms of trade and a joint European approach to borderless problems' (VVD, 1998); 'The future of the Netherlands is in Europe.' (CDA, 1994).

27. For example, 'Yes to the environment and work – No to the EU! A vote for MP is also a vote for a strong and clear resistance to the EU in the Swedish parliament.' [ownership] (MP, 1994); 'More money for education and health care. Less money to the military; to the EU's bureaucracy and to vanity projects.' [choice] (MP, 1998); 'V says a firm no to the EU. We will work against an EU membership. More opponents to the EU are needed in parliament – only this can stop the hollowing out of the Swedish laws and of the Swedish welfare policies that was initiated by the EES-agreement. [ownership]' (V, 1994); 'V advocates for a stronger pan-European co-operation. The EU can't solve these problems (i.e. issues of human rights; arms reduction; the environment; unemployment; welfare cuts)' [choice] (V, 1998); 'We want to broaden and deepen co-operation in all areas.' [choice] (SAP, 1998); 'We'll also bring the Social Democratic values of freedom; equality and solidarity to the EU, to the UN and to other progressive governments around the world//...//[W]e'll be the strong voice for peace; for human and trade union rights; for equality; disarmament; jobs and responsibility for the environment.' [ownership] (SAP, 2010).

28. For example, 'We will make sure that Sweden is not part of the common currency.' (CP, 1994); 'Sweden shall push for increased demands and for binding EU legislations on vehicle emissions//...//We want to continue to simplify

and improve these regulations' (CP, 2010); '[M]embership is an important precondition for jobs in Sweden//...//Being on the outside makes it a lot harder to attract investment.' (FP. 1994); 'Yes to the Euro. Sweden shall introduce the Euro as a currency. A new referendum should therefore take place during the next parliamentary period.' (FP, 2010); 'Through a referendum the Swedish people shall decide on whether or not Sweden will become a member of the EC. The result shall be followed regardless if it's a 'Yes' or a 'No'//...//European co-operation means that KD will work for peace; the environment; combat unemployment and take up the fight against drugs and substance abuse.' (KD, 1994); '[T]he EU and Sweden must take the lead in this work (ie: to limit the environmental problems associated with modernisation in the Third World).' (KD, 2002).

29. 'Sweden shall concentrate its' efforts on supporting the Baltic states' and Poland's desires to become members.' (SAP, 1998).

30. 'As an organisation, the EU cannot just replicate the way that other international organisations or nation-states work. The EU must develop its own working procedures; increase levels of transparency in the decision-making process and its effectiveness in common undertakings. To further develop these forms of governance are important parts of our engagement with the EU.' (SAP, 2002)

31. 'We'll also bring the Social Democratic values of freedom; equality and solidarity to the EU, to the UN and to other progressive governments around the world//...//[W]e'll be the strong voice for peace; for human and trade union rights; for equality; disarmament; jobs and for responsibility for the environment.' (SAP, 2010).

32. 'M is *the* party for Europe in Sweden. We want to and can lead Sweden into further European co-operation//...//We do not hesitate regarding Sweden's direction.' (M, 1991); 'We want to be part of the process that forms the future of European co-operation. It presupposes a government that can uphold Sweden's role in the new Europe and that can contribute towards the development of a Europe of nations.' (M, 1994); 'The politics of low inflation has become accepted in the 1990s. This achievement will be consolidated through Sweden's full membership in the economic and monetary union. We want to introduce the Euro as quickly as possible. Sweden's influence is strengthened by quickly establishing our intention to introduce the Euro.' (M, 1998); 'Sweden shall be a part of the EU's core and push for a type of co-operation that is open, effective, dynamic and well anchored among the European citizens//...//' (M, 2010).

33. 'V says a firm no to the EU. We will work against an EU membership. More opponents to the EU are needed in parliament – only this can stop the hollowing out of the Swedish laws and of the Swedish welfare policies that was initiated by the EES-agreement.' (V, 1994); 'We will work against an EU membership and the adjustments that have been made towards the currency union' (V, 1998); 'It's the government, not the parliament, that represents Sweden in the EU//...//that's why it's even more important who is part of it. A Leftist government must respect the various fundamental views on the EU.' (V, 2002); 'The EU must become more democratic and less centralised.' (V, 2006).

34. 'We strive for a Europe that co-operates on environmental policy; arms reduction and on essential social rights. We strive for trade to be characterised by solidarity, and do not accept the EC's high tariffs towards the rest of the world or the asylum policies which state that a 'No' in one country means a 'No' in another.' (MP, 1991); 'A vote for MP is also a vote for a strong and clear resistance to the EU in the Swedish parliament.' (MP, 1994); 'Society must become more democratic. That's why we don't accept that more and more power ends up in the EU's bureaucracy, or with international capital.' (MP, 1998); 'The EU must become more democratic and less centralised.' (MP, 2010).

35. 'We will make sure that Sweden stands aside from the common currency.' (CP, 1991); 'Sweden will not take part in a Common Defence Force.' (CP, 1994); 'The EU has not done enough so far to improve the European environment.' (CP, 1998); 'CP pushes for the EU to become a global actor and a leader on questions that concern sustainable development; human rights; women's rights; democratic development; conflict resolution and peace' (CP, 2010).

36. 'Sweden must become a full member of the EC as soon as possible.' (FP, 1991); 'A Swedish membership is an important precondition for jobs.' (FP, 1994); 'EMU membership' (FP; 1998); 'It's urgent to introduce the Euro, even in Sweden.' (FP, 2002); 'Enlargement must continue.' (FP, 2006); 'The EU's refugee policy must become more humane than it is today.' (FP, 2010).

37. 'Membership of the EC is the expression of an ideological connection to peace and to belonging in Europe.' (KD, 1991); 'European co-operation means that KD will work for peace; for the environment; combat unemployment and take up the fight against drugs and substance abuse.' (KD, 1994); 'Sweden shall work to implement majority decisions [on the EU level] which can lead to a reduction in gashouse emissions and other environmentally harmful substances// ... //Sweden shall actively work for this tax reform in the EU as well (i.e. a tax that increases the cost for environmentally harmful activities).' (KD, 1998); '[T]he EU and Sweden must take the lead in this work (ie: to limit the environmental problems associated with modernisation in the Third World).' (KD, 2002); 'Develop an EU level policy for global development which provides a clear focus for poverty reduction and that prevents the EU from acting in a way that would go against this development.' (KD, 2010).

38. 'Sweden shall work to implement majority decisions [on the EU level] which can lead to a reduction in gashouse emissions and other environmentally harmful substances// ... //' (KD, 1998).

39. 'In recent years, the asylum and immigration policies have become increasingly repressive// ... //For GA this cannot continue. We ask for fundamental adjustments in these areas' (GA, 1999).

40. E.g. 'The economic world is dominated by the North and as such the North is responsible for the socio-economic and cultural upheaval in many Third World countries. We therefore cannot just slam the door on these asylum seekers' (GA, 1991); 'The UN Convention on Children should be fully implemented, in letter as well as in spirit. Provide more places in specialised shelters so that each minor can get specific care and support. The federal

government and the communities should come to an agreement on the reception of unaccompanied minors.' (GA, 2003); 'The illegal influx of people should definitely be avoided through a more rigorous prosecution policy. The control of illegal workers in the construction sector should be extended to other sectors as well. There should be strict quotas on foreign workers but they should also take into account the needs of the concerned sectors. The internal labour market situation will be assessed' (CD&V, 1991); 'Finally, CD&V wishes for strict procedures for assessing political asylum claims and that the distinction between economic and political refugees is maintained.' (CD&V, 1995); 'We choose a new perspective on migration. But it is clear that these flows in the globalised world will only increase. For Open VLD, immigration is not a negative nor a threatening phenomenon. People who come here want to work and contribute to our prosperity//...//We opt for a European system where investors and people with employment are paired according to the needs of the job market so that they can live here and work. For those that do not immediately fit these criteria, our society must be open but in accordance with the quotas agreed upon within the EU. People in this category should preferably migrate to our country having already acquired the necessary language and vocational skills in the country where they come from. Open VLD continues to fight the abuse of the asylum and family reunification systems//Controlled immigration is based on European quotas.' (Open Vld, 2007)

41. For example, 'GA continues to call for a generous asylum policy where the procedures are carefully followed and where the rights of the Refugee Convention are fully respected.' (GA, 1995); 'There must be a full legal status for unaccompanied minors.' (GA, 2007); 'Sp.a continues to endorse the Geneva Convention. Anyone who, because of a well-founded fear of persecution within the meaning of the Convention, must leave his country of origin is entitled to asylum.' (Sp.a, 1991); 'Legal and illegal people, these are terrible words. But they are also the reality. Not everyone can come here and not everyone can stay here.' (Sp.a, 2007); 'CD&V will implement sound, balanced and properly managed rules and procedures regarding the different [asylum and refugee] statutes.' (CD&V, 2003); 'We also work towards a European approach for a common asylum and migration policy.' (CD&V, 2010); 'The majority proved to be unfounded. These people had other reasons for migrating here. It is therefore necessary to carry out an active "refugee policy"' (Open Vld, 1991); 'The abuse of the family reunification route will be countered.' (Open Vld, 2003); 'Open VLD remains opposed to the collective, or automatic, regularisation of failed asylum seekers or illegal migrants. All applications must be individually examined.' (Open Vld, 2010).

42. 'Sp.a continues to endorse the Geneva Convention. Anyone who, because of well-founded fear of persecution within the meaning of the Convention, must leave his country, is entitled to asylum.' (Sp.a., 1991).

43. '[P]ersons not recognised as refugees but who may also be unreturnable because their safety cannot be guaranteed, must obtain a temporary residence status [here]. Expulsions must be consistent and continue to take place but always with the greatest respect for the individual. Initiatives that

encourage the voluntary departure of failed asylum seekers should definitely be reinforced.' (CD&V, 1999)

44. 'For example, 'It is of course the case that we would continue to guarantee the possibility of asylum to an alien who fears persecution because of race, nationality, religion, membership of a particular social group or political opinion, but PS also acknowledges that Belgium has no capacity to absorb the masses of people that are fleeing for economic reasons. We therefore consider it necessary to strengthen the efforts made by the government to further cut the procedural time for recognising a refugee status.' (PS, 1991); 'PS will pay particular attention to the status of children based on the Convention on the Rights of the Child.' (PS, 1999); 'Reinterpret the concept of "refugees". Treat all applicants with dignity and ensure the integrity of the asylum procedure.' (Ecolo, 1999); 'Enhance the protection of vulnerable groups, including that of the unaccompanied minors.' (Ecolo, 2007); 'Do you know that 100,000 potential refugees have entered our country in the past seven years, and that most of them have stayed illegally? Do you think that the abuse of the immigration system is under control?// ... //If you want firm and responsible policies where more efforts are made against illegal migrants// ... //then choose us.' (MR, 1995)

45. '[T]o stabilise migration flows this will by definition require a model of sustainable co-development for the entire globe [ownership]// ... //Ecolo wants to strengthen the control measures and the disincentives to hire foreign workers illegally. The law should penalise employers much more severely.' [choice]. (Ecolo, 1991).

46. 'Stop immigration and return those who betray our hospitality. Immigration is not in itself a security issue but has become one due to the Socialist/Christian Democratic government's lack of courage. Rather than deciding on what to do, they have chosen to let the situation deteriorate to a point when it has become explosive.' (MR, 1991)

47. 'A specific problem concerns the influx of refugees, which is as much the result of economic underdevelopment as it is due to a lack of democracy. True to its tradition but also because of capacity issues, CDH wants to accelerate the process of recognising the refugee status' (CDH, 1991).

48. '[A]n intelligent integration policy must be accompanied by an on-going control of flows, including and ensuring the effective repatriation of rejected applicants and one that works through the files that have accumulated and that have caused a significant administrative delay.' (CDH, 1995).

49. 'In accordance with our international commitments, we are strong supporters of the asylum system and that political refugees should be recognised// ... //On the other hand, illegal immigration must be combated.' [ownership]; 'Beyond these internal measures, the response to those in search of a better future must be sought in economic cooperation so as to encourage and facilitate economic and human development, and democracy in their countries of origin.' [Noc] (MR, 2003).

50. 'Like any other member state, the management of migration is seen from an essentially defensive angle but this approach also has limitations. The number of migrants trying to enter our country – legally as well as illegally – is growing. This is why it will be necessary to develop a comprehensive and balanced approach. It does not imply the absence of defensive

measures however. They should instead be strengthened and include an implementation strategy of preventative measures in the countries of origin.' [ownership]; 'More globalisation means more migration. These international issues affect all countries in the world.' [Noc] (MR, 2007).

51. '[W]e want a comprehensive approach [to illegal migration], particularly taking into account the causes of such movements and that Belgium provides a humane and consistent returns policy. This will include negotiating agreements with countries of origin so they can control their borders better// . . .//As for regularisation// . . .//it should remain exceptional. Each year, the ministry regularises between 8,000 and 11,000 people. This policy must be denounced.' [ownership]; 'MR wants a common [European] policy on legal immigration which allows the Union to meet the demands of the labour market.' [choice] (MR, 2010).

52. '[I]mmigration rules will remain clear, firm and fair/// . . .//Britain has a long record of providing a home for such people, and it is important that we maintain this position. But asylum should not be an alternative route to immigration// . . .//The primary purpose rule, which split families and did nothing to stop abuse, has been ended. A right of appeal for family visitors has been introduced.' (Labour, 2001); 'We will also regularly review immigration policy// . . .//Asylum seekers, in particular, have been treated in a disgraceful manner by both Labour and the Conservatives' (Lib Dems, 2001).

53. 'Britain is made up of many ethnic communities. Conservatives believe that we are richer and stronger for it.' (Conservatives, 2001).

54. For example, 'A new Act will guarantee sanctuary to genuine refugees but prevent bogus applications for asylum.' (Labour, 1992); 'Every country must have firm control over immigration and Britain is no exception.' (Labour, 1997); 'We are modernising our asylum and immigration system; and we will take the necessary measures to protect our country from international terrorism// . . .//We need skilled workers. So we will establish a points system for those seeking to migrate here.' (Labour, 2005); 'Asylum claims are back down to early 1990s levels, and the cost of asylum support to the taxpayer has been cut by half in the last six years.' (Labour, 2010); 'We will introduce improved welfare and legal rights for genuine asylum seekers and establish substantive rights of appeal.' (Lib Dems, 1992); 'We will reform current immigration laws so as to enable genuine family reunions.' (Lib Dems, 1997); 'We will not pander to fear and prejudice. We offer fair and effective policies over the distinct issues of asylum and immigration.' (Lib Dems, 2005); 'Introduce a regional points-based system to ensure that migrants can work only where they are needed. We need to enforce any immigration system through rigorous checks on businesses and a crackdown on rogue employers who profit from illegal labour.' (Lib Dems, 2010); '[I]n the new Parliament we must there reintroduce the Asylum Bill, opposed by Labour and the Liberal Democrats, to create a faster and more effective system of determining who are genuine politics refugees and who are not.' (Conservatives, 1992); 'We will ensure that, while genuine asylum seekers are treated sympathetically, people do not abuse these provisions to avoid normal immigration controls.' (Conservatives, 1997); 'Conservatives will restore common sense to Britain's asylum procedures. A safe haven, not a soft touch, on asylum.' (Conservatives, 2001); 'But if those benefits are to continue to flow we

need to ensure that immigration is effectively managed, in the interests of all Britons, old and new//This Government has lost effective control of our borders. More than 150,000 people (net) come to Britain every year, a population the size of Peterborough. Britain has reached a turning-point. That is why a Conservative Government will bring immigration back under control. We will introduce health checks for immigrants in order to curb the spread of diseases such as TB and to protect access to our NHS. It is, after all, a national health service not a world health service. People coming to Britain for over 12 months from outside the EU will be required to undergo a full medical test. And anyone settling permanently here from outside the EU will have to demonstrate that they have an acceptable standard of health and that they are unlikely to impose significant costs or demands on Britain's health system.' (Conservatives, 2005); '[I]mmigration today is too high and needs to be reduced. We do not need to attract people to do jobs that could be carried out by British citizens, given the right training and support. So we will take steps to take net migration back to the levels of the 1990s – tens of thousands a year, not hundreds of thousands// ... //A Conservative government will strengthen the system of granting student visas so that it is less open to abuse.' (Conservatives, 2010)

55. For example, 'Under these circumstances it will be wise to keep refugee policy as it currently is.' (SP, 1994) [ownership]; 'Labour migration, from the new member states and beyond, should be better regulated.' (SP, 2006) [choice]; 'Whoever thinks that rich countries can close their borders to the arrival of immigrants cherishes illusions.' (GL, 1994) [ownership]; 'In the reception of asylum seekers, the vulnerability of children should be taken into account.' (GL, 2006) [choice]; 'Under the new Aliens Act, PvdA is committed to the strict but fair rules that will be implemented.' (PvdA, 2002) [ownership]; 'PvdA is in favour of the selective admission of migrant workers.' (PvdA, 2010) [choice]; 'The right to protection as well as the European directives must be central to our asylum policy.' (D'66, 2010) [ownership]; 'The asylum procedure should be significantly improved.' (D'66, 1998) [choice]; 'Our migration policy is in four parts: (1) integration (2) restriction (3) combating discrimination and (4) encourage return migration.' (VVD, 1998) [ownership]; 'VVD wants an honest and restrictive immigration policy.' (VVD, 2010) [choice]; 'The Netherlands must, in accordance with the relevant international conventions, provide a fair and humane policy for the victims of fundamental human rights violations.' (CDA, 1998) [ownership]; 'Within the European context it should be possible to reunite families whose members have ended up in different countries.' (CDA, 1998) [choice].

56. For example, '[We] do not accept// ... //[the EC's] asylum policies which state that a "No" in one country means a "No" in another.' (MP, 1991); 'We want to create more legal options for migration into the EU// ... //we want to have an amnesty for undocumented migrants.' (MP, 2010); 'V wants a generous interpretation of the asylum legislation.' (V, 2006); 'In our vision of the future, society is free from racism and Sweden has a humane asylum and refugee policy that conforms to existing regulations and international conventions.' (V, 2010); 'Diversity enriches and is an asset which should be taken care of.' (SAP, 2002); 'All employees should be treated equally regardless if they come from Ronneby; Riga or Rotterdam.' (SAP, 2010).

57. 'Sweden does not live up to a decent and humanitarian treatment of refugees, and should instead have a more generous refugee policy.' (MP, 2002); 'There have been deficiencies in the Swedish immigration process for a long time, and that is why we want an amnesty for undocumented migrants.' (MP, 2010); 'Sweden's refugee policy// ...//is a failure from a humanitarian point of view// ...//Children are being deported which runs contrary to the conventions that our country has signed up for.' (V, 1998).

58. For example, 'We must change the reception strategy for refugees so that they have the possibility to work and be independent// ...//the consequences of harsher asylum policies are disastrous.' (FP, 1991); 'Even during a time of crisis, Sweden must be prepared to take on those who are fleeing.' (FP, 1994); 'People who are forced to flee must be given help and Sweden should be a refuge for them.' (FP, 1998); 'We can't afford to be without migrants. We need new ideas and we need entrepreneurship. That's why we have to deal with exclusion and segregation but also why we need to make it possible for more people to come here.' (FP, 2002); 'International solidarity and a humane refugee policy are cornerstones within the social-liberal tradition.' (FP, 2006); 'FP has been pushing for a liberalisation of the labour migration legislations.' (FP, 2010).

59. For example, 'Asylum policies should be generous and based on solidarity// ...//The situation of children seeking asylum should be paid special attention to.' (CP, 1991); 'We need more people to come to live and work here, not just because of the labour deficit in certain sectors but also because people live longer and work fewer years.' (CP, 2006); 'We want to revoke the decision that was taken in Dec. 1989. This also means that we should accept refugee-type reasons and war refusals as being legitimate grounds for asylum'. (KD, 1991); 'All countries should take their share of the responsibility and offer protection to those who are fleeing.' (KD, 2010).

60. 'Refugee policy must be more effective.' (CP, 1994); 'In cases where conflict cannot be prevented we must show solidarity with those who are fleeing' (KD, 2002); 'Sweden shall be open to people fleeing oppression and persecution// ...//.' (KD, 2010).

61. For example, 'We should have a humane refugee policy.' (SAP, 1991); 'Sweden's refugee policy should be humane, lawful and characterised by solidarity.' (SAP, 2002); 'Our refugee policy should be humane and characterised by solidarity// ...///those in need of protection should find sanctuary in our country.' (SAP, 2006); 'More newcomers// ...//should be able to establish themselves on the labour market.' (SAP, 2010).

62. For example, 'We want to increase the possibilities of migrating for work purposes.' (M, 1991) [choice]; 'Sweden needs a more up-to-date refugee policy. The skills and knowledge base that immigrants bring must be better cared for.' (M, 1991) [ownership]; 'Those who have a job offer should have the right to settle in our country.' (M, 2002) [choice]; 'Sweden continues to be a sanctuary for those that are persecuted and are in need of asylum.' (M, 2002) [ownership].

Bibliography

Abiri, E (2000) 'The changing praxis of "generosity": Swedish refugee policy during the 1990s', *Journal of Refugee Studies* 13(1): 11–28.

Abts, K, Heerwegh, D and Swyngedouw, M (2009) 'Sources of Euroscepticism: utilitarian interest, social distrust, national identity and institutional distrust', *World Political Science Review* 5(1): 1–26.

Ackland, R and Gibson, R (2013) 'Hyperlinks and networked communication: a comparative study of political parties online', *International Journal of Social Research Methodology* 16(3): 231–244.

Adams, J and Merrill III, S (1999) 'Modeling party strategies and policy representation in multiparty elections: why are strategies so extreme?', *American Journal of Political Science* 43(3): 765–791.

Adams, J and Somer-Topcu, Z (2009) 'Policy adjustment by parties in response to rival parties' policy shifts: spatial theory and the dynamics of party competition in twenty-five post-war democracies', *British Journal of Political Science* 39(4): 825–886.

Adams, J, Clark, M, Ezrow, L and Glasgow, G (2004) 'Understanding change and stability in party ideologies: do parties respond to public opinion or to past election results?', *British Journal of Political Science* 34(4): 589–610.

Adams, J, Clark, M, Ezrow, L and Glasgow, G (2006) 'Are niche parties fundamentally different from mainstream parties? The causes and the electoral consequences of Western European parties' policy shifts, 1976–1998', *American Journal of Political Science* 50(3): 513–529.

Alonso, S and Claro da Fonseca, S (2012) 'Immigration, left and right', *Party Politics* 18(6): 565–884.

Ålund, A and Schierup, C-U (1991) *Paradoxes of multiculturalism* (Avebury: Aldershot).

Anderson, B (1983) *Imagined communities: reflections on the origin and spread of nationalism* (London: Verso).

Anderson, CJ and Kaltenthaler, KC (1996) 'The dynamics of public opinion toward European integration, 1973-93', *European Journal of International Relations* 2(2): 175–199.

Archer, C (2000) 'Euroscepticism in the Nordic region', *Journal of European Integration* 22(1): 87–114.

Arian, A and Shamir, M (1983) 'The primarily political functions of the left-right continuum', *Comparative Politics* 15(2): 139–158.

Aspinwall, M (2000) 'Structuring Europe: powersharing institutions and British preferences on European integration', *Political Studies* 48(3): 415–442.

Aspinwall, M (2002) 'Preferring Europe: ideology and national preferences on European integration', *European Union Politics* 3(1): 81–111.

Aspinwall, M (2007) 'Government preferences on European integration: an empirical test of five theories', *British Journal of Political Science* 37(1): 89–114.

Bache, I, George, S and Bulmer, S (2011) *Politics in the European Union* (Oxford: Oxford University Press).

Baker, D (2001) 'Britain and Europe: the argument continues', *Parliamentary Studies* 54(2): 276–288.

Baker, D, Gamble, A, Seawright, D and Bull, K (1999) 'MPs and Europe: Enthusiasm, circumspection or outright scepticism?', *British Elections & Parties Review* 9(1): 171–185.

Bakker, R, de Vries, C, Edwards, E, Hooghe, L, Jolly, S, Marks, G, Polk, J, Rovny, J, Steenbergen, M and Vachudova, M (2012) 'Measuring party positions in Europe: the chapel hill expert survey trend file, 1999–2010', unpublished ms.

Baldwin-Edwards, M (1991) 'Immigration after 1992', *Party & Politics* (19(3): 199–212.

Bale, T (2003) 'Cinderella and her ugly sisters: the mainstream and extreme right in Europe's bipolarising party systems', *West European Politics* 26(3): 67–90.

Bale, T (2006) 'Between a soft and hard place? The Conservative Party, valence politics and the need for a new 'Euroscepticism', *Parliamentary Affairs* 59(3): 385–400.

Bale, T (2008) 'Turning round the telescope. Centre-right parties and immigration and integration policy in Europe', *Journal of European Public Policy* 15(3): 315–330.

Bale, T (2010) *The Conservative Party: from Thatcher to Cameron* (Cambridge: Polity Press).

Bale, T, Green-Pedersen, C, Krouwel, A, Luther, K-R and Sitter, N (2010) 'If you can't beat them, join them? Explaining social democratic responses to the challenge from the populist radical right in Western Europe', *Political Studies* 58(3): 410–426.

Banks, R (2000) 'Europeanising the reception of asylum seekers: the opposite of welfare state politics' in Geddes, A and Bommes, M (eds.) *Immigration and Welfare: Challenging the Borders of the Welfare State* (New York: Routledge): 146–167.

Batory, A and Sitter, N (2004) 'Cleavages, competition and coalition-building: agrarian parties and the European question in Western and East Central Europe', *European Journal of Political Research* 43(4): 523–546.

Bélanger, É and Meguid, B (2008) 'Issue salience, issue ownership, and issue-based vote choice', *Electoral Studies* 27(3): 477–491.

Belavusau, U (2008) 'The case of Laval in the context of the post-enlargement EC law development', *German Law Journal* 9(12): 1279–1308.

Bennie, LG, Curtice, J and Rüdig, W (1994) 'Liberal, social democrat or liberal democrat? Political identity and British centre party politics', *British Elections and Parties Yearbook* 4(1): 148–166.

Benoit, K and Laver, M (2007) 'Estimating party policy positions: comparing expert surveys and hand-coded content analysis', *Electoral Studies* 26(1): 90–107.

Betz, H-G (1994) *Radical right-wing populism in Western Europe* (New York: St. Martin's Press).

Bevelander, P (2004) *Immigration patterns, economic integration and residential segregation: Sweden in the late 20th century* (Malmö: Malmö Högskola).

Bieler, A (2002) 'The struggle over EU enlargement: a historical materialist analysis of European integration', *Journal of European Public Policy* 9(4): 575–597.

Biernacki, P and Waldorf, D (1981) 'Snowball sampling: problems and techniques of chain referral sampling', *Sociological Methods and Research* 10(2): 141–163.

Bjurner, A (2003) 'Sweden' in Ojanen, H (ed.) *Neutrality and Non-alignment in Europe Today* (FIIA Report 6: Helsinki): 41–46.

Blomqvist, P (2004) 'The choice revolution: privatization of the Swedish welfare services in the 1990s', *Social Policy and Administration* 38(2): 139–155.

Blomqvist, P and Green-Pedersen, C (2004) 'Defeat at home? Issue-ownership and social democratic support in Scandinavia', *Government and Opposition* 39(4): 587–613.

Bomberg, E (2002) 'The Europeanisation of Green parties: exploring the EU's impact', *West European Politics* 25(3): 29–50.

Boréus, K (2006) *Diskrimineringens retorik: en studie av svenska valrörelser 1988–2002* (Stockholm: Fritzes).

Borevi, K (2002) *The welfare state in a multicultural society* (Stockholm: Elanders Gotab).

Börzel, TA and Risse, T (2008) 'Revisiting the nature of the beast – politicization, European identity, and postfunctionalism: a comment on Hooghe and Marks', *British Journal of Political Science* 39(1): 217–220.

Bousetta, H (2009) 'Multinational federalism and immigrant multiculturalism in Brussels' in Zapata-Barrero, R. (ed.) *Immigration and Self-Government of Minority Nations* (Brussels: P.I.E. Peter Lang), 87–103.

Boswell, C (2003) *European migration policies in flux: changing patterns of inclusion and exclusion* (Oxford: Wiley-Blackwell).

Boswell, C and Hough, D (2008) 'Politicizing migration: opportunity or liability for the centre-right in Germany?', *Journal of European Public Policy* 15(3): 331—349.

Brandorf, M, Esaiasson, P and Håkansson, N (1996) 'Svenska valfrågor. Partiernas valdebatt 1902–1994', *Statsvetenskaplig tidskrift* 99: 1–36.

Breugelmans, SM and van de Vijver, F (2004) 'Antecedents and components of majority attitudes toward multiculturalism in the Netherlands', *Applied Psychology* 53(3): 400–422.

Breunig, C and Luedtke, A (2008) 'What motivates the gatekeepers? Explaining governing party preferences on immigration', *Governance: An International Journal of Policy, Administration, and Institutions* 21(1): 123–146.

Broughton, D and Donovan, M (eds.) (1999) *Changing party systems in Western Europe* (London: Pinter).

Bucken-Knapp, G (2009) *Defending the Swedish model: social democrats, trade unions and labor migration policy reform* (Lanham, MD: Lexington Books).

Budge, I (1994) 'A new spatial theory of party competition: uncertainty, ideology and policy equilibria viewed comparatively and temporally', *British Journal of Political Science* 24(4): 443–467.

Budge, I (2000) 'Expert judgements of party policy positions: uses and limitations in political research', *European Journal of Political Research* 37(1): 103–113.

Budge, I (2001) 'Validating the manifesto research group approach. Theoretical assumptions and empirical confirmations' in Laver, M (ed.) *Estimating the Policy Positions of Political Actors* (London: Routledge): 50–65.

Budge, I and Farlie, D (1978) 'The potentiality of dimensional analyses for explaining voting and party competition', *European Journal of Political Research* 6(2): 203–231.

Budge, I and Farlie, D (1983) *Explaining and predicting elections. Issue effects and party strategies in twenty-three democracies* (London: George Allen and Unwin).

Budge, I and Pennings, P (2007) 'Do they work? Validating computerised word frequency estimates against policy series', *Electoral Studies* 26(1): 121–129.

Budge, I, Klingemann, H-D, Volkens, A, Bara, J and Tanenbaum, E (2001) *Mapping policy preferences. Estimates for parties, governments and electors 1945–1998* (Oxford: Oxford University Press).

Camia. V and Caramani, D (2012) 'Family meetings: ideological convergence within party families across Europe, 1945–2009', *Comparative European Politics* 10(1): 48–85.

Carmines, E and Stimson, J (1993) 'On the evolution of political issues' in Riker, W (ed.) *Agenda formation* (Ann Arbor, MI: University of Michigan Press): 151–68.

Castles, S and Davidson, A (2000) *Citizenship and migration: globalization and the politics of belonging* (Basingstoke: Palgrave).

Castles, S and Miller, MJ (2003) *The age of migration* (Basingstoke: Palgrave MacMillan).

Charteris-Black, J (2006) 'Britain as a container: immigration metaphors in the 2005 election campaign', *Discourse and Society* 17(5): 563–581.

Christensen, D-A (1996) 'The left-wing opposition in Denmark, Norway and Sweden: cases of Euro-phobia?', *West European Politics* 19(3): 525–546.

Chong, D and Druckman, JN (2007) 'A theory of framing and opinion formation in competitive elite environments', *Journal of Communications* 57(1): 99–118.

Clark, M (2009) 'Valence and electoral outcomes in Western Europe, 1976–1998', *Electoral Studies* 28(1): 111–122.

Clark, NT and Lipset, SM (1991) 'Are social classes dying?', *International Sociology* 6(4): 397–410.

Corbetta, P, Cavazza, N and Roccatto, M (2009) 'Between ideology and social representations: four theses plus (a new) one on the relevance and the meaning of the political left and right', *European Journal of Political Research* 48(5): 622–641.

Corluy, V, Marx, I and Verbist, G (2011) 'Employment chances and changes of immigrants in Belgium: the impact of citizenship', *Journal of Comparative Sociology* 52(4): 50–368.

Cousins, C (1998) 'Social exclusion in Europe: paradigms of social disadvantage in Germany, Spain, Sweden and the United Kingdom', *Policy and Politics* 26(2): 127–146.

Cowles, MA and Smith, M (2000) *The state of the European Union Vol. 5: risks, reform, resistance, and revival* (Oxford: Oxford University Press).

Cox, GW (1990) 'Centripetal and centrifugal incentives in electoral systems', *American Journal of Political Science* 34(4): 903–935.

Creswell, JW and Miller, DL (2000) 'Determining validity in qualitative inquiry', *Theory and Practice* 39(3): 124–130.

Crowson, NJ (2011) *Britain and Europe: a political history since 1918* (London: Routledge).

Crum, B (2007) 'Party stances in the referendums on the EU constitution: causes and consequences of competition and collusion', *European Union Politics* 8(1): 61–82.

Daalder, H (1984) 'In search of the center of European party systems', *The American Political Science Review* 78(1): 92–109.

Dahlström, C (2004) *Nästan välkomna. Invandrarpolitikens retorik och praktik* (Almost welcome. Rhetoric and practice in immigrant policy) (Gothenburg: Department of Political Science).

Dahlström, C and Esaiasson, P (2011) 'The immigration issue and anti-immigrant party success in Sweden 1970–2006: a deviant case analysis', *Party Politics* 18(3): 1–22.

Dahlström, C and Sundell, A (2012) 'A losing gamble. How mainstream parties facilitate anti-immigrant party success', *Electoral Studies* 31(2): 353–363.

Dalton, RJ (1996) 'Political cleavages, issues, and electoral change' in Leduc, L, Niemi, RG and Norris, P (eds.) *Comparing Democracies: Elections and Voting in Global Perspective* (CA: Sage Publications): 319–342.

Dalton, RJ (2002) 'Political cleavages, issues and electoral change' in LeDuc, L, Niemi, RG and Norris, P (eds.) *Comparing Democracies 2: New Challenges in the Study of Elections and Voting* (London: Sage): 189–209.

Dalton, RJ and Wattenberg, MP (2000) *Parties without partisans. Political change in advanced industrial democracies* (Oxford: Oxford University Press).

Dandoy, R (2009) 'Comparing party manifestos in Belgium: the multi-national challenge', taken from http://sciencespo.site.ulb.ac.be/dossiers_membres/dandoy-regis/fichiers/dandoy-regis-publication66.pdf; accessed on 16/10/2013.

Davis, DW and Davenport, C (1999) 'Assessing the validity of the postmaterialism index', *The American Political Science Review* 93(3): 649–664.

De Cleen, B (2009) 'Popular music against extreme right populism: the Vlaams Belang and the 0110 concerts in Belgium', *International Journal of Cultural Studies* 12(4): 577–595.

De Graaf, ND, Heather, A and Need, A (2001) 'Declining cleavages and political choices: the interplay of social and political factors in the Netherlands', *Electoral Studies* 20(1): 1–15.

De Lange, S (2007) 'A new winning formula? The programmatic appeal of the radical right', *Party Politics* 13(4): 411–435.

Della Porta, D and Diani, M (2006) *Social movements: an introduction* (Oxford: Blackwell).

Denman, R (1996) *Missed chances: Britain and Europe in the twentieth century* (London: Cassel).

Deschouwer, K (2009) *The politics of Belgium* (Basingstoke: Palgrave).

Deschouwer, K (2013) 'Party strategies, voter demands and territorial reform in Belgium', *West European Politics* 36(2): 338–358.

Deschouwer, K and van Assche, M (2005) 'It goes (almost) without saying: Europe in the Belgian parties', unpublished manuscript taken from http://aei.pitt.edu/3297/; accessed on 02/10/2013.

Deschouwer, K and van Assche, M (2008) 'Hard but hardly relevant: Party-based Euroscepticism in Belgium' in Szczerbiak, A and Taggart, P (eds.) *Opposing Europe: The Comparative Party Politics of Eurscepticism* (Oxford: Oxford University Press): 75–92.

Devine, F (2002) 'Qualitative methods' in Marsh, D and Stoker, G (eds.) *Theory and methods in political science* (Basingstoke: Palgrave): 197—230.

Dinas, E and Gemenis, K (2010) 'Measuring parties' ideological positions with manifesto data: a critical evaluation of the competing methods', *Party Politics* 16(4): 427–450.

Downs, A (1957) *An economic theory of democracy* (New York: Harper).

Downs, WM (2001) 'Pariahs in the midst: Belgian and Norwegian parties react to extremist threats', *West European Politics* 24(3): 23–42.

Dronkers, J and Vink, MP (2012) 'Explaining access to citizenship in Europe: how citizenship policies affect naturalization rates', *European Union Politics* 13(3): 390–412.

Dummett, A (2005) 'United Kingdom' in Baubock, R, Ersboll, E, Groendijk, K and Waldrauch, H (eds.) *Acquisition and loss of nationality, volume 2: comparative analyses* (Amsterdam: University of Amsterdam Press): 551–580.

Dummett, A and Nicol, A (1990) *Subjects, citizens, aliens and others: nationality and immigration law* (Evanston: Northwestern University Press).

Duyvendak, JW and Scholten, P (2012) 'Deconstructing the Dutch multicultural model: a frame perspective on Dutch immigrant integration policymaking', *Comparative European Politics* 10(3): 266–282.

Eichenberg, RC and Dalton, RJ (1993) 'Europeans and the European community: the dynamics of public support for European integration', *International Organization* 47(4): 507–534.

Ekberg, J (1999) 'Immigration and the public sector: income effects for the native population in Sweden', *Journal of Population Economics* 12(3): 411–430.

Ekberg, J (ed.) (2004) Egenförsörjning eller bidragsförsörjning? Invandrarna, arbetsmarknaden och välfärdsstaten (SOU 2004:21), Stockholm.

Elff, M (2007) 'Social structure and electoral behaviour in comparative perspectives: the decline of social cleavage in Western Europe revisited', *Perspectives on Politics* 5(2): 277–294.

Ellison, N (2011) 'The Conservative Party and the "big society" in Holden, C, Kilkey, M and Ramia, G (eds.) *Social policy review 23: analysis and debate in social policy* (Bristol: The Policy Press): 45–63.

Ennser, L (2012) 'The homogeneity of West European party families: the radical right in comparative perspective', *Party Politics* 18(2): 151–171.

Entorf, H and Minoiu, N (2005) 'What a difference immigration policy makes: a comparison of PISA scores in Europe and traditional countries of immigration', *German Economic Review* 6(3): 355–376.

Entzinger, H (1985) 'The Netherlands' in Hammar, T (ed.) *European immigration policy* (Cambridge: Cambridge University Press): 50–89.

Entzinger, H (2003) 'The rise and fall of multiculturalism: the case of the Netherlands' in Joppke, C and Morawska, E (eds.) (2003) *Toward assimilation and citizenship: immigrants in liberal nation-states* (Basingstoke: Palgrave MacMillan): 59–87.

Enyedi, Z (2008) 'The social and attitudinal basis of political parties: cleavage politics revisited', *European Review* 16(3): 287–304.

Enyedi, Z and Deegan-Krause, K (2010) 'Introduction: the structure of political competition in Western Europe', *West European Politics* 33(3): 415–418.

Evans, G (1998) 'Euroscepticism and Conservative electoral support: how an asset became a liability', *British Journal of Political Science* 28(4): 573–590.

Evans, G, Heath, A and Lalljee, M (1996) 'Measuring left-right and libertarian-authoritarian values in the British electorate', *The British Journal of Sociology* 47(1): 93–112.

Faist, T (1994) 'How to define a Foreigner? The symbolic politics of immigration in German partisan discourse, 1978–1992', *West European Politics* 17(2): 50–71.

Favell, A (1998) *Philosophies of integration: immigration and the idea of citizenship in France and Britain* (Basingstoke: Palgrave MacMillan).

Fennema, M (2000) 'Legal repression of extreme-right parties and racial discrimination' in Koopmans, R and Statham, P (eds.) *Challenging immigration and ethnic relations politics* (Oxford: Oxford University Press): 119–145.

Fitzmaurice, J (1992) 'The extreme right in Belgium: recent developments', *Parliamentary Affairs* 45: 300–308.

Flanagan, SC and Lee, A-R (2003) 'The new politics, culture wars, and the authoritarian-libertarian value change in advanced industrial democracies', *Comparative Political Studies* 36(3): 235–270.

Flood, C (2009) 'Dimensions of Euroscepticism', *Journal of Common Market Studies* 47(4): 911–917.

Florence, E and Martinello, M (2005) 'Social science research and public policies: the case of immigration in Belgium', *International Journal of Multicultural Societies* 7(1): 49–67.

Forster, A (2002) 'Anti-Europeans, anti-marketeers and Eurosceptics: the evolution and influence of Labour and Conservative opposition to Europe', *Political Quarterly* 73(3): 299–308.

Franklin, M (1992) 'The decline of cleavage politics' in Franklin, M, Mackie, T and Valen, H (eds.) *Electoral change: Responses to evolving social and attitudinal structures in Western countries* (Cambridge: Cambridge University Press): 383–405.

Franzmann, S and Kaiser, A (2006) 'Locating political parties in policy space: a reanalysis of party manifesto data', *Party Politics* 12(2): 163–188.

Freeman, G (1995) 'Modes of immigration politics in liberal democratic states', *International Migration Review* 29(4): 881–902.

Freeman, G (1997) 'Immigration as a source of political discontent and frustration in Westerns democracies', *Studies in Comparative International Development* 32(3): 42–64.

Freeman, G (2006) 'Immigrant labour and working-class politics: the French and British experiences' in Messina, AM and Lahav, G (eds.) *The immigration reader: exploring politics and policies* (London: Lynne Reiner): 150–170.

Fukuyama, F (1992) *The end of history and the last man* (New York: Free Press).

Gabel, MJ and Huber, JD (2000) 'Putting parties in their place: inferring party left-right ideological positions from party manifestos data', *American Journal of Political Sciences* 44(1): 94–103.

Geddes, A (2000) *Immigration and European integration: towards fortress Europe?* (Manchester: Manchester University Press).

Geddes, A (2003) *The politics of migration and immigration in Europe* (London: Sage).

Gemenis, K (2012) 'Proxy documents as a source of measurement error in the comparative manifestos project', *Electoral Studies* 31(3): 594–604.

George, AL and Bennett, A (2005) *Case studies and theory development in social sciences* (MA: MIT Press).

Gibney, M and Hansen, R (2005) 'United Kingdom' in Gibney, M and Hansen, R (eds.) *Immigration and asylum: from 1900 to the present* (Oxford/Santa Barbara: ABC-CLIO): 506–507.

Gifford, C (2009) 'The UK and the European Union: dimensions of sovereignty and the problem of Eurosceptic Britishness', *Parliamentary Studies* 63(2): 1–18.

Giljam, M and Oscarsson, H (1996) 'Mapping the Nordic party space', *Scandinavian Political Studies* 19(1): 25–44.

Givens, T and Luedtke, A (2004) 'The politics of European Union immigration policy: institutions, salience and harmonization', *Policy Studies Journal* 32(1): 145–165.

Glyn, A and Wood, S (2001) 'Economic policy under New Labour: how social democratic is the Blair government?', *The Political Quarterly* 72(1): 50–66.

Gordon, P (1985) *Policing immigration: Britain's internal controls* (London: Pluto Press).

Gould, A (1999) 'The erosion of the welfare state: Swedish social policy and the EU', *Journal of European Social Policy* 9(2): 165–174.

Gowland, D, Turner, A and Wright, A (2010) *Britain and European integration since 1945: on the sidelines* (Abingdon: Routledge).

Granberg, D and Holmberg, S (1986) 'Political perception among voters in Sweden and the U.S.: analyses of issues with explicit alternatives', *The Western Political Quarterly* 39(1): 7–28.

Green, J (2007) 'When voters and parties agree: valence issues and party competition', *Political Studies* 55(3): 629–566.

Green, J and Hobolt, SB (2008) 'Owning the issue agenda: party strategies and vote choices in British elections', *Electoral Studies* 27: 460–474.

Green-Pedersen, C (2004) 'Center parties, party competition, and the implosion of party systems: a study of centripetal tendencies in multiparty systems', *Political Studies* 52(2): 324–341.

Green-Pedersen, C (2007) 'The growing importance of issue competition: the changing nature of party competition in Western Europe', *Political Studies* 55(3): 607–628.

Green-Pedersen, C and Krogstrup, J (2008) 'Immigration as a political issue in Denmark and Sweden', *European Journal of Political Research* 47(5): 610–634.

Green-Pedersen, C and Odmalm, P (2008) 'Going different ways? Rightwing parties and the immigrant issue in Denmark and Sweden', *Journal of European Public Policy* 15(3): 367–381.

Grendstad, G (2003) 'Comparing political orientations: grid-group theory versus the left-right dimension in the five Nordic countries', *European Journal of Political Research* 42(1): 1–21.

Grofman, B (2004) 'Downs and two-party convergence', *Annual Review of Political Science* 7(25): 25–46.

Gstöhl, S (2002) 'Scandinavia and Switzerland: small, successful and stubborn towards the EU', *Journal of European Public Policy* 9(4): 529–549.

Hammar, T (1985) *European immigration policy: a comparative study* (Cambridge: Cambridge University Press).

Hammar, T (1999) 'Closing the doors to the Swedish Welfare state' in Brochmann, G and Hammar, T (eds.) *Mechanisms of immigration control. A comparative analysis of European regulation policies* (Oxford: Berg): 169–203.

Hampshire, J (2005) *Citizenship and belonging: immigration and the politics of demographic governance in post-war Britain* (Basingstoke: Palgrave).

Hampshire, J (2013) *The politics of immigration: contradictions of the liberal state* (Cambridge: Polity Press).

Hansen, R (1999) 'The Kenyan Asians, British politics, and the commonwealth immigrants act, 1968', *The Historical Journal* 42(3): 809–834.

Hansen, R (2000) *Citizenship and immigration in post-war Britain* (Oxford: Oxford University Press).

Hansen, R and King, D (2000) 'Illiberalism and the new politics of asylum: liberalism's dark side', *The Political Quarterly* 71(4): 396–403.

Harmel, R and Gibson, RK (1995) 'Right-libertarian parties and the "new values" a re-examination', *Scandinavian Political Studies* 18(2): 97–118.

Harmsen, R (2004) 'Euroscepticism in the Netherlands: stirrings of dissent' in Harmsen, R and Spiering, M (eds.) *Euroscepticism: party politics, national identity and European integration* (Amsterdam/New York: Editions Rodopi): 99–126.

Harmsen, R (2005) *A dual exceptionalism? British and French patterns of Euroscepticism in wider comparative perspective* (Oxford: Centre for the Study of Democratic Government) taken from http://oxpo.politics.ox.ac.uk/materials/national_identity/Harmsen_Paper.pdf; accessed on 30/09/2013.

Harmsen, R and Spiering, M (2004) 'Introduction: Euroscepticism and the evolution of European political debate' in Harmsen, R and Spiering, M (eds.) *Euroscepticism: party politics, national identity and European integration* (Amsterdam/New York: Editions Rodopi): 13–37.

Haste, H (2006) 'Assets, aliens or asylum seekers? Immigration and the United Kingdom', *Prospects* 36(3): 327–341.

Hatton, TJ (2009) 'The rise and fall of asylum: what happened and why?', *The Economic Journal* 119(535): 183–213.

Hayton, R (2010) 'Towards the mainstream? UKIP and the 2009 elections to the European Parliament', *Politics* 30(1): 26–35.

Heath, AF, Jowell, RM and Curtice, JK (2001) *The rise of New Labour: party policies and voter choices* (Oxford: Oxford University Press).

Heffernan, R (2001) 'Beyond Euro-scepticism: exploring the Europeanisation of the Labour Party since 1983', *Political Quarterly* 72(2): 180–189.

Helbling, M, Hoeglinger, D and Wuest, B (2010) 'How political parties frame European integration', *European Journal of Political Research* 49(4): 496–521.

Hinnfors, J, Spehar, A and Bucken-Knapp, G (2011) 'The missing factor: why social democracy can lead to restrictive immigration policy', *Journal of European Public Policy* 19(4): 1–19.

Hix, S (1999) 'Dimensions and alignments in European Union politics: cognitive constraints and partisan responses', *European Journal of Political Research* 35(1): 69–106.

Hix, S and Lord, C (1997) *Political parties in the European Union* (New York: St. Marin's).

Hobolt, S (2008) *The dynamics of issue diversity in the party rhetoric*, OCSID Working Paper OCSID _03 (Oxford centre for the study of inequality and democracy: Oxford University) taken from http://ocsid.politics.ox.ac.uk/publications/index.asp; accessed on 30/09/2013.

Holian, DB (2004) 'He's stealing my issues! Clinton's crime rhetoric and the dynamics of issue ownership', *Political Behaviour* 26(2): 95–124.

Hollifield, J (1992) *Immigrants, markets and states: the political economy of postwar Europe* (Cambridge, MA: Harvard University Press).

Hooghe, L (2007) 'What drives Euroskepticism?: party-public cueing, ideology and strategic opportunity', *European Union Politics* 8(1): 5–12.

Hooghe, L and Marks, G (2007) 'Sources of Euroscepticism', *Acta Politica* 42(2): 118–127.

Hooghe, L, Bakker, R, Brigevich, A, de Vries, C, Edwards, E, Marks, G, Rovny, J and Steenbergen, M (2010) 'Reliability and validity if measuring party positions: the chapel hill expert surveys of 2002 and 2006', *European Journal of Political Research* 49(5): 687–703.

Hooghe, L, Marks, G and Wilson, C (2002) 'Does left/right structure party positions on European integration?', *Comparative Political Studies* 35(8): 962–989.

Hopkins, J (2009) 'Party matters: devolution and party politics in Britain and Spain', *Party Politics* 15(2): 179–198.

Huber, J and Inglehart, R (1995) 'Expert interpretations of party space and party locations in 2 societies', *Party Politics* 1(1): 73–111.

Hunger, U (2001) 'Party competition and inclusion of immigrants in Germany', *German Policy Studies* 1(3): 302–330.

Hussain, AM (2001) *British immigration policy under the Conservative government* (Aldershot: Ashgate).

Hylarides, P (2001) 'The Netherlands: from Euroscepticism to Europhoria', *Contemporary Review 279*(1629): 225–231.

Inglehart, R (1971) 'The silent revolution in post-industrial societies', *American Political Science Review* 65(4): 991–1017.

Inglehart, R (1977) *The silent revolution: changing values and political styles among Western publics* (Princeton, NJ: Princeton University Press).

Inglehart, R (1990) *Culture shift in advanced industrial society* (Princeton, NJ: Princeton University Press).

Inglehart, R (1997) *Modernization and postmodernization: cultural, economic, and political change in 43 societies* (Princeton, NJ: Princeton University Press).

Inglehart, R (2008) 'Changing values among Western publics from 1970–2006', *West European Politics* 31(1–2): 130–146.

Inglehart, R and Klingemann, HD (1987) 'Party identification, ideological preference and the left-right dimension among Western mass publics' in Budge, I, Robertson, D and Hearl, DJ (eds.) *Ideology, strategy and party changes: spatial analyses of post-war election programmes in 19 democracies* (Cambridge: Cambridge University Press): 243–273.

Ireland, P (2000) 'Reaping what they sow: institutions and immigrant political participation in Western Europe' in Koopmans, R and Statham, P (eds.) *Challenging immigration and ethnic relations politics* (Oxford: Oxford University Press): 233–283.

Irving, REM (1979) 'Christian democracy in post-war Europe: conservatism writ-large o distinctive political phenomena?', *West European Politics* 2(1): 53–68.

Irwin, GA and Thomassen, J (1975) 'Issue-consensus in a multi-party system: voters and leaders in the Netherlands', *Acta Politica* 10(4): 389–420.

Jacobs, D (1999) 'The debate over enfranchisement of foreign residents in Belgium', *Journal of Ethnic and Migration Studies* 25(4): 649–663.

Jadot, C (2012) *Do all roads lead to the same Europe? Reconsidering the pro-/anti-integration yardstick to measure national party positions towards the EU: the case of Belgium*, taken from http://www.uaces.org/pdf/papers/1240/jadot.pdf; accessed on 16/01/2013.

Jagers, J and Walgrave, S (2007) 'Populism as political communication style: an empirical study of political parties' discourse in Belgium', *European Journal of Political Research* 46(3): 319–345.

Jahn, D (2010) 'Conceptualizing left and right in comparative politics: towards a deductive approach', *Party Politics* 17(6): 745–765.

Jahn, D and Storsved, A-S (1995) 'Legitimacy through referendum? The nearly successful domino-strategy of the EU referendums in Austria, Finland, Sweden and Norway', *West European Politics* 18(4): 18–37.

Jansen, G, Evans, G and de Graaf, ND (2013) 'Class voting and left-right party positions: a comparative study of 15 Western democracies, 1960–2005', *Social Science Research* 42(2): 376–400.

Johansson, K-M and Raunio, T (2001) 'Partisan responses to Europe: comparing Finnish and Swedish political parties', *European Journal of Political Research* 39(2): 225–249.

Jones, B and Baumgartner, F (2005) *The politics of attention: how government prioritizes attention* (Chicago: University of Chicago Press).

Jones, E (1999) 'Is "competitive" corporatism an adequate response to globalisation. Evidence from the low countries', *West European Politics* 22(3): 159–181.

Jonung, L (2004) To be or not to be in the Euro? Benefits and costs of monetary unification as perceived by voters in the Swedish euro referendum 2003 (MPRA Paper No. 1334), taken from http://mpra.ub.uni-muenchen.de/1334/1/MPRA_paper_1334.pdf; accessed on 09/01/2013.

Jupp, J (2005) 'Race, ethnicity, immigration and the British general election', *People and Place* 13(3): 15–20.

Karapin, R (1999) 'The politics of immigration control in Britain and Germany: subnational politicians and social movements', *Comparative Politics* 31(4): 423–444.

Karp, JA and Banducci, SA (2002) 'Issues and party competition under alternative electoral systems', *Party Politics* 8(1): 123–141.

Katz, R (2008) 'Euroscepticism in parliament: a comparative analysis of the European and National Parliaments' in Szczerbiak, A and Taggart, P (eds.) *Opposing Europe: the comparative party politics of Eurscepticism* (Oxford: Oxford University Press): 151–181.

Katz, R and Mair, P (1995) 'Changing models of party organization and party democracy: the emergence of the cartel party', *Party Politics* 1(1): 5–28.

Kicinger, A (2004) *International migration as a non-traditional security threat and the EU responses to this phenomenon*, CEFMR working paper (Warsaw: Central European Forum for Migration Research), taken from http://www.cefmr.pan.pl/docs/cefmr_wp_2004-02.pdf; accessed on 07/09/2011.

Kite, C (2006) 'The domestic background: public opinion and party attitudes towards integration in the Nordic countries' in Bailes, A, Herolf, G and Sundelius, B (eds.) *The Nordic Countries and the European Security and Defence Policy* (Oxford: Oxford University Press): 99–107.

Kitschelt, H (1988) 'Left-libertarian parties: explaining innovation in competitive party systems', *World Politics* 40(2): 194–234.

Kitschelt, H (1994) *The transformation of European social democracy* (Cambridge: Cambridge University Press).

Kitschelt, H (2000) 'Citizens, politicians, and party cartellizations: political representation and state failure in post-industrial democracies', *European Journal of Political Research* 37(2): 149–179.

Kitschelt, H. (2004) *Diversification and reconfiguration of party systems in postindustrial democracies* (Bonn, Germany: Friedrich Ebert Stiftung).

Kitschelt, H and McGann, A (1995) *The radical right in Western Europe. A comparative analysis* (Ann Arbor, MI: University of Michigan Press).

Klingemann, H-D (1987) 'Electoral programmes in West Germany 1949–1980: explorations in the nature of political controversy' in Budge, I, Robertson, D and Hearl, D (eds.) *Ideology, strategy, and party change: spatial analyses of post-war election programmes in 19 Democracies* (New York: Cambridge University Press): 294–323.

Klingemann, H-D, Volkens, A, Bara, J, Budge, I and Macdonald, M (2006) *Mapping policy preference II: estimates for parties, electors and governments in Eastern Europe, the European Union and the OECD, 1990–2000* (Oxford: Oxford University Press).

Knutsen, O (1990) 'The materialist/post-materialist value dimension as a party cleavage in the Nordic countries', *West European Politics* 13(2): 258–274.

Knutsen, O (1995a) 'The impact of old politics and new politics value orientations on party choice: a comparative study', *Journal of Public Policy* 15(1): 1–63.

Knutsen, O (1995b) 'Value orientations, political conflicts and left-right identification: a comparative study', *European Journal of Political Research* 28(1): 63–93.

Koopmans, R (2010) 'Trade-offs between equality and difference: immigrant integration, multiculturalism and the welfare state in cross-national perspective', *Journal of Ethnic and Migration Studies* 36(1): 1–26.

Koopmans, R, Statham, P, Giugni, M and Passy, F (2005) *Contested Citizenship: immigration and cultural diversity in Europe* (Minneapolis: University of Minnesota Press).

Kopecky, P and Mudde, C (2002) 'The two sides of Euroscepticism: party positions on European integration in East Central Europe', *European Union Politics* 3(3): 297–326.

Kriesi, H (2007) 'The role of European integration in national election campaigns', *European Union Politics* 8(1): 83–108.

Kriesi, H and van Praag Jr, P (1987) 'Old and new politica: the Dutch peace movement and the traditional political organizations', *European Journal of Political Research* 15(3): 319–346.

Kriesi, H, Grande, E, Lachat, R, Dolezal, M, Bornschier, S and Frey, T (2006) 'Globalisation and the transformation of the national political space: six European countries compared', *European Journal of Political Research* 45(6): 921–956.

Kymlicka, W (1995) *Multicultural citizenship* (Oxford: Oxford University Press).

Lahav, G (1997) 'Ideological and party constraints on immigration attitudes in Europe', *Journal of Common Market Studies* 35(3): 307–406.

Lahav, G and Courtemanche, M (2011) 'The ideological effects of framing threat on immigration and civil liberties,' *Political Behavior* 34(3): 477–505.

Lane, J-E and Ersson, S (1991) *Politics and society in Western Europe* (London: Sage).

Laver, M and Hunt, B (1992) *Party and policy competition* (London: Routledge).

Lawler, P (1997) 'Scandinavian exceptionalism and European Union', *Journal of Common Market Studies* 35(4): 565–594.

Layton-Henry, Z (1980) *Conservative Party politics* (Basingstoke: Palgrave).

Layton-Henry, Z (1994) 'Britain: the would be-be zero-immigration country' in Cornelius, WA, Martin, PL and Hollifield, J (eds.) *Controlling immigration: a global perspective* (Stanford: Stanford University Press): 273–297.

Leconte, C (2010) *Understanding Euroscepticism* (London: Palgrave Macmillan).

Lijphart, A (1975) *The politics of accommodation: pluralism and democracy in the Netherlands* (Berkeley: California University Press).

Lindahl, R and Naurin, D (2005) 'Sweden: the twin faces of a Euro-outsider', *Journal of European Integration* 27(1): 65–87.

Lindvall, J and Rothstein, B (2006) 'Sweden: the fall of the strong state', *Scandinavian Political Studies* 29(1): 47–63.

Linhart, E and Shikano, S (2009) 'Ideological signals of German parties in a multi-dimensional space: an estimation of party preferences using the CMP data', *German Politics* 18(3): 301–322.

Lipset, S and Rokkan, S (1967) 'Cleavage structures, party systems, and voter alignments: an introduction' in Lipset, S and Rokkan, S (eds.) *Party systems and voter alignments: cross national perspectives* (New York: The Free Press): 1–64.

Loobuyck, P and Jacobs, D (2006) 'The Flemish immigration society: political challenges on different levels' in Haenens, L, Hooghe, M, Vanheule, D and Gezduci, H (eds.) *'New' citizens, new policies? Developments in diversity policy in Canada and Flanders* (Gent: Academia Press): 105–124.

Lubbers, M and Scheepers, P (2005) 'Political versus instrumental Euro-scepticism', *European Union Politics* 6(2): 223–242.

Lucardie, P and Napel, H-M (1994) 'Between confessionalism and liberal conservatism: the Christian Democratic parties in Belgium and the Netherlands' in Hanley, D (ed.) *Christian Democracy in Europe* (London: Pinter): 51–71.

Lucassen, J and Penninx, R (1997) *Newcomers, immigrants and their descendants in the Netherlands 1550–1995* (Amsterdam: Het Spinhuis).

Luedtke, A (2011) 'Uncovering European Union immigration legislation: policy dynamics and outcomes', *International Migration* 49(2): 1–27.

Lundh, C and Ohlsson, R (1994) *Från arbetskraftsimport till flyktinginvandring* (Stockholm: SNS Förlag).

MacDonald, I and Blake, N (1995) *MacDonald's immigration law and practice* (London: Butterworths).

Mair, P (1989) 'Continuity, change and the vulnerability of party', *West European Politics* 12(4): 169–187.

Mair, P (2008) 'Electoral volatility and the Dutch party System: a comparative perspective', *Acta Politica* 43(2–3): 235–253.

Manners, I and Sorensen, C (2007) *New political contestation in the European Union* (DIIS Brief: Copenhagen).

Marks, G and Wilson, C (2000) 'The past in the present: a cleavage theory of the party responses to European integration', *British Journal of Political Science* 30(3): 433–449.

Martinello, M (2003) 'Belgium's immigration policy', *International Migration Review* 37(1): 225–232.

Martiniello, M (1995) *Migration, Citizenship and Ethno-National Identities in the European Union* (Avebury: Aldershot).

Martiniello, M (2012) 'Immigrant integration and multiculturalism in Belgium' in Taras, Raymond (ed.) *Challenging multiculturalism: European models of diversity* (Edinburgh: Edinburgh University Press): 120–138.

Martinello, M and Rea, A (2003) *Belgium's immigration policy brings renewal and challenges (Country Profiles.)* (Washington, DC: Migration Policy Institute), taken from http://www.migrationinformation.org/Profiles/display.cfm?ID=164; accessed on 18/01/2013.

Massetti, E (2009) 'Explaining regionalist party positioning in a multidimensional ideological space: a framework for analysis', *Regional and Federal Studies* 19(4–5): 501–531.

Mayring, P (2000) 'Qualitative content analysis' in Flick, U, von Kardoff, E and Steinke, A (eds.) *Companion to qualitative research* (London: Sage): 266–270.

Meguid, B (2005) 'Competition between unequals: the role of mainstream party strategy in niche party success', *American Political Science Review* 90(3): 347–359.

Menon, A (2004) 'Britain and European integration: the view from within', *Political Quarterly* 75(3): 285–317.

Merrill III, S (1995) 'Discriminating between the directional and proximity spatial models of electoral competition', *Electoral Studies* 14(3): 273–287.

Messina, A (1985) 'Race and party competition in Britain: policy formation in the post-consensus period', *Parliamentary Affairs* 38(4): 423–436.

Messina, A (1989) *Race and party competition in Britain* (Oxford: Oxford University Press).

Messina, A (2007) *The logics and politics of post-WWII migration in western Europe* (New York: Cambridge University Press).

Mielants, E (2006) 'The long-term historical development of racist tendencies within the political and social context of Belgium', *Journal of Comparative Sociology* 47(3–4): 313–334.

Miles, L (2001) 'Sweden in the European Union: changing expectations?, *Journal of European Integration* 23(4): 303–333.

Miljan, T (1977) *The reluctant Europeans: the attitudes of the Nordic countries towards European integration* (London: C. Hurst and Co.).

Money, J (1999) *Fences and neighbors. The political geography of immigration control* (Cornell University Press).

Mudde, C (1999) 'The single-issue party thesis: extreme right parties and the immigration issue', *West European Politics* 22(3): 182–197.

Mudde, C (2004) 'The populist zeitgeist', *Government and Opposition* 39(4): 541–563.

Mudde, C (2007) *Populist radical right parties in Europe* (Cambridge: Cambridge University Press).

Müller-Rommel, F (2002) 'The lifespan and the political performance of green parties in Western Europe', *Environmental Politics* 11(1): 1–16.

Mycock, A (2009) 'British citizenship and the legacy of empire', *Parliamentary Affairs* 63(2): 1–17.

Norris, P (2005) *Radical right: voters and parties in the electoral market* (Cambridge: Cambridge University Press).

Odmalm, P (2005) *Migration policies and political participation* (Basingstoke: Palgrave Macmillan).

Odmalm, P (2011) 'Political Parties and "the Immigration Issue": Issue ownership in Swedish Parliamentary Elections 1991-2010', *West European Politics* 34(5): 1070–1091.

Odmalm, P (2012) 'Party competition and positions on immigration: strategic advantages and spatial locations', *Comparative European Politics* 10(1): 1–22.

Oliver, DG, Serovich, JM and Mason, TL (2005) 'Constraints and opportunities with interview transcription: towards reflection in qualitative research', *Social Forces* 84(2): 1273–1289.

Page Moch, L (2003) *Moving Europeans: Migration in Western Europe since 1650* (Bloomington and Indianapolis: Indiana University Press).

Patton, MQ (2002) *Qualitative research and evaluation methods* (London: Sage).

Pauwels, T (2011) 'Explaining the strength decline of the populist radical right Vlaams Belang in Belgium: the impact of permanent opposition', *Acta Politica* 46(1): 60–82.

Pelizzo, R (2003) 'Party positions or party direction? An analysis of party manifesto data', *West European Politics* 26(2): 67–89.

Pellikaan, H, van der Meer, T and de Lange, S (2003) 'The road from a depoliticized to a centrifugal democracy', *Acta Politica* 38(1): 1–27.

Pellikaan, H, van der Meer, T and de Lange, S (2007) 'Fortuyn's legacy: party system change in the Netherlands', *Comparative European Politics* 5(3): 282–302.

Penninx, R (2005) 'Bridges between research and policy? The case of post-war immigration and integration policies in the Netherlands', *International Journal of Multicultural Societies* 7(1): 33–48.

Perlmutter, T (1996) 'Bringing parties back in: comments on "modes of immigration politics in liberal democratic societies"', *International Migration Review* 30(1): 375–388.

Petrocik, J (1996) 'Issue ownership in presidential elections with a 1980 case study', *American Journal of Political Science* 40(3): 825–850.

Phalet, K and Swyngedouw, M (2003) 'Measuring immigrant integration: the case of Belgium', *Studi Emigrazione/Migration Studies* XL (152): 773–803.

Poguntke, T (2012) 'Towards a new party system: the vanishing hold of the catch-all parties in Germany', *Party Politics* (Published online before print 30 October 2012, doi: 10.1177/1354068812462925): 1–20.

Pontusson, J (1988) 'The triumph of pragmatism: nationalisation and privatisation in Sweden', *West European Politics* 11(4): 129–140.

Prop. 1990/91: 195 *(Regeringens proposition 1990/91:195 om aktiv flykting- och immigrationspolitik m.m.) (Governmental Bill 1990/91:195).*

Raunio, T (2007) 'Softening the persistent: Euroscepticism in the Nordic EU countries', *Acta Politica* 42(2–3): 191–210.

Ray, L (1999) 'Measuring party orientations towards European integration: results from an expert survey', *European Journal of Political Research* 36(2): 283–306.

Raymond, C (2011) 'The continued salience of religious voting in the United States, Germany and Great Britain', *Electoral Studies* 30(1): 125–135.

Riaño, Y and Wastl-Walter, D (2006) 'Historical shifts in asylum policies in Switzerland: between humanitarian values and the protection of national identity', *Refugee Watch* 27: 1–18.

Riker, W (1996) *The strategy of rhetoric: campaigning for the American constitution* (New Haven, CT: Yale University Press).

Ring, H (1995) 'Refugees in Sweden: inclusion and exclusion in the welfare state' in Miles, R and Thränhardt, D (eds.) *Migration and European integration: the dynamics of inclusion and exclusion* (London: Pinter): 159–177.

Ringmar, E (1998) 'Re-imagining Sweden: the rhetorical battle over EU membership', *Scandinavian Journal of History* 23(1–2): 45–63.

Roggeband, C and Vliegenthart, R (2007) 'Divergent framing: the public debate on migration in the Dutch parliament and media, 1995–2004', *West European Politics* 30(3): 524–548.

Rose, R (1964) 'Parties, factions and the tendencies in Britain', *Political Studies* 12(1): 33–36.

Russell, A and Fieldhouse, E (2005) *Neither left nor right? The Liberal Democrats and the electorate* (Manchester: Manchester University Press).

Russell, A, Fieldhouse, E and MacAllister, I (2002) 'The anatomy of Liberal support in Britain, 1974–1997', *British Journal of Politics and International Relations* 4(1): 9–74.

Rydgren, J (2002) 'Radical right populism in Sweden: still a failure, but for how long?', *Scandinavian Political Studies* 25(1): 27–56.

Rydgren, J (2004) 'Mechanisms of exclusion: ethnic discrimination in the Swedish labour market', *Journal of Ethnic and Migration Studies* 30(4): 697–716.

Rydgren, J (2005) 'Is extreme right-wing populism contagious? Explaining the emergence of a new party family', *European Journal of Political Research* 44 (3): 413–437.

Sartori, G (1976) *Parties and party systems* (New York: Cambridge University Press).

Schall, CE (2004) 'In the absence of conflict: the role of immigration discourse in the lack of extreme right success in Sweden', taken from http://www.ssc .wisc.edu/~cschall/Absence%20of%20Conflict-shortversion.doc; accessed on 30/09/2013.

Schattschneider, E (1960) *The semi-sovereign people: a realist's view of democracy in America* (New York: Holt, Rinehart and Winston).

Schattschneider, E (2009) [1942] *Party government* (3rd edition) (New Brunswick: New Jersey).

Scheffer, P (2011) 'The open society and its believers' in: McTernan, M (ed.) *Exploring the cultural challenges to social democracy: anti-migration populism, identity and community in an age of insecurity* (London: The Policy Network): 61–70.

Scholten, P (2009) 'The coproduction of immigrant integration policy and research in the Netherlands: the case of the Scientific Council for Government Policy', *Science and Public Policy* 36(7): 561–573.

Scholten, P (2010) *Framing immigrant integration: Dutch research-policy dialogues in comparative perspective* (Amsterdam: Amsterdam University Press).

Scholten, P (2012) 'Agenda dynamics and the multi-level governance of intractable policy controversies: the case of migrant integration policies in the Netherlands', *Policy Sciences* 46(3): 217–236.

Schuster, L (2000) 'A comparative analysis of the asylum policy of seven European governments', *Journal of Refugee Studies* 13(1): 118–132.

Schain, MA (2008) *The politics of immigration in France, Britain, and the United States: a comparative study* (Basingstoke: Palgrave).

Sinardet, D (2010) 'From consociational consciousness to majoritarian myth: Consociational democracy, multi-level politics and the Belgian case of Brussels-Halle-Vilvoorde', *Acta Politica* 45(3): 346–369.

Sitter, N (2001) 'The politics of opposition and European integration in Scandinavia: is Euro-scepticism a government-opposition dynamic?', *West European Politics* 24(4): 22–39.

Sitter, N (2002) *Opposing Europe: Euro-scepticism, opposition and party competition*, SEI Working Paper No. 56/Opposing Europe Research Network Paper No. 9 (Sussex European Institute: ISSN 1350–4649).

Smith, J (2008) 'Toward consensus? Centre-right parties and immigration policy in the UK and Ireland', *Journal of European Public Policy* 15(3): 415–431.

Soininen, M (1999) 'The "Swedish Model" as an institutional framework for immigrant membership rights', *Journal of Ethnic and Migration Studies* 25(4): 685–702.

Solomos, J (2003) *Race and racism in Britain* (Basingstoke: Palgrave).

SOU 1991:1 *Flykting- och immigrationspolitiken betänkande. Sammanfattning av utredningen SOU 1991:1* (Official Report Swedish Government; *Asylum and immigration policies. Summar of investigation SOU 1991:1*).

SOU 2006:87 *Arbetskraftsinvandring till Sverige – förslag och konsekvenser* (Official Report Swedish Government; *Labour migration to Sweden – suggestions and consequences*).

Soysal, Y (1998) *Limits of citizenship: migrants and postnational membership in Europe* (Chicago: University of Chicago Press).

Spång, M (2008) *Svensk invandringspolitik i demokratiskt perspektiv* (Current Themes in IMER Research: Malmö University).

Spencer, IRG (1997) *British immigration policy since 1939: the making of multi-racial Britain* (London: Routledge).

Spiecker, B and Steutel, J (2001) 'Multiculturalism, pillarization and liberal civic education in the Netherlands', *International Journal of Educational Research* 35(3): 293–304.

Spiering, M (2004) 'British Euroscepticism', *European Studies* 20(1): 127–149.

Spies, D and Franzmann, ST (2011) 'A two-dimensional approach to the political opportunity structure of extreme right parties in Western Europe', *West European Politics* 34(5): 1044–1069.

Statham, P and Geddes, A (2006) 'Elites and the "organised public": who drives British immigration politics and in which direction?', *West European Politics* 29(2): 248–269.

Statham, P, Koopmans, R, Giugni, M and Passy, F (2005) 'Resilient or adaptable Islam?: Multiculturalism, religion and migrants' claims-making for group demands in Britain, the Netherlands and France', *Ethnicities* 5(4): 427–459.

Steenbergen, M and Marks, G (2007) 'Evaluating expert surveys', *European Journal of Political Research* 46(3): 37–366.

Stokes, DE (1963) 'Spatial models of party competition', *American Political Science Review* 57: 368–377.

Sundberg, J (1999) 'The enduring Scandinavian party system', *Scandinavian Political Studies* 22(3): 221–241.

Swyngedouw, M (1998) 'The extreme right in Belgium: of a non-existent Front National and an omnipresent Vlaams Blok' in Betz, H-G and Immerfall, S (eds.) *The new politics of the right: neo-populist parties and movements in established democracies* (New York: St Martin's Press): 59–77.

Taggart, P (1998) 'A touchstone of dissent: Euroscepticism in contemporary Western European party systems', *European Journal of Political Research* 33(3): 363–388.

Taggart, P and Szczerbiak, A (2002) *The party politics of Euroscepticism in EU member and candidate states* SEI Working Paper No 51/Opposing Europe Research Network Working Paper No 6 (Sussex European Institute: ISSN 1350–4649).

Taggart, P and Szczerbiak, A (2008) 'Introduction: researching Euroscepticism in European party systems: a comparative and theoretical research agenda' in

Taggart, P and Szczerbiak, A (eds.) *Opposing Europe: the comparative party politics of Euroscepticism* (Oxford: Oxford University Press): 1–28.

Tashakkori, A and Teddlie, C (1998) *Mixed methodology: combining qualitative and quantitative approaches* (London: Sage).

Teney, C, Jacobs, D, Rea, A and Delwit, P (2010) 'Ethnic voting in Brussels: voting patterns among ethnic minorities in Brussels (Belgium) during the 2006 local elections', *Acta Politica* 45(3): 273–297.

Thomassen, JJA (2005) *The European voter: a comparative study of modern democracies* (Oxford: Oxford University Press).

Thorpe, A (1997) *The history of the British Labour Party* (Basingstoke: MacMillan).

Thränhardt, D (2009) 'Conflict, consensus, and policy outcomes: immigration and integration in Germany and the Netherlands' in Koopmans, R and Statham, P (eds.) *Challenging immigration and ethnic relations politics: comparative European perspectives* (Oxford: Oxford University Press): 162–187.

Timmermans, A and Breemans, G (2012) 'Morality issues in the Netherlands: coalition politics under pressure' in Engeli, I, Green-Pedersen, C and Thorup Larsen, L (eds.) *Morality politics in Western Europe: parties, agendas and policy issues* (Basingstoke: Palgrave): 35–62.

Toshkov, D and de Haan, L (2013) 'The Europeanization of asylum policy: an assessment of the impact of asylum applications and recognition rates', *Journal of European Public Policy* 29(5): 661–683.

Tromp, B (1989) 'Party strategies and system change in the Netherlands', *West European Politics* 12(4): 82–97.

Urwin, DW (1970) 'Social cleavages and political parties in Belgium: problems of institutionalization', *Political Studies* 18(3): 320–340.

Usherwood, S (2002) 'Opposition to the European Union in the UK: the dilemma of public opinion and party management', *Government and Opposition* 37(2): 211–230.

Van Biezen, I (2012) 'Constitutionalizing party democracy: the constitutive codification of political parties in post-war Europe', *British Journal of Political Science* 42(1): 187–212.

Van der Brug, W (2004) 'Issue ownership and party choice', *Electoral Studies* 23(2): 209–233.

Van der Brug, W and Van Spanje, J (2009) 'Immigration, Europe, and the "new" cultural dimension', *European Journal of Political Research* 48(3): 309–334.

Van Donselaar, J (1995) *De staat paraat? De bestrijding van extreme-rechts in West-Europa* (Amsterdam: Babylon-De Geus).

Vanheule, D and Witlox, F (2010) 'Asylum legislation and asylum applications: a geographical analysis of Belgian asylum policy by country of origin (1992–2003)', *International Migration* 48(1): 129–147.

Van Kersbergen, K (1994) 'The distinctiveness of Christian Democracy' in Hanley, D (ed.) *Christian Democracy in Europe* (London: Pinter): 31–51.

Van Kersbergen, K and Krouwel, A (2008) 'A double-edged sword! The Dutch centre-right and the "foreigners issue" ', *Journal of European Public Policy* 15(3): 398–414.

Van Rie, T, Marx, I and Horemans, J (2011) 'Ghent revisited: unemployment insurance and union membership in Belgium and the Nordic countries', *European Journal of Industrial Relations* 17(2): 125–139.

Van Spanje, J (2010) 'Contagious parties: anti-immigration parties and their impact on other parties' immigration stances in contemporary Western Europe', *Party Politics* 16(5): 563–586.

Van Spanje, J and van der Brug, W (2007) 'The party as pariah: the exclusion of anti-immigration parties and its effect on their ideological positions', *West European Politics* 30(5): 1022–1040.

Vasta, E (2007) *Accommodating diversity: why current critiques of multiculturalism miss the point.* Working Paper, WP-07-53 (Centre of Migration, Policy and Society: University of Oxford).

Vermeulen, F and van Heelsum, A (2009) 'Immigrant organisations in Amsterdam' in Nell, L and Rath, J (eds.) *Ethnic Amsterdam: immigrants and urban change in the twentieth century* (Solidarity and Identity Series) (Amsterdam: Amsterdam University Press): 145–158.

Vermeulen, H and Penninx, R (2000) *Immigrant integration: the Dutch case* (Amsterdam: Het Spinhuis).

Vink, M and Meijerink, F (2003) 'Asylum applications and recognition rates in EU member states 1982–2001: a quantitative analysis', *Journal of Refugee Studies* 16(3): 297–315.

Wagner, M (2012) 'Defining and measuring niche parties', *Party Politics* 18(6): 45–864.

Walgrave, S and Nuytemanns, M (2009) 'Friction and party manifesto change in 25 countries, 1945–98', *American Journal of Political Science* 53(1): 190–206.

Weakliem, DL (1991) 'The two lefts? Occupation and party choice in France, Italy, and the Netherlands', *American Journal of Sociology* 96(6): 1327–1361.

Widfeldt, A (1996) 'Sweden and the European Union: implications for the Swedish party system' in Miles, L (ed.) *The European Union and the Nordic Countries* (London: Routledge): 99–114.

Widfeldt, A (2007) 'The Swedish parliamentary election of 2006', *Electoral Studies* 26(4): 797–837.

Widgren, J (1982) *Svensk invandrarpolitik: en faktabok* (Lund: Liber Laromedel).

Wolinetz, S (1988) *Parties and party systems in liberal democracies* (New York: Routledge).

Yanasmayan, Z and Foblets, M-C (2010) *Country report Belgium* (The INTEC project. Integration and naturalisation tests: the new way to European Citizenship), taken from http://www.humanrights.dk/files/pdf/INTEC/Belgium%20Intec%20final.pdf; accessed on 04/10/2013.

Interviews

Belgium

GA 1, 23/09/13
GA 2, 17/09/13
Ecolo 1, 29/07/13
Sp.a 1, 11/07/13
Sp.a 2, 17/07/13
PS 1, 25/07/10
PS 2, 25/07/10
PS 3, 25/07/10
CD&V 1, 04/03/10
CD&V 2, 01/06/10
MR 1, 26/02/10
Open VLD 1, 21/07/10
Open VLD 2, 22/07/10

Britain

Conservatives 1, 16/09/10
Conservatives 2, 10/06/10
Conservatives 3, 2/07/10
Conservatives 4, 25/02/10
Conservatives 5, 15/09/10
Conservatives 6, 11/05/10
Conservatives 7, 09/09/10
Conservatives 8, 31/08/10
Conservatives 9, 16/03/11
Labour 1, 9/12/09
Labour 2, 13/11/09
Labour 3, 29/03/11
Labour 4, 18/11/09
Lib Dems 1, 21/07/10
Lib Dems 2, 13/12/10
Lib Dems 3, 17/06/10
Lib Dems 4, 4/11/10
Lib Dems 5, 14/06/11

The Netherlands

SP 1, 06/11/12
SP 2, 9/07/13
GL 1, 28/06/13
PvdA 1, 02/02/10

PvdA 2, 11/02/10
PvdA 3, 11/02/10
CDA 1, 11/02/10
CDA 2, 12/05/10
CDA 3, 18/05/10
CDA 4, 18/05/10
VVD 1, 08/02/10
VVD 2, 27/06/13
VVD 3, 11/07/13
D'66 1, 18/07/13

Sweden

V 1, 21/08/09
V 2, 01/09/09
V 3, 18/08/09
V 4, 28/08/09
MP 1, 20/08/09
MP 2, 28/08/09
SAP 1, 27/08/09
SAP 2, 01/09/09
SAP 3, 31/08/09
SAP 4, 02/09/09
M 1, 26/08/09
M 2, 26/08/09
M 3, 18/08/09
KD 1, 18/08/09
KD 2, 22/08/09
FP 1, 19/08/09
FP 2, 25/08/09
FP 3, 25/08/09
CP 1, 27/08/09
CP 2, 20/08/09
CP 3, 19/08/09
CP 4, 02/09/09

Index

asylum seekers and refugees, 5–6, 16, 24–5, 28, 33–4, 48, 53, 58, 61–2, 66–7, 70–2, 74, 76–7, 79, 82–4, 86–90, 92–4
authoritarianism, 9–10, 43, 85

citizenship, 20–1, 30, 34–5, 41–2, 45, 47–8, 53–4, 59
conflicting ideological 'pulls', 4, 6, 12–14, 16, 26, 64–6, 69, 81, 94–7, 107, 110, 112–14

the environment, 1–2, 9, 12, 21, 23, 25, 41, 57, 66, 71–2, 75, 94
equality, 9, 21, 36, 54, 57, 60, 63, 68–9
the EU
    competition on, 3–7, 10–14
    degrees of conflict on, 5, 31–2, 38–41, 48–51, 55–8
    explaining modes of competition on, 3, 14–16
    measuring manifesto positions on, 23–4
Euroscepticism, 3, 5, 11, 14, 16, 23, 31–2, 39, 50, 55, 57, 75–77, 80, 87, 92

free market, 4, 8, 68, 81, 93

GAL/TAN dimension
    meaning of, 9–10
    operationalisation of, 20–3
    relevance of, 10, 14, 16, 73–5, 85, 90, 93

ideological bear trap, 115
ideology
    changing nature of, 1, 6, 10, 97, 112
    relevance of, 2, 4, 13–14, 16, 80, 88, 112–13

immigration
    competition on, 4, 10–14, 30
    degrees of conflict on, 5–6, 32–8, 41–8, 51–5, 58–62
    explaining modes of competition on, 3, 16
    measuring manifesto positions on, 24–5
integration, 5, 9, 20–1, 23, 25, 32–8, 40, 42, 44, 46–7, 49, 50–1, 53–7, 89, 107
internationalism, 13, 44, 57, 71, 89
interviews, 26–8
issue ownership
    meaning of, 2–3, 15
    in relation to party competition, 6, 15–16, 28, 97–100, 101–6

labour market, 4, 8, 11, 18, 20, 25–6, 28, 35–6, 42, 51, 53–5, 59–60, 63, 72, 75, 77, 87–9
labour migration, 16, 24, 34, 48, 52–3, 59–61, 70–1, 74–7, 82–4, 88–9, 94

mainstream parties
    in Belgium, 17
    in Britain, 17
    in the Netherlands, 17
    in Sweden, 17

nationalism, 9–10, 21, 37–8, 47, 66, 79, 82, 88
neutrality, 30, 49, 55–7

party competition
    changes to the modes of, 3, 6, 9, 97, 112, 116
    ideology's relevance for, 2, 73, 97, 107, 114, 116
    institutional effects on, 13–14, 32, 34, 40, 52, 95, 107, 112, 114–15

party competition – *continued*
   spatial explanations for, 2, 14
   valence explanations for, 3, 14–15
party manifestos
   Chapel Hill Expert Survey, 7, 25–6
   Comparative Manifestos Project, 7,
     25–6
   limitations of, 18
   usefulness of, 18
populist radical right parties
   challenges posed by, 3–6, 13, 30,
     33–4, 49, 51, 62, 115
   impact on mainstream party
     competition by, 4–6, 51

sovereignty, 4, 9, 12, 31, 39–41, 47,
   49, 57, 63, 65, 71, 81–2,
   84, 113
state interventionist/free market
   dimension
   meaning of, 8–10
   operationalisation of,
     18–20
   relevance of, 2, 8, 10–12

taxes, 11, 20, 23, 37, 72, 84, 87

welfare-state chauvinism, 82

CPI Antony Rowe
Chippenham, UK
2018-06-25 22:44